ARISTOTLE
AS POET

ARISTOTLE AS POET

The Song for Hermias and Its Contexts

Andrew Ford

OXFORD
UNIVERSITY PRESS
2011

OXFORD
UNIVERSITY PRESS

Oxford University Press, Inc., publishes works that further
Oxford University's objective of excellence
in research, scholarship, and education.

Oxford   New York
Auckland   Cape Town   Dar es Salaam   Hong Kong   Karachi
Kuala Lumpur   Madrid   Melbourne   Mexico City   Nairobi
New Delhi   Shanghai   Taipei   Toronto

With offices in
Argentina   Austria   Brazil   Chile   Czech Republic   France   Greece
Guatemala   Hungary   Italy   Japan   Poland   Portugal   Singapore
South Korea   Switzerland   Thailand   Turkey   Ukraine   Vietnam

Copyright © 2011 by Oxford University Press

Published by Oxford University Press, Inc.
198 Madison Avenue, New York, New York 10016
www.oup.com

Oxford is a registered trademark of Oxford University Press
All rights reserved. No part of this publication may be reproduced,
stored in a retrieval system, or transmitted, in any form or by any means,
electronic, mechanical, photocopying, recording, or otherwise,
without the prior permission of Oxford University Press.

Library of Congress Cataloging-in-Publication Data
Ford, Andrew Laughlin.
Aristotle as poet : the song for Hermias and its contexts / Andrew L. Ford
p. cm.
ISBN 978-0-19-973329-3
1. Aristotle. 2. Poetry–Early works to 1800. I. Title.
PN1040.A53F67 2010
881'.01—dc22   2010000006

1 3 5 7 9 8 6 4 2
Printed in the United States of America
on acid-free paper

For Annabelle and Viviane

quand j'ai été père ... —Balzac

CONTENTS

Abbreviations — xix

1. The Text — 1
   Aristotle: The Song for Hermias — 1
   Sources and First Reading — 3

2. History and Context — 9
   Deconstructing Atarneus: Questions of Method — 10
   Constructing Hermias: The Erythraean Inscription — 17
   The End of Hermias: Theopompus's *Letter to Philip* — 21

3. Performance and Occasion — 27
   Commemorative Epigrams: Aristotle and Simonides — 29
   Book Epigrams: Theocritus of Chios — 35
   Texts and Things: Herodotus on Hermotimus — 41

4. Performance and Context — 45
   Witnesses: Callisthenes' *Hermias* — 48

Sources: Hermippus's *On Aristotle*	54
Authenticity: "Aristotle's" *Apology*	60
5. Genres of Poetry	**69**
Lyric Genres from Plato to Alexandria	71
Impious Song: The Paean to Lysander	80
Paean, Hymn, *Skolion*?	86
6. Kinds of Hymn	**91**
Hymnic Form: Ariphron's Paean to Health	91
Hymnic Flexibility: Pindar's Fourteenth Olympic Ode	97
Hymns in Hexameters: "Homer" and Aristotle	105
7. Ethos	**113**
Ethos in Debate: An Attic *Skolion* and a Poem by Sappho	114
Ethos in Protreptic: Aristotle's Hymn to Hermias, vv. 1–8	121
Ethos in Epiphany: Immortal Virtue in Sophocles' *Philoctetes*	127
8. Reading	**137**
Troping: πολύμοχθος in Euripides and Bacchylides	138
Mythologizing: Hymn to Hermias, vv. 9–16	144
Immortalizing: Hymn to Hermias, vv. 17–21	147
9. Endurance	**157**
Memorial: Aristotle's Elegiacs to Eudemus	160
Survival: A Letter from Plato	166
NOTES	173
BIBLIOGRAPHY	217
GENERAL INDEX	233
INDEX OF PASSAGES DISCUSSED	239

PREFACE

People are often surprised to hear that Aristotle wrote poetry, naturally thinking of him in the first instance as a philosopher and indeed as one of the greatest thinkers in the ancient world. In fact, Aristotle composed enough poetry to fill two papyrus rolls in the ancient collections of his works, for it was not unusual that a well-educated gentleman of his day should be able to come up with a verse or song to grace special occasions. What is very surprising is the story told about one of his poems, for the sources that preserve the text also tell us that it came near to costing the philosopher his life. This lyric, one of only two to survive complete, will be the central thread in the study that follows, which combines a close reading of that work with an attempt to understand its remarkable reception. Though very little of Aristotle's poetic output survives, I hope thereby to cast further light on his relation to the Greek lyric tradition and to the musical culture of the later fourth century.

The poem—strictly speaking, the lyric to a brief song—commemorates Hermias of Atarneus, ruler of a small principality in the northeast corner of the Aegean. In the late 340s BCE,

Hermias, who had been Aristotle's student, patron, and father-in-law, became entangled in the tensions between the Persian Empire to his east and a rising Macedon to his west. When Hermias was captured by the Persian king and put to death around 341, Aristotle composed an ode in praise of his friend's character. My original aim had been to call attention to this text, which is relatively little discussed today, and to place it within the Greek literary tradition. This I have done mainly in the latter part of the book. But my project expanded as I found myself drawn into a very old debate about which genre the poem belonged to: strictly speaking, was this a dirge for Hermias, a eulogy, a hymn, a drinking song, or some combination of these? The question may sound academic, except that it seems to have meant enough to some of Aristotle's contemporaries that they were willing to threaten him with trial and execution on account of it. This episode is usually thought to have occurred after the death of Alexander the Great in 323 BCE when a wave of anti-Macedonian sentiment swept through Greece. In Athens, where Aristotle was teaching, his long-standing relations with the regime (his father had been the physician of Alexander's grandfather and he himself had been the young king's tutor) would have been a liability. Political agitators, we are told, began to accuse the foreign-born philosopher (from Stagira in northern Greece) of being too sympathetic to tyrants, and the song for Hermias was brought forth as a prime piece of evidence. According to the version preserved in Athenaeus (who wrote around five centuries after the event), a religious official of Demeter's Eleusinian mysteries teamed up with an Athenian politician to charge that Aristotle's song, ostensibly a lament for his friend, was actually a kind of hymn implying that Hermias had become a god. This was impiety in itself, the priest might urge, and the politician could add that such a song revealed a person unsympathetic to Athenian ideals of democratic equality. Both could buttress their case by recalling the trial of Socrates, who had been put to death on charges that included impiety in 399. We are not told whether the case against Aristotle ever came to trial, but it seems that the threat of legal action was real enough, for he left Athens for good in 323, reportedly explaining that he was leaving, "lest the Athenians sin twice against Philosophy."[1]

A modern reader may well ask if such a story, like Aristotle's *bon mot*, is too good to be true. Due scrutiny of the sources will follow, but it seemed to me that a reading of Aristotle's poem that put this information aside as unreliable or irrelevant could hardly be called complete. Indeed, it seemed to me impossible even to construe the text without considering these matters, for they bear directly on our view of what the poem is trying to do. The story of the trial also raises questions about Greek literary culture in Aristotle's time. Is it credible that an Athenian jury—which typically included hundreds of people selected at random—should have cared whether the song was a hymn or not? What was the prosecution thinking in launching such an attack, and how did they understand the text? We may also wonder about the relation between Aristotle the literary theorist and the wider public: How is it possible that he of all people could have opened himself up to a charge of misapplying generic rules? The Prince of Philosophers was, after all, also the Prince of Critics, and his lectures on *Poetics* had set out with exemplary clarity the system of literary genres on which most ancient and much modern literary criticism is based. He least of anyone should have erred in the question of what was a hymn and what wasn't. Finally, if we doubt the story of the trial, ought we also to reject the poem as a later fabrication?

Such reflections led me to include in my literary analysis a wider view that took in the song's contexts, including its early reception and transmission. Coming to terms with the words seemed to require understanding the circumstances under which they were composed, presumably shortly after 341; and some idea of how such songs might circulate seemed necessary to understand how a personal lyric could have become a public scandal, as it seems to have in 323. In addition, once the question of the song's authenticity arises, we must give some thought to its later transmission, in particular asking about the circumstances under which a genuine song of Aristotle's might have been recorded and preserved. The result has been a rather extended piece of exegesis, but one that I hope is justified both by the intrinsic interest of the song and by the interpretative issues it raises; one of the pleasures in reading old poems is that the basic process of making sense of the words can provide heightened examples of the choices that arise in literary reading generally.

Aristotle's song for Hermias ought in fact to be recognized as a landmark in the history of Greek literature, because it is one of the very first lyric poems for which we have substantial evidence—in some cases going back to contemporaries—for how and where it was composed, performed, and received. We usually read early Greek poems knowing next to nothing about their authors and nothing about the people to whom they refer (except, of course, what the poems themselves tell us). But Aristotle's song comes down to us along with considerable information about its author, subject, and the responses of early audiences; we thus have an opportunity to supplement a reading we might give of it as an isolated, authorless fragment with one that can place it rather precisely within the political, religious, and musical cultures of the late classical age. Acknowledging that this agenda will draw me into areas beyond my expertise, and that literary theory has made the old tactic of putting texts in historical context a less than straightforward affair, I nonetheless hope that this attempt to see a lyric "in the round," as it were, may be a useful case study for the more frequent occasions when evidence is lacking to trace a poem's background in detail.

In my literary interpretations I have been guided by the first question that comes up when people hear that Aristotle wrote poetry: "Really? What's it like?" I know of no other way to say what the song is like than to set it beside other poems in the tradition, both those that closely resemble it—Ariphron's lyric in praise of health is the best-known example—and those that bring out its distinctive qualities by contrast. I end up comparing a far wider range of texts than earlier scholars have cited—from Sapphic stanzas through Sophoclean trimeters, taking in both "high" and "popular" verse and prose genres as well—but I submit each as illuminating specific aspects of Aristotle's text while being worth a fresh look in its own right.

The book is organized to place Aristotle's poem first, so that readers can come back to it repeatedly, as the text does. It is followed by my translation and a brief run-through of its contents, a first reading designed to register its principal themes and tropes as they would have unfolded before an ancient audience. I then turn to the evidence for Hermias and his relations with Aristotle and consider how it may affect our interpretation of the poem. Chapter 2 walks the story back to its sources very carefully, for the "historical" texts we use to understand a "literary" text are rarely straightforward and have contexts themselves to be considered. Chapter 3 takes up Aristotle's only other poem to survive complete, an epigram he composed about Hermias's death, which is reported to have been inscribed on a monument in Delphi. This and other related epigrams will make us confront the worrying gap that may arise between textual accounts of an event or object and the posited event or object itself. Despite these complexities, and despite some definitely spurious sources, I conclude in chapter 4 that we should accept Aristotle's song for Hermias as authentic, even though attempts to specify a single original performative context remain speculative. At this point we will turn from the song's contexts to the song, which I hold is best approached by following Aristotle's accusers and asking: What is its genre? The first of the next two chapters sketches the traditional Greek system for recognizing forms of lyric (a topic that deserves more attention than it has received); the second argues for the flexibility and negotiability of a song's genre in actual practice. My interest in genre is not judicial—to determine the literary category to which the work properly "belongs"— but historical, looking at genres as epitomes of cultural norms and observing how they influence the meanings of songs and govern their circulation through society. Only if we appreciate the close connection between Greek conceptions of genre and the occasions of social life can we understand why Aristotle's accusers could have expected to arouse a jury's indignation at this alleged hymn. Chapter 7 begins a re-reading of the Hermias song, now seen against the panorama of Greek song types that constituted Aristotle's literary horizon. Here and in chapter 8 we will be in a position to see this poem and others like it in a new way. Even if the sources for the story turn out not to be trustworthy in all details, they can bring the text into focus by calling attention to aspects of it that provoked divergent and apparently heated interpretations. And even if some ancient readers seem to have misconstrued the text deliberately, this bizarre episode in the history of its interpretation is an important reminder that we cannot wish away our historical distance and see the work stripped of all partisan construal and temporal obfuscation. Indeed, we cannot draw a sharp line separating modern understandings of Aristotle's song from the chain of its ancient receptions, for the lyric has only reached us by being recorded again and again, each time under a particular conception of its meaning and value. That ongoing process of reception and interpretation is considered in the final chapter.

I should say here that I regard the perspectives I bring to bear as complementary without pretending that they combine to reveal the poem's final and definitive meaning. It would be naïve to claim that putting a poem in its historical context is sufficient to determine its "correct" interpretation, however this be defined. Nor is my aim to understand the poem as an expression of Aristotle's psychology or to discover in it his personal response to events in his life. For me, the value of exploring the poem's history and the responses it drew from its audiences is that they enrich our perception of it as a specific cultural artifact, as a work of art produced in a unique time and place.[2] Historicizing also allows us to read the song's language against the language of the time and so to catch its "contemporary" accents, for all poems begin as contemporary poetry. The payoff for reading the lyric in light of its contexts is a more fine-tuned appreciation for its verbal dynamics. It will be seen that the song modulates through a variety of lyric styles and that it shifts the picture it gives of itself as it unfolds. For such reasons I will decline to pin it down in the end to a single historical context or a single genre; what seemed more important was to follow its changing meanings throughout its dynamic career, from the time it arose among the circle of Hermias's intimates until it passed, after a contentious entry into the public sphere, into antiquarian compilations such as that of Athenaeus, where we can read it today. What follows, then, is less an exhaustive historical analysis or final literary interpretation than notes toward a biography of a song.

A poem by "the master of those who know" can hardly be expected to have passed unnoticed among scholars of Greek literature, and my debts to earlier treatments of this poem ought to be acknowledged. It will be clear from my discussion that I have found especially useful Wilamowitz (1893), Bowra (1938), Jaeger (1948), and Renehan (1982), though I have not agreed with them on all points. What I have tried to add to these indispensable studies is a more constant awareness of

Aristotle's poem as a piece for performance, as a song (a μέλος or ἀοιδή), which is what the Greeks would have called it. We have Aristotle's words because they were written down and then read, re-read, and re-copied; but their form shows that they were made as part of a song, a melodic work designed to be performed, re-performed, and remembered. (Accordingly, I use the term *poem* in what follows when considering Aristotle's lyric in its function as a written text, and *song* when thinking of it as a performance piece.) Keeping this fact in mind adds important dimensions to our understanding of the words that remain and of the meanings they took on through history. In sorting through the traditions about Aristotle, I have learned much from Düring's superb collection, in particular what value there is in "source criticism" properly done. This old approach was out of fashion when I was in school, in part because it could be seem naively positivistic to seek to track down the "sources" of great books. But the learning and intelligence displayed in such works as Wormell (1935) on the tradition about Hermias, Bollansée (2001) on Hermippus, and Harding (2006) on Didymus, along with, of course, the fundamental work of Wilamowitz and Jacoby, command respect; if we cannot aspire to recover all or even the key sources that lie behind a given work, such scholarship can be of great help in recognizing the ways in which texts and songs were used, passed around, and preserved in the ancient world.

Finally, I would not have ventured so far into fields of scholarship in which I was little more than a novice if I had not known I could rely on learned friends for help. Of those who read and commented on this book in manuscript, I thank first Douglas Lane Patey, my long-standing ideal reader on these matters. Nearby is M. B. E. Smith, whose bracing criticisms led me to omit many weak arguments and strengthen what I could not omit. My colleague Michael Attyah Flower lavished on me his deep and subtle knowledge of Greek history and its sources. It was a pleasure to be able to impose on the kindness of Marco Fantuzzi, whose imaginative and learned criticism I have long admired. Vayos Liapis was similarly generous with his detailed knowledge and tactful sense of poetry, as was the versatile and thoughtful Marek Wecowski. Last but not least, Pauline LeVen's valuable suggestions were marked by the same originality and independence she displayed in the fine dissertation she wrote with me on fourth-century Greek lyric. My manuscript was supported at a crucial stage by Stefan Vranka of Oxford University Press; he secured helpful readers' reports and contributed many wise suggestions on repeated readings of the manuscript. Thanks to them all, my text has been purged of errors, inaccuracies, and infelicities of expression, while being enriched with references to primary and secondary literature. I thank them most warmly and avow with equal warmth that the defects that remain are mine alone.

ABBREVIATIONS

CA   J. U. Powell, ed. *Collectanea Alexandrina*. Oxford: Clarendon Press, 1925.

CEG   P. A. Hansen, ed. *Carmina epigraphica Graeca saeculorum vii-v a. Chr. n.* (Texte und Kommentare xii). Berlin and New York: De Gruyter, 1983.

DK   H. Diels and W. Kranz, eds. *Die Fragmente der Vorsokratiker*, edition. 3 vols. Berlin: Weidmann, 1952.

DL   Diogenes Laertius, *Lives of Eminent Philosophers (Vitae philosophorum)*, ed. M. Marcovich and H. Gärtner. Stuttgart and Leipzig: Teubner, 1999.

FGrH   F. Jacoby, *Fragmente der Griechischen Historiker*. Leiden: Brill, 1923–.

Fr(r).   fragment(s) in the edition specified

IEG   M. L. West, ed. *Iambi et elegi Graeci*, 2nd edition. 2 vols. Oxford: Clarendon Press, 1989–1992.

LSJ   H. G. Liddell, R. Scott, and H. S. Jones, *A Greek English Lexicon*. 9th ed. Oxford: Clarendon Press, 1925–1940.

PMG   D. Page, ed. *Poetae melici Graeci*. Oxford: Clarendon Press, 1962.

PMGF	M. Davies, ed. *Poetarum melicorum Graecorum fragmenta*, vol. 1. Oxford: Clarendon Press, 1991.
RE	A. Pauly, G. Wissowa, W. Kroll, eds. *Real-Encyclopädie der classischen Altertumswissencschaft*. Stuttgart: J. B. Metzler, 1893–.
Rose	V. Rose, ed. *Aristotelis qui ferebantur librorum fragmenta*, 3rd ed. Leipzig: Teubner, 1886.
SH	H. Lloyd-Jones and P. Parsons, eds. *Supplementum Hellenisticum*. Berlin: W. de Gruyter, 1983.
Test(t).	testimonium (-ia) in the edition specified
TrGF	B. Snell, R. Kannicht, and S. Radt, eds. *Tragicorum Graecorum Fragmenta*, 5 vols. Göttingen: Vandenhoeck & Ruprecht, 1971–2004.
Wehrli	Fritz Wehrli, ed. *Die Schule des Aristoteles*, 2nd ed. 10 vols. and 2 suppl. Basel: Schwabe, 1967–1974.

Chapter 1

The Text

Aristotle: The Song for Hermias

ἀρετὰ πολύμοχθε γένει βροτείῳ,
   θήραμα κάλλιστον βίῳ,
σᾶς πέρι, παρθένε, μορφᾶς
   καὶ θανεῖν ζαλωτὸς ἐν Ἑλλάδι πότμος
   καὶ πόνους τλῆναι μαλεροὺς ἀκάμαντας·   5
τοῖον ἐπὶ φρένα βάλλεις
   καρπὸν ἰσαθάνατον χρυσοῦ τε κρείσσω
καὶ γονέων μαλακαυγήτοιό θ' ὕπνου.
σεῦ δ' ἕνεκεν ‹καὶ› ὁ δῖος
   Ἡρακλῆς Λήδας τε κοῦροι   10
πόλλ' ἀνέτλασαν ἐν ἔργοις
   σὰν [ἀγρεύ]οντες δύναμιν.
σοῖς τε πόθοις Ἀχιλεὺς Αἴας τ' Ἀίδαο δόμους ἦλθον·
σᾶς δ' ἕνεκεν φιλίου μορφᾶς Ἀταρνέος   15
   ἔντροφος ἀελίου χήρωσεν αὐγάς.

τοιγὰρ ἀοίδιμος ἔργοις,
    ἀθάνατόν τέ μιν αὐξήσουσι Μοῦσαι,
Μναμοσύνας θύγατρες, Δι-
    ὸς ξενίου σέβας αὔξου–   20
σαι φιλίας τε γέρας βεβαίου.

O Virtue of great toil for humankind,
    the fairest quarry in life,
for your shape, maiden,
    even to die is an enviable fate in Greece
and to endure pains, consuming, unrelenting;   5
such is the fruit you cast into hearts,
    immortal-like, better than gold,
than breeding, than sleep with its soft beams.

For your sake even that godly
    Heracles and the sons of Leda   10
endured much in their exploits
    on the track [?] of your power;
in longing for you Achilles and
    Ajax entered the house of Hades;
for the sake of your dear shape, Atarneus'   15
    nursling left the rays of the sun bereft.

Hence he will be a subject of song on account of his exploits,
    and the Muses will grow him into immortality,
those daughters of Memory,
    making grow reverence for Zeus,   20
god of guest-friends, and the rewards of steadfast friendship.

Sources and First Reading

The Greek text above is taken from the standard modern edition of Greek lyric poetry by Denys Page (with one supplement at v. 12).[1] It is based on three ancient sources: the oldest is a commentary from the second half of the first century BCE on a speech attributed to Demosthenes; the commentary was composed by Didymus, an extremely productive and well-read scholar who worked in Alexandria.[2] In elucidating a speech (most probably the *Fourth Philippic*, 10.32) that alluded to Hermias, Didymus recalls certain points in his career and quotes Aristotle's song. The fullest account of the incidents surrounding the poem is given by Athenaeus, writing around the beginning of the third century CE. He quotes it near the end of his *Learned Banqueters* (Douglas Olsen's translation of *Deipnosophistai*), a long fictional account of an impossibly brilliant dinner conversation that Athenaeus composed by pillaging earlier works of antiquarian scholarship (Book 15, 696A-697B). Sometime later in the third century, Diogenes Laertius also quoted the poem in the account of Aristotle that he composed for his *Lives of the Philosophers*. These sources differ in small ways, and the question of what sources they used will be taken up in due course.

Page is responsible for the colometry of the text above, the ragged right- and left-hand margins meant to demarcate the musical phrases of the original; in the Didymus papyrus, the poem is written *en bloc*, as lyric poetry was often transcribed in the Hellenistic age.[3] The patterning of short and long syllables shows that the song consists of a single stanza, composed in a fairly common kind of rhythm for which modern scholars have devised the term *dactylo-epitrite*. We do not know enough to say whether dactylo-epitrites were associated with a specific range of emotions or themes, but a leading expert in Greek metrics has noted that in the fourth century the rhythm was characteristic of what he terms "educated bourgeois lyric."[4] As a performance piece, it should be conceptualized as a short, single-stanza song—dactylo-epitrites were always sung—with a melody unique to that song. It is dogma that goes back to the ancients that this meter implies that the song was for choral performance; the dialect suits this possibility, since it has the light Doric coloration that was conventional in choral odes. But I shall argue below that there is no reason the song could not have been performed or at least re-performed as a solo piece.

My rather literal translation follows the line numbers and punctuation of Page's text, though for convenience I have inserted spaces in the translation to signal the song's three main conceptual periods. As an introduction to the poem, let us follow Aristotle's words and themes as they would have unfolded before an ancient audience, bearing in mind that Greek audiences were familiar with a vast body of songs, many known by heart, and were capable of delighting in new variations on old themes. This is to postpone a synoptic examination of the work's structure, giving it a first hearing, so to speak, as an event that would have played out in time.[5]

No hearing occurs without expectations, and so the question of how the song sounded to an ancient audience raises for the first time the question of genre. Prima facie, Aristotle's song begins very much like a hymn, which is to say that its formal components can be paralleled in innumerable Greek songs composed to praise a divinity.[6] Hymnic style begins with the very first word, *areta*, a vocative that at once invokes and personifies "virtue." (I take over, with some misgiving, this traditional translation of *areta* because it is less awkward than a more precise rendering would be, such as "human excellence," which is the way the word is often rendered in Aristotle's ethical treatises. What is crucial to bear in mind is that Greek "virtue" has not the moral or sexual connotations the word later acquired from its use in

Christian literature. In the context of a praise song, the best definition of *areta* may be that of Russell and Wilson, who base it on Aristotle's rhetorical and ethical works: *aretê* is "the power to provide and protect good things, and to confer great benefits.")[7] In form, *areta* cues us to expect the Doric dialect (slightly different from the pronunciation *aretê* in Athens); that is, the following speech will not be everyday, unmarked talk. Songs with touches of Doric were characteristic of Greek cult hymns, though all we can infer from this formal detail is that the song presents itself as suitable to be sung by a choir and at a cult site, not that it was ever actually put to use in that way.

The hymnic rhetoric continues as the vocative is followed, as regularly in hymns, by an epithet: Aristotle calls upon not any form of Virtue but the one characterized by great struggling, literally "of many toils." He then gets down to the main business of the hymn, praise of the divinity, for as in many Greek hymns, the principle here is *do ut des*: the poet gives praise so that the god may be gracious in return.[8] Aristotle fills the first sixteen verses with praise of *Areta* as the most desirable object of human aspiration. This praise is articulated into two parts, with the end of the first movement marked by a priamel in vv. 6–9, a figure of speech common in praise poetry that lists items in ranked order to set off the merits of the object of praise.[9] Virtue is thus presented as more desirable than wealth or noble ancestry, more alluring than physical pleasure. Aristotle's version of this figure is made eminently apprehensible by being shaped as a tricolon crescendo in which the third element is given capping force by being expanded. (As in, "our Lives, our Fortunes, and our sacred Honor.") Here the word translated "with soft beams," a sesquipedalian and archaic-sounding epithet, rounds out the first conceptual period with sleep and at the same time brings the performer to a metrical pause in which to take a breath.

The second period (vv. 9–16) "proves" the claims of the first by adducing a series of admirable figures who spent their lives in the service of Virtue. These exemplary heroes are organized chronologically—Heracles and the Disokouroi did their deeds before the Trojan War in which Achilles and Ajax won glory—and metaphysically: Heracles is Zeus's son, as were Castor and Pollux, the male offspring of his intercourse with Leda; of the Trojan pair, Achilles had the goddess Thetis for a mother, while Ajax was fully mortal. We are thus thinking in terms of time and noble ancestry when a third example comes up, which we may suspect will be the last, since the number three proved to mean closure in the priamel. In all respects the third item (v. 15) surprises: Aristotle names only one figure, and he leaps from heroes of old to a contemporary and friend, an abrupt move from *muthos* to *logos*, from more than mortal figures to the "nursling of Atarneus."

Things conform a little less strictly to the hymnic program as our song begins its third period after v. 16. In the poem's argument, Hermias's devotion to *Areta* is the culminating proof of her worth and so belongs to the hymnic agenda of praise. At the same time—and here one begins to see an opening for Aristotle's critics—Aristotle is also praising Hermias, implying that his travails, which are put on a par with the mythical exploits of heroes, make him worthy to be remembered like them. And so the third movement inaugurates a shift in focus, as what began sounding like a hymn to a divine principle modulates to sound like a song of praise directed at a fellow mortal. This shift in focus is arguably also a shift in genre, since in Aristotle's day there was a long-standing and widely respected tradition that outstanding human achievement deserved to be celebrated in song, but that songs for mortals should keep their praise at a level below that which is offered to the gods. The distinction between hymns in praise of gods and songs for mortals was preserved in the popular terminology of Aristotle's day, which called a song celebrating human achievement an *enkômion*, literally a "revel song" sung by a band of cheering young men on a carouse. The Greeks knew well that revels can become rowdy—"For he's a jolly good fellow" can quickly turn into "as nobody will deny!"—and so encomia were expected to temper praise with pious warnings against excess. An illustration is Pindar's victory songs, which in their day were usually called *enkômia* (as will be seen in chapter 5): almost any Pindaric epinician will show how insistently he blends glorification of athletic triumph with warnings that the happy victor should not be misled by success to think himself more than mortal.

In turning to praise Hermias, therefore, Aristotle entered into the unwritten encomiastic contract. And indeed in v. 17, he resorts to a common encomiastic *topos* when he declares that Hermias's extraordinary qualities make him worthy to be celebrated in song, adding that the Muses, the daughters of Memory, will make Hermias "immortal" (v. 18). Once again, Aristotle's enemies may prick up their ears, but there is nothing impious here. If Aristotle offers his friend the highest form of praise a mortal could hope for, it is also quite a conventional compliment, even stereotypical by this time; there is nothing novel in the idea of achieving immortality through song, which already had a long tradition behind it when Homer spoke of Achilles winning "unwithering fame" in the *Iliad* (9.189). The rhythm of the poem underscores Aristotle's appeal to traditional ideas of poetic immortalization, for verses 13-14, describing Hermippus' epic predecessors, come near to a dactylic hexameter, the canonical meter of epic.

Aristotle's song contains a minor surprise, since many (though not all) hymns would close with a petition of some kind. This ostensible hymn, however, includes no prayer, unless its closing expectation that Hermias's excellence will be remembered is taken as a request that he meet his due reward. At the end of the song Aristotle's rhetoric becomes a little involuted and may seem overwrought, and when the Muses' celebration of Hermias turns out to be a song increasing the honor of Zeus we may lose sight of whether we are praising Virtue, Hermias, or Zeus. Later I will argue that Aristotle was not losing control here but was deliberately and conscientiously pushing poetic forms to a limit. For now, it will be agreed that at no point does he explicitly say that Hermias has or will become a god. Though, as we will see, some of the heroes mentioned managed in some stories to overcome death, Aristotle is clear that the immortality Hermias will enjoy will be in poetry, not on Olympus. Wilamowitz said that only a calumniator could call this a *paean* to Hermias, and almost all modern commentators agree that the charge of impiety was baseless.[10] To the extent that the poem is a hymn, it is a paean to human excellence personified, which we will see was a perfectly conventional conceit. Yet a closer reading will show that things are not altogether simple and that the song does contain a sort of hymn to Hermias hovering just beneath the surface. The poem is more artful in its stance than has been shown so far, but this must be made to appear, paradoxically, by turning away from the text for a moment and thinking about the culture from which it came.

Chapter 2

History and Context

Two prose texts about Hermias from this period remind us that Aristotle's neat little piece had a public: one is an inscription recording a treaty concluded in Hermias's name, the other a contemptuous dismissal of him by a contemporary observer of the political scene. These diametrically opposed sketches of Hermias provide a background that can illuminate Aristotle's words, but show as well that reconstructing the historical context of a song is not simple: it is clear that the texts we use to reconstruct the context of a poem need themselves to be contextualized. Even when we can put our hands on tangible firsthand traces of the historical actors—as in Hermias's inscription—we are not in touch with rock-solid reality but with partisan representations that need situating and often decoding. Certain postmodern strains in current criticism would accordingly suggest that we regard Hermias as, so to speak, a figure of speech, a verbal sign that we decode by referring to other signs without ever getting to "the truth" of things. The force of such arguments must be acknowledged: the people referred to by our texts are indeed known to us only through a concatenation of other texts, and it is hard to leap the gap from words to reality. But I will argue in the following section that to concede that context is not something easily reconstructed from texts does not require reducing the people in the story to the status of signifieds or regarding their doings and sufferings as merely linguistic interactions in the texts recalling them.[1]

Deconstructing Atarneus: Questions of Method

Methodological difficulties in contextualizing works of literature are particularly acute for readers of early Greek poetry because our historical knowledge is so thin. A Latinist colleague asks me with only partly feigned exasperation why, when you place before Hellenists one of their subtle lyric texts, they start spinning out a historical novel about how it was composed and performed—matters that are usually impossible to know for certain and arguably irrelevant to an appreciation of the work as a poem. One might reply that we are only following the lead of our Greek texts, which typically refer to the contexts and occasions of their performance, and of the Greek scholarly tradition, which typically defined kinds of lyric according to the occasions at which they might be performed. But it remains true that after the poststructuralist criticism of the 1970s and 1980s we can no longer speak of historical context as if it were something straightforwardly "out there" behind the texts and easy to reach. The problems for readers of ancient literature are really two: one is pragmatic, the result of the fact that historical evidence is usually rare and is very often contaminated by the texts it would be used to explain; the other is theoretical, having to do with postmodern objections to the way the relation between text and context is conceived. I think readers of Greek poetry need not be defeated by the second set of objections and that we can, and should, cope with the first.

A simple, I hope not too simple, way to bring out the theoretical problems with adducing the historical context of a poem is to pose the question: What in Aristotle's text directs us to look away from it for information? There is just one place that will give pause to readers who find contextualization problematic or irrelevant—the phrase "Atarneus' nursling" in v. 15. The expression is a cipher without some reference to a historically specific place—a town that was situated on the northwestern coast of Turkey, near the modern town of Dikili. Only if we know this can we know, having consulted other texts, that Aristotle refers to Hermias, who ruled Atarneus from around the middle of the fourth century. The little puzzle is easily enough solved, but solved it must be because this verse is the only time that Hermias is named in the poem, a poem whose purpose seems to be to celebrate him.

If it is agreed that the phrase "nursling of Atarneus" sends us outside the text, it must be conceded that appealing from text to context is easier said than done. Over recent decades, the traditional practice of reading literary works in relation to their historical contexts has been regarded as highly problematic. A main basis for such reservations derives from principles of structural linguistics: reference works not by words pointing to things in the world but by one linguistic signifier directing us to other signifiers, which send us to other signifiers in turn. "Atarneus" sends us to Hermias, but we only know who Hermias was from historical documents, that is, from more texts. The impasse that ensues is epitomized in the slogan, taken over from Jacques Derrida, that there is no "outside" the text, by which it is meant that there is never a leaping of the gap between sign and referent.[2] Note that what drives Aristotle's reader to think of fourth-century history is not simply the fact that Atarneus and Hermias are proper nouns—for so are Heracles, Achilles, and Zeus. These names also set the reader a challenge insofar as they are not words to be found in dictionaries; but mythological figures do have a definition of a sort, that is, a more or less stable mythology that determines whether we regard Aristotle's use of them as correct or solecistic, as plausible or paradoxical. Names like "Zeus" and "Achilles" thus show that proper names can sometimes function like ordinary words and need not call us to a specific person or point in history. From a poststructuralist perspective, it is hard to see that Hermias and Atarneus are much different; just as we know Heracles only from Homer, Euripides, Ovid, and so on, the "historical" Hermias for a modern reader may be no more than the nexus of a number of more or less convergent stories in Didymus, Athenaeus, Diogenes, and so on.[3] Mythological personages thus provide an apt illustration of the view that the person behind a proper name is to be found not in historical fact but in text—in the sum total of the things that have been said under that name and found acceptable and memorable. Aristotle was free, then, to bring Atarneus into his poem, even as he was free to bring in mythological figures. But history, as Mae West might have said, had nothing to do with it.

Postmodern reading holds further that reference in texts is not only inescapably intralinguistic but also endless, so that we create meaning only by arbitrarily breaking into this sign-to-sign relay. It happens that our phrase can illustrate this point as well. We hear from Himerius of Bithynia, a public orator of Roman Imperial times, that Atarneus was the name of a king of Mysia who founded the city (*Oration* 40.40-1 Colonna). A deconstructionist would be happy to accept this testimony that the one historical name in our poem, "Atarneus," properly belongs not to the city but to its founder, and that it is only the linguistic process of metonymy, a process of *transferring* meaning, that fixes the word onto the physical place as its true and "proper" name. Nor would such a reading be discomfited by the fact that the story could be told the other way round: a historian experienced in foundation legends will read Himerius suspecting that the toponym came first and suggested a name for the founding king when such a figure was wanted. As often, we are not in a position to know. Behind one name lies another, and behind that name lies another still. The little riddle in "Atarneus' nursling" turns out to be hard to solve after all, and the would-be historicist reader ends up reading like a postmodern, going from text to text.

The argument can become metaphysical, but pragmatically speaking there is no denying that the word "Atarneus" now has purely linguistic content—the city no longer survives, having been abandoned a few centuries after Hermias (or so at least we are informed by another text, Pausanias's *Description of Greece* 7.2.11). Deconstruction compensates for this rather bleak (and, after a while, repetitive) insight by usefully highlighting the ways by which texts create an illusion of extra-textual realities out of purely linguistic resources. In this, it can help the reader of poetry, often raising beguiling paradoxes in the process. For example, on a deconstructive reading, the problem with Aristotle's poem is not, as his accusers charged, that he collapsed the distinction between man and god by composing a hymn to his friend, but that he naively assumed there was a difference between these signifiers when, linguistically, Zeus, Achilles, and Hermias are all on the same level.

I find a deconstructive approach inadequate to give a full account of these texts, though I recognize that it can be effective at unmasking tricks of *logos*. Its value derives, I think, from the fact that deconstruction is a form of rhetorical criticism, albeit an extreme one that insists that *all* language—not excluding "the" and "a"—is figurative, allusive, not referential. But for the classical rhetorician, *logos* is only one of three aspects of speech that require analysis; the task of reading should also pay attention to the *ethos*, the speaker's character suggested by the words, as well as to *pathos*, the impression meant to be created in the audience. We will see that crucial aspects of Aristotle's poem emerge only when we consider these latter two aspects, taking it as a speech that projects a certain sort of character—not only in Hermias but also in the poet who ventures to praise him—and as an address that has particular designs on its audience's state of mind. Bringing to light the *ethos* and *pathos* of the poem will prove to be the main reason for not adopting the postmodern view, because it puts us too much out of sympathy with what Aristotle is trying to say and do in the poem. At this point, however, we need only argue that a rhetorical reading of the song militates against obliterating Hermias's historical status. For it is only as the name of a historical individual, of a figure who is *not* a myth, that Hermias works in the rhetoric of the piece: his name can only cap the series of devotees to Virtue by being different in kind from them. Only by referring to a historical Hermias can Aristotle succeed in the evident ambition of his poem to add a name to the canon of heroes. It is left to deconstruction to claim that Aristotle's attempt to separate myth from history was in vain, but it is not an option to say he did not try.

If we have defended the claim that the word "Atarneus" is not fully legible without a historical gloss, it still remains to say what role such knowledge should have in appreciating the poem as a work of literature. Much, indeed most Greek lyric poetry is studded with proper names about which we know nothing from other sources; in some cases we cannot decide whether these names referred to actual historical persons or were archetypal names for stock figures celebrated in song. (Pity the future historicizing critic who tries to track down the original Yankee Doodle Dandy.) Why should it matter, then, that in the case of Aristotle's song we happen to have external evidence about its honoree? It is not obvious that this adventitious knowledge obliges us to interpret this poem in its context. These details might interest historians of the northeast Aegean but not necessarily readers of poetry.

Knowledge of a poem's historical references might be regarded as gratuitous information, an extra nuance to be savored by those so inclined, except that historical glossing is sometimes inseparable from the basic task of construing the text.[4] Again, the phrase "nursling of Atarneus" affords a compact example: we will see that some contemporaries disputed Hermias's lineage and legitimacy, claiming he was a slave and a barbarian from Bithynia.[5] In this light, the metaphor "nursling" could be read as a deliberate counterassertion, rooting Hermias in the soil of Atarneus as a native. Support for the assumption that legitimacy was at issue can be taken from the similar way in which Himerius introduces him, "Hermias of Atarneus by birth" (Ἑρμείας Ἀταρνεὺς γένος, *Or.* 40.40).[6] Whether we take Aristotle's "nursling" as a pregnant locution can again be thought optional, but once admitted, considerations of context tend to extend beyond glossing names and affect the meaning of other parts of the text. For example, the mention in v. 4 that dying for virtue is accounted "an enviable fate in Greece" gains an extra reason to be in the text if read as an assertion that Hermias, far from being a barbarian, shared Greek values. The curiously expressed thought in vv. 4–5—for the sake of virtue, "even to die is an enviable fate in Greece / and to endure pains"—also seems less curious if contextualized. It sounds anticlimactic, having mentioned that people will die for Virtue, to add that they are willing to suffer for her as well. One "immanentist" explanation of this arrangement is to cite the trope of *husteron proteron* ("second things first"), a feature of many Greek poems and narratives by which what is logically the second of two connected elements is mentioned before the first. Identifying a trope is more than labeling a textual curiosity, for it adduces a host of parallel cases that reassure us that we are not misconstruing the words. But naming a trope is never a complete interpretation, for we still can ask why Aristotle would use *husteron proteron* here. One possible explanation might rely on reports that Hermias died after being tortured by the Persian king. If we take v. 3 as a tactful paraphrase of this painful (and, in Greek eyes, shameful) fact, then the *husteron proteron* emphasizes Hermias's bearing up under torture as on at least an equal footing with accepting death as signs of Virtue's appeal.[7]

These readings might be debated, but we should only be debating the extent and not the fact that the text of Aristotle's song had particular verbal resonance in the world for which it was composed, and that though this world is gone, the words bear ineradicable marks of the historical context from which they came. I would like to close this methodological discussion by saying that I know of no more significant and far-reaching advance in humanistic studies of the twentieth century than structuralism's elaboration of the systematic processes (the *langue*) that underlie and make meaningful each individual act of speech (*parole*) or sign-making. James Redfield has well drawn some of the implications of this development for criticism: "Social analysis is the necessary precondition of literary criticism because poetry implies culture just as *parole* implies *langue*."[8] Much current criticism in the vein called cultural studies would agree when Redfield adds, "Poetic language is wonderfully dual, conflicted, rich and self-extending language, but it is language—an elaboration of a human collective—so reading a poem is learning the language and learning the culture that shaped the language to be reshaped." But the *reading* of poetry, the making of meanings from its words, cannot confine itself to the structural or even poststructural level. On this basis I aim to bring out the linguistic processes and cultural ideologies at work in the song without denying the agency of individual actors—especially Aristotle the poet, but also his readers and misreaders, along with those who transmitted his text.

No doubt many historical meanings are now buried beyond our power to excavate, but that is of course no reason not to register the ones we can see. Moreover, even when the historical motivations underlying certain phrases have been dropped from the tradition, they can make their presence felt in the text to the extent that, in their time, they influenced the way that the poem was made or affected the way that it was received and remembered. In this indirect way, even the hidden past can exert a formal influence, and such influences can only be legible if one is looking for them. I do not claim that Hermias was the "onlie begetter" of this song or that a complete knowledge of his life is essential to understanding it; but I urge that we proceed on the assumption that the poem would not exist, or would not exist in the form we know, were it not for his life and friendship with Aristotle.

Constructing Hermias: The Erythraean Inscription

The ancient sources for Hermias's life differ radically. As noted, the paragon of virtue that appears in Aristotle's portrait is countered in other early accounts that revile Hermias not only as a eunuch, a slave, and a barbarian, but also as a ruthless and bloodstained tyrant. This is unsurprising; an unelected, unconstitutional strongman, Hermias had to maintain power between a restive Persian Empire to his east and competing Greek interests to the west and south.[9] Indeed, Didymus was moved to insert an excursus on Hermias into a Demosthenic commentary precisely because accounts about the autocrat had become so contradictory (Didymus col. 4.60–65). He seems to have taken control in Atarneus around the middle of the fourth century when he succeeded, some suggested by assassination, Eubulus, the previous ruler and his erstwhile patron.[10] Eubulus began in Bithynia and may have owed his rise in station to a wave of revolts in the late 360s by the satraps of Anatolia against the Persian king Artaxerxes II (reigned 404–359/358). In these changing times a number of minor figures succeeded in installing themselves as independent dynasts.[11] Eubulus had been a banker, and Hermias's name is from Hermes, a good patron god for exchange and commerce.

For a long time in its earlier history, the area of Atarneus had been controlled by Chios, and it is notable that some of Hermias's most determined early detractors come from the island.[12] One prominent antagonist was the historian Theopompus of Chios, who, in an open letter addressed to Philip of Macedon, smeared Hermias as a repulsive person and a dangerously aggressive ruler. On the other side, Hermias's supporters include several Peripatetics in addition to Aristotle; they were indebted to him for his hospitality and so had reason to portray him as an ideal student of philosophy.[13] Aristotle's song for Hermias, then, must be regarded in some respect at least as a piece of propaganda. The fact that Theopompus appears to concede that Hermias has a certain "reputation" (*doxa* at Didymus col. 5.23) that has reached Philip indicates that the tyrant's story was of more than local interest, and when we come to consider the monument Aristotle dedicated to Hermias at Delphi, it will be easy to see that at least part of his agenda in his commemorative acts was to project an image of Hermias and his character that did not reflect badly on his school. As much as acquaintance with Aristotle's other writings may impress us with his integrity, he was of course no impartial witness, and in defending an associate he was also defending himself and his profession. The philosopher himself was hardly immune to slander.[14] We know this best from one of Aristotle's defenders of the early Roman period, Aristocles of Messene in Sicily, a Peripatetic historian of philosophy who was generously excerpted by Eusebius in his *Preparation for the Gospels*. Aristocles found it convenient to deal with the many texts slandering Aristotle by breaking their authors down into those who knew him, those who read those who knew him, and the rest of the crowd.[15] An indication of some themes raised in these writings can be seen in Aristocles' remark that Aristotle incited this resentment "because of his friendships with kings and the sheer superiority of his writings" (*Praep. Ev.* 15.2.11).

The written record nowhere provides a "straight" historical account to which we can turn to detect historical evasions or distortions in our poem.[16] One of our oldest pieces of evidence for Hermias's career is an inscription discovered in Smyrna (modern Izmir), whose tangible reality is not to be confused with objectivity. The inscription records in 33 lines a treaty between that city and Hermias's government at Atarneus.[17] At the time of the treaty, Hermias has already established himself along the coast of Asia Minor around 60 miles north of Chios and seems to be trying to extend his influence to the south by forming an alliance with Erythrae, an Ionian mainland city just opposite Chios. The treaty is thus to be dated sometime when he was in control, that is, 350–342 BCE. The most striking aspect of the inscription is that it is between "the Erythraeans" on one side and "Hermias and his companions" on the other (*hetairoi*, repeated in lines 2–3, 10–11, 14–15, 20–21, 25). Some have inferred from the phrase that Hermias had adopted some form of constitutional rule, in line with the favorable tradition, found in Philodemus and Didymus, that Hermias "softened his tyranny" under the influence of Aristotle and other students of Plato.[18] This idealizing view, powerfully advanced in Werner Jaeger's account, would harmonize with the representation of

Hermias found in a prose eulogy for him that was composed by Aristotle's nephew, Callisthenes of Olynthus (to be discussed below). According to Callisthenes, Hermias died wishing to have word sent "to his friends and companions" that he had done nothing unworthy of philosophy (Didymus col. 6.15–16). We know nothing specific about the form of Hermias's government, but it may be naive to infer a sort of enlightened power-sharing from the inscription's "companions." The term could easily have been a euphemism for the inner council or bodyguard with which ancient autocrats were wont to surround themselves. The poetry of Pindar, for example, shows that the tyrants and monarchs of the archaic period allowed their paid wise men to describe themselves as the "friends" (*philoi*) or "guest-friends" (*xenoi*, see below) or even *hetairoi* of the king.[19] All we can say for sure is that Hermias's "companions" must be seen as a piece of acceptable self-representation by the ruling power. The inscription itself (lines 32–33) directs that a copy be put on display in both cities; Hermias will set up his copy in the sanctuary (*hieron*) of Atarneus, the founding hero of the city (Himerius, *op. cit.*). The placement of the stone in itself asserts the legitimacy of the autocrat.

The texts about Hermias that we have, then, can be divided into two main camps. One side presents him as a cut-throat and tyrant who tried to cover up his crimes and ignoble origins by cultivating famous wise men as toadies; the Peripatetics suggest that he died as a martyr to philosophy and so set the stage for his portrayal by moderns as a fledgling philosopher-king.[20] Historians who are familiar with the full range of evidence can best balance these traditions and give reasons for preferring one side or the other. My own view is that neither extreme will do: the former portrait is clichéd and the latter unconvincingly idealized. In the long tradition of Greek monarchs who included "wise men" in their entourage, the actions of Hermias strike me as particularly intelligible if we regard him as a harbinger of the

Hellenistic age, one of those rulers who were willing—partly out of personal taste and conviction and partly for political reasons—to establish a place for men of culture to gather and so let the world know that civilization flourished in their city.

Although there are basic questions about Hermias that we cannot answer with certainty, to write him off as a retrievable historical individual puts us too out of sympathy with the poem's ambition to recall and praise him. It would certainly be a convenient policy in dealing with archaic Greek poems to bracket historical questions about the proper names they mention; and it is true that it little matters to the force of the poem which portrait of Hermias is historically accurate. Yet once the full import of the poem is in view, it will be clear that a pervasive skepticism takes a metaphysical view fundamentally at odds with Aristotle's and makes us unable to grasp his point. I turn, then, to the evidence for Hermias's fall and his relations with Aristotle, promising only that the reader will understand Aristotle's song better by reading other texts among which it raised its voice and against which it claimed a place.

The End of Hermias: Theopompus's *Letter to Philip*

In 348/7 Plato died, and Aristotle left Athens for a sojourn abroad that would last a dozen years. The two events have often been connected, but we simply do not know why Aristotle left or even whether it was before or after his mentor died. Many have seen significance in the fact that Speusippus and not he was chosen to take over as head of the Academy. The implication that Aristotle's departure signaled some kind of falling out with the Academy has appealed to ironists and critics of the philosopher, but may be a fabrication *post hoc ergo propter hoc*.[21] Speusippus was, after all, Plato's nephew, and we may be wrong to expect that there would have been evident "academic" standards for choosing a successor: the Academy was in many ways unprecedented as an institution of higher learning that was not identified with its lead teacher and so had to find its own way in developing a plan for succession.[22] A quite different explanation for Aristotle's leaving the city is that in 348 Athens became uncomfortable for people with Macedonian connections: that year Philip sacked and razed Olynthus, a one-time Athenian ally, and anti-Macedonian riots broke out in the city. Demosthenes rode such passions to prominence as the leader of a nationalist, anti-Macedonian party and his *Olynthiac Orations* stressed Macedonian iniquity repeatedly to the public.[23] The issue was still a sore point in 306, well after Aristotle's death, when Demochares delivered a speech "Against the Philosophers," charging that Aristotle had collaborated with Philip by indicating which Olynthian families were the richest and ripest for plunder.[24]

Things are a little clearer if we change the question and ask why, when he left, Aristotle first headed for Asia Minor and Hermias. It seems likely that Hermias and Aristotle had prior connections to judge from the fact that Aristotle was, as Didymus puts it, "treated like family" (col. 5.63: οἰκειότατα διέκειτο). The Augustan-age scholar Strabo reports that Hermias had studied in Athens, whether at Plato's Academy or with Aristotle; this is contradicted by a letter attributed to Plato (the Sixth) in which the writer says he has never met Hermias; Platonic epistles are always open to being doubted, but it seems to me that the position of tyrant was not one that could easily be attained or maintained through long absences.[25] Aristotle is more likely to have known Hermias through family connections he had in Atarneus. At the risk of seeming a romantic novelist, I point out some suggestive connections that the tradition records. Some ancient biographies say it was a man from Atarneus called

Proxenus who took charge of Aristotle when his father died; this Proxenus would have been the one who shipped Aristotle off when he was seventeen to study under Plato at Athens. It may be worrisome how aptly named this helping figure is (something like, "ambassador" or "consul"), and we shall later have to consider the possibility of his being a creature of the Aristotle legend. But there can be no doubt that Aristotle was especially close to Hermias; at some point he married Pythias, recorded as the tyrant's niece or adopted daughter. Aristotle and Pythias had a daughter also called Pythias, who is mentioned in the philosopher's will as recorded in Diogenes Laertius. Indeed, that document assigns a certain Nicanor to be guardian to the younger Pythias (whom he eventually married), and an attractive conjecture by C. M. Mulvaney identifies Nicanor as the son of Proxenus of Atarneus and Aristotle's older sister Arimneste.[26]

Apart from these shadowy but possibly close familial ties, the fact that when he went east Aristotle found himself in the company of several sympathetic students of philosophy inclines me to think that he anticipated something like the substantial hospitality Hermias could afford. Hermias made Assos, Atarneus's port city to the west (modern Behramkale in Turkey), available to him and his fellows for research.[27] We do not know who else exactly was in Assos, but Theophrastus, Aristotle's student, collaborator, and eventual successor in the Lyceum, was certainly not far—if not in Assos, then just opposite on Lesbos. Nearby to the northeast, Erastos and Koriskos, two of Aristotle's fellows at the Academy, had gone to teach philosophy in their home town of Sepsis on the slopes of Mount Ida. The Platonic letter mentioned above seems to be the teacher's recommendation of these young scholars to the care of the prince. Aristotle might have also have been accompanied by his nephew Callisthenes. Callisthenes, to whom we will return, is said to have been the grandson of Proxenus of Atarneus and Arimneste.

Whatever it was that first brought philosopher and tyrant together, there is no doubt that Hermias was interested in philosophy and specifically in the philosophy of Plato's school. This shows clearly through a hostile source, Theopompus of Chios, who circulated, apparently toward the end of the 340s, an open letter to King Philip designed to blacken Hermias's reputation. The following extract, quoted in a relatively tattered part of Didymus's papyrus, is spoken with scornful irony:

[Εὐνοῦχος μ(ὲν) γ(ὰρ) ἦν, ὡσαύ]τως δὲ χαρίεις κ(αὶ) φιλ[όκαλ]ος γε[γον]ώς, κ(αὶ) [βάρβ]αρος μ(ὲν) ὢν μ(ετὰ) τῶν Π[λατω]νείων [φ]ιλο[σο]φεῖ, δοῦλος δ(ὲ) γενόμ(εν)ος ἀ[δ]ηφάγοις ζεύγεσιν ἐν ταῖς πανηγύρεσιν ἀγωνίζεται

[although a eunuch (?)], he has become a charming man of taste; and though he is a barbarian he philosophizes with the followers of Plato; born a slave, he competes at the Panhellenic games with chariots that cost so much.[28]

Theopompus's language need not imply that Hermias visited the Academy but could refer to his relations with Aristotle and such fellow philosophers who were near Assos, these being for all practical purposes still "Platonists."[29] His point in any case is that Hermias's philosophizing is pretentious, an attempt to pose as a man of culture when he was in reality a debased barbarian slave. It seems to be true that, whatever Hermias's devotion to ideas may have been, having wise men in one's court was a source of what Pierre Bourdieu called "cultural capital." The fact that Theopompus puts Hermias's philosophizing on a par with his adopting refined manners and competing in the Greek games suggests that philosophizing could be, in the fourth century, what athletics had been in the sixth—a way for autocrats on the margins of the Greek world to present themselves to that world as civilized, enlightened, and legitimate rulers.[30]

Such as it may have been, the school of Atarneus proved short-lived. In 342 Aristotle was summoned by Philip to Pella to take charge of the education of the prince Alexander. He spent seven years at the Macedonian court and finally returned to Athens (after a visit to his hometown) in 335. It was while Aristotle was in Pella in the late 340s that Hermias's always precarious political situation turned perilous. The great king of Persia, now Artaxerxes III Ochus (reigned 358–338), became concerned that Hermias was intriguing with Philip of Macedon; Philip could use Atarneus as a foothold if he decided to attack Asia, as some Greeks were urging him to do (and as Alexander in fact did in 334). It has even been suspected that when Aristotle showed up in Atarneus in 347 he was acting as a secret agent for Philip.[31] In his *Fourth Philippic*, Demosthenes speaks as if there is no doubt that Hermias had entered into a pact with Philip, but all we can say is that such negotiations would have been prudent on Hermias's part in the 340s.[32] His position depended on Persian acquiescence, for Atarneus lay within Dascyleum, the Persian satrapy in northwest Anatolia. Persia had been reasserting itself, notably in the reconquest of Egypt in 343/342 for which expedition the general was Hermias's friend, Mentor of Rhodes. This minor player in our story had been made satrap of Asia Minor and was the brother-in-law of Artabazos, who had been installed as satrap of Dascyleum by Artaxerxes II.[33] Thus it was that Artaxerxes III was able to reach down and use Mentor to trick Hermias and deliver him into his hands in Susa, probably in 341. This event is what attracted Demosthenes' notice, apparently in the time between Hermias's capture and his death.[34] As a rabid opponent of Philip, he was happy to think that Hermias would betray their mad conspiracy; the *Fourth Philippic* calls Hermias "the agent and accomplice of everything which Philip plans against the King [of Persia]" and hopes that "the King will hear the whole business . . . from the very person who carried it out and was responsible for it" (10.32). In the event, Hermias seems to have betrayed nothing, despite being tortured and, on some accounts, mutilated.

Chapter 3

Performance and Occasion

Having noticed some early documents from Hermias's career, we turn to the poetry his death elicited. I begin not with Aristotle's song but with a short epigram he composed in Hermias's memory and an epigram responding to this by a contemporary poet, Theocritus of Chios. To take up these poems, however, is not to move at last from talking about historical context to texts, for these texts propose contexts and occasions for their own performance that we must take into account in interpreting them. This returns me to the argument with my colleague mentioned above, and my position that, although our reconstructions of performative contexts for Greek poems must be tentative and sometimes speculative, we cannot fail to attempt such reconstructions because the words of the poems often call them forth by alluding to their own situations of performance. Unlike most modern Western lyric, Greek lyric poems typically present themselves not as private meditations but as speeches made in social circumstances. They create meaning by projecting a persona by whom such words might be spoken and also occasions at which they might appropriately be delivered. Though Aristotle and his peers were obviously highly literate and literary, poetry was still in his day predominantly an art to be heard, and the occasions at which a song was presented could exert a powerful influence on how it was received and interpreted. For this reason, many Greek songs find ways to construct for themselves preemptively ideal occasions in which they would be the perfect thing to say. Context thus must be considered not only as a hard reality out in the world against which songs echoed—actual places, occasions, and audiences before whom they were performed—but also as a projection of the song by which it hoped to secure a favorable reception. Our approach to occasions and contexts, then, must be partly historical—considering the social realities that gave the words of a poem particular relevance and resonance—and partly rhetorical—allowing that the poetic language could do a great deal to situate the audience and shape their perception of the event.

Context in this sense is integral to interpreting the song for Hermias because it is not too much to say that the genre of a Greek poem was effectively the same as the occasions for which it was appropriate. The question of contexts of performance is thus tied to that of genre, and when we come to consider Aristotle's trial we will have to ask how far his song's meaning and genre changed when the lyric was brought into the courtroom. For the present, however, I want to pursue the idea of context and occasion as something projected by the poem, partly a reflection of the importance of social conventions in a still vital performative culture and partly a rhetorical construct, an imagined world and set of expectations that the performance itself brought about and fulfilled. Epigrams would seem to be easy to discuss in these terms: the obvious context is the physical site where the inscribed stone is set; the occasion nothing particular at all, just the chance of a passerby happening upon the words. It will be seen that things are not so simple on both counts, and I will propose that with Theocritus's counter-epigram and possibly with Aristotle's original we have to allow for the possibility that we are dealing with book-epigrams, fictional representations of stones, locales, and their inscriptions. Considering the verses in these terms will put us in a better position to ask in the following chapter what was the original context or contexts for Aristotle's song for Hermias.

Commemorative Epigrams: Aristotle and Simonides

When Hermias was killed, Aristotle was still in Pella supervising Alexander's education; it is likely that news of his death came quickly to the capital and that it was from Macedon that Aristotle decided to make a public response, indeed to let his view of the matter be heard throughout the Greek world. Diogenes Laertius's *Life* tells us that Aristotle had a statue (*andrias*) erected for Hermias at the sanctuary of Delphi, and quotes the pair of elegiac couplets he had inscribed beneath it:[1]

> τόνδε ποτ' οὐχ ὁσίως παραβὰς μακάρων θέμιν ἁγνὴν
>   ἔκτεινεν Περσῶν τοξοφόρων βασιλεύς,
> οὐ φανερᾷ λόγχῃ φονίοις ἐν ἀγῶσι κρατήσας,
>   ἀλλ' ἀνδρὸς πίστει χρησάμενος δολίου.

> This man was once upon a time impiously and sinfully
>   slain by the king of the bow-bearing Persians,
> winning his victory not in an open test of deadly strength
>   but by trust placed in a treacherous man.

A biographical question, naive and unanswerable though it may be, may provide the quickest way into the specificity of this verse: In view of the fact that Hermias and Aristotle had been so close, do we find the tone of the couplets too cool? Verse epitaphs were certainly able to strike a plangent, personal note that is often the more forceful for being compressed; but here Aristotle deliberately focuses not on the loss of his close friend and benefactor but on his despicable enemies. The text stresses the king's impiety and conflates his execution of Hermias with the treachery of Mentor. Context counts for much in Greek poetry, even for epigrams meant to last for generations, and it seems that this poem was situated in a Panhellenic sanctuary primarily to broadcast the perfidy of Persia.

Aristotle's public tone, more indignant than grieving, should not mask the deep bond that this dedication represents. We can see this if we understand that the relationship between Aristotle and Hermias was of a very special kind that the Greeks called *xenia*, a form of ritualized friendship greatly illuminated in Gabriel Herman's 1987 study. Traditionally translated as "sacred hospitality" or the "guest-host relationship," *xenia* named a broad set of mutual obligations between any benefactor and beneficiary, obligations that were underwritten by no less a god than *Zeus xenios*, "Zeus the god of guest-friends." Herman points out that the services typically rendered by *xenoi* could include setting up funerary stones for one's *xenos* and composing poems to express one's affection. Although it was impossible for Hermias to get a proper burial among family and friends, Aristotle could do the next best thing and erect a kind of cenotaph for him. In addition, a monument afforded a blank slate for verse, and so Aristotle took the opportunity to execute a *xenos*' duty to set the record straight and spell out just who the villain was in this episode. Pindar, a supreme singer of the ties of hospitality, could have been describing Aristotle's agenda: "I am a *xenos*: warding off blame that obscures, I come to my dear friend as with streams of water to proclaim his true glory" (ξεῖνός εἰμι · σκοτεινὸν ἀπέχων ψόγον, / ὕδατος ὧτε ῥοὰς φίλον ἐς ἄνδρ' ἄγων / κλέος ἐτήτυμον αἰνέσω).[2] Delphi was an obvious choice for these purposes: seat of one of Greece's most famous oracles and host of the prestigious Pythian games, it attracted visitors from the entire Greek world and a little beyond. There they could read—or have read to them by guides—inscriptions on the monuments that adorned the sanctuary and lined the road leading to Apollo's temple. One of the examples Herman mentions, a votive plaque put up by Xenophon of Athens in a treasury built by the Athenians along Delphi's sacred way, suggests in the name of its dedicatee how deeply the ethic lay: "For Proxenos, for he was a *xenos*." In addition, Delphi had taken on an extra symbolic role as a symbol of Greek unity in the face of Persian invasions in the early fifth century. Hence Aristotle's condemnation of Eastern treachery was appropriate to the locale.

The context in which this poem was exposed is reflected in its metrical form, and here I think of form not only from the point of view of artistic shaping but also as a device facilitating the circulation and survival of poetry. Of course, Aristotle's choice of elegiac couplets was dictated by a centuries-old tradition of Greek epitaphs; but tradition settled on elegiacs for these purposes with reason. First of all, elegiacs are easy to memorize: their dactylic rhythms have much in common with the great warhorse of Greek verse, the hexameter, but elegiacs are even more regular in closing each couplet with an identical heptasyllabic rhythmic unit. For the same reason, they are easy to read, and because they require no melody to be recited, they can be re-performed after being read or heard once or twice. The result is that, though the stone may stay in place, its message can be widely dispersed by passersby. In these respects, Aristotle's inscribed *verse* for Delphi is fundamentally different from the *song* he composed to Virtue, even though we call both "poems." The *words* of a *song* might be read off a page, as in the Didymus papyrus, but one will not be able to perform it without learning the melody; without this melody, the rhythms of the song—which were unique to that song—are far less easily memorized or even perceived. I shall return to this basic difference in the two types of rhythmical composition when I come to Aristotle's song, but for the present observe that not only is a poet's choice of form made in light of what convention and context demand but that convention and context have favored certain forms because of the way they are able to move among people. To maintain a sense of song and poetry as machines for social communication, we ought not to lump together every text that can be metrically scanned in some broad and homogeneous notion of "poetry."[3] It was as readable, recitable *verse* that Aristotle's mini-message was memorized by readers or those within earshot of readers and carried away from this international meeting place.

Re-performance is also built into the rhetoric of the piece: as phrased, the inscription can be taken in two ways, as a label attached to an object on the spot or as a script for a more portable speech act. As a label, as information carved on a statue base, the stone "speaks" the verse in the sense that it imparts to the viewer the story behind the monument; such "speaking monuments" are very common in the rhetoric of Greek tombstones. But the addition of a little particle, "once upon a time . . . " (ποτε), which is found in other commemorative inscriptions, makes the words performable in another way.[4] The adverb transforms the verse from a label affixed to a stone into something that can be said by an onlooker at some distant time, indeed something that can be said on an indefinite number of occasions in the future. The reader no longer speaks in the name of the stone, vocalizing its message, but adopts the persona of a local exegete or tourist who may stand before the monument—the deictic force of "this" in v. 1 is strong in Greek—and declare what it is. This aspect of the text makes every reading of it a re-play, a re-dedication of the original act of inscription that can be re-enacted with no end in sight. As performed, the words are moreover not only a speech act but something of a curse. It is worth recalling that epigrams were designed to be recited aloud rather than silently read, and the Greeks were always aware that their word for glory (κλέος) meant "something heard"; "renown" meant re-naming and re-hearing. Hence every reader/performer of this text ensured that the name of Persia lived in infamy, her impiety literally resounding again.

Aristotle thus contrived for his Delphic monument a message that was at once authoritatively rooted to the spot and re-playable, even portable. Our last observation is that it may have been fictional as well. Consider, for example, the epithet "bow-bearing": this may be taken to hint at Persian cowardice, if the bow be given its traditional force as a symbol of unheroic fighting—the antithesis of Homeric warfare at close quarters with swords and spears. On the other hand, gods can be "bow-bearing" as well, and the epithet is found of divinities in earlier poetry, including Delphi's own Apollo. The choice between these two flavors of the epithet is between reading Aristotle's epigram as an attempt to transcribe a historical event in conventional form and language or as an attempt to extend and innovate within the tradition of monumental epigrams. In favor of the latter possibility is the fact that the same form of the epithet is found in the same metrical position in an epigram attributed to Simonides, Greece's most famous memorializing lyric poet. "Bow-bearing" also modifies the Persians (called "Medes" in fifth-century parlance) in a pair of elegiacs that purport to celebrate their defeat by the Athenians at the river Eurymedon in 468 BCE:

Οἵδε παρ' Εὐρυμέδοντά ποτ' ἀγλαὸν ὤλεσαν ἥβην
μαρνάμενοι Μήδων τοξοφόρων προμάχοις

αἰχμηταί, πεζοί τε καὶ ὠκυπόρων ἐπὶ νηῶν·
κάλλιστον δ' ἀρετῆς μνῆμ' ἔλιπον φθίμενοι.

> These men once upon a time lost their youth by gleaming Eurymedon
> contending with the champions of the bow-bearing Medes,
> warriors, both foot soldiers and on swift-faring ships;
> they left behind the finest memorial of *aretê* when they died.

The unresolved debate about whether these lines, which are preserved only in a late anthology, were actually inscribed on a monument or were what Page calls "a later literary exercise" only makes clearer that the "memorial" (μνῆμα) left behind at the end is figurative; more than any stone that may have stood near Eurymedon, it is the verse itself that works as a "reminder" (μνημεῖον) of these excellent dead.[5]

Aristotle's epigram too, although the deictic pronoun leading off the poem would seem to tie it to a stone, has undoubtedly had life apart from "this" monument, circulating in oral re-performance and making Persian perfidy resound among hearers who would never set eyes on the stone (as it continues to do this day). Once the "this" is allowed to be fictional, one might question whether there was a "real" stone at all, for no trace of this monument has ever been found. In other words, we may underestimate the power of Aristotle's rhetoric when we assume as realists that some actual monument, now lost, lies behind Diogenes' quotation rather than crediting the poetic "this" of the verse with generating our belief in a stone on which the text was first inscribed. After all, in the fourth century, Greek poetry had begun to explore the genre of artificial and consciously ironic "book epigrams" that feature so prominently in Hellenistic literature.[6] In a book epigram the "Here lies ... ," which functions as true a deictic in inscribed epitaphs, becomes a conventional marker of the genre, its meaning ironically reversed to "not here," "not on this page." I raise the issue not because there is a particular reason to doubt Diogenes' word, but to call attention to the fact that Aristotle's language in the poem is at once thoroughly conventional and at the same time capable of shaping our conceptions of the world that it ostensibly points to.[7] If occasion and context can powerfully affect the meaning given a poem, poetic language can do a good deal to determine the contexts and occasions we imagine for it as well—almost to the point of producing a stone out of thin air.

Book Epigrams: Theocritus of Chios

Whether it was ever inscribed or not, Aristotle's epigram would have spread at least as widely by passing from mouth to mouth as by being read in situ. By either route, the brief and pointed poem made its way across the Aegean and came to the attention of a Chian politician and poet called Theocritus. No friend of Hermias or of the philosopher, he issued a sharp reply in kind:

Ἑρμίου εὐνούχου τε καὶ Εὐβούλου τόδε δούλου
    σῆμα κενὸν κενόφρων τεῦξεν Ἀριστοτέλης,
ὃς διὰ τὴν ἀκρατῆ γαστρὸς φύσιν εἵλετο ναίειν
    ἀντ' Ἀκαδημείας βορβόρου ἐν προχοαῖς.

For Hermias, the eunuch and slave of Eubulus
    empty-headed Aristotle made this empty tomb;
doing honor to his unrestrained belly, he chose to dwell
    in outpourings of slime rather than in the Academy.

The elegiacs, preserved for us by Didymus and Diogenes, among others, are a faux-epitaph, an alternate inscription for Hermias's monument.[8] Posing as an inscription on the same ("this") cenotaph on which Aristotle wrote, Theocritus's epigram is a kind of graffito scrawled over the original. At the same time, the verses are crafted so as to be rewarding in oral performance. The stunning first line has nine of fourteen syllables composed of *ou-* sounds, and the second is neatly divided between *k*'s and nasals in the first half and *t*'s and sibilants in the second. One assumes such a flourish of assonance could sound savagely taunting. It is also noteworthy that Theocritus's opening alliteration, with the line-ending *doulou*, picks up the *doliou* ("deceptive") that ended Aristotle's epigram, suggesting that his own text would "play" very neatly if it followed a recitation of that verse.

Theocritus's is a "book epigram," a fictional epitaph never inscribed; he was known as a satirist and his witticisms were collected in a book by an otherwise unknown figure called Bryon or Ambryon.[9] Literariness can be contagious, for when Theocritus took it up he ensured that Aristotle's verse—whether or not an original was actually carved anywhere—entered the world of performative epigrams as well. As such, both texts became subject to minor variation or adaptation in re-performance. For example, it is a notable detail that Theocritus says Aristotle's poem was on a tomb (a *sêma*), whereas Diogenes speaks of a statue (*andrias*).[10] We should not put much weight on either as historical evidence: there is no reason to assume that Theocritus's *sêma* represents eye-witness testimony; conversely, Diogenes' "statue" may be an inference from the initial τόνδε, "this man," he found in his version of the text. Complicating any attempt to settle the question is the fact that we are examining the operations of a highly traditional language of poetic commemoration in which words and phrases of a given metrical shape tended to be easily substitutable for each other in a line. For an audience of such poetry of variety-within-limits, it made little difference whether Theocritus was misremembering or modifying his precursor text in order to set up a pun. *Sêma* suits Theocritus's second verse better than would the roughly synonymous and isometric *mnêma* ("memorial") because one did speak in Greek metaphor of an empty *sêma*, a cenotaph, but less readily of an "empty" memorial or statue. There are in fact visible traces of the oral circulation that these epitaphs enjoyed in the transmission of Theocritus's text. Consider, for example, the minor variations in the way its first two lines are recorded. Diogenes Laertius, citing "Ambryon's" *On Theocritus* gives (5.11):

Ἑρμίου εὐνούχου ἠδ' Εὐβούλου ἅμα δούλου
σῆμα κενὸν κενόφρων τεῦξεν Ἀριστοτέλης

Of Hermias, eunuch and slave to Eubulus at once,
    empty-headed Aristotle wrought an empty tomb [*sêma*].

Didymus, citing the same *On Theocritus* but attributing it to "Bryon," gives:

Ἑρμίο[υ] εὐ[νούχου τ]ε κ(αὶ) Ε[ὐβούλου τόδε] δούλου
σῆμα κ[ενὸν] κενό[φρων] θῆκεν Ἀριστο]τέλης

Of Hermias, eunuch and slave to Eubulus, this
    is the empty tomb [*sêma*] empty-headed Aristotle erected.

Eusebius, quoting Aristocles, gives:

Ἑρμείου εὐνούχου τε καὶ Εὐβούλου τόδε δούλου
μνῆμα κενὸν κενόφρων θῆκεν Ἀριστοτέλης

> Of Hermeias [sic], eunuch and slave to Eubulus, this
> is the empty monument [*mnêma*] empty-headed Aristotle
> erected.

Among several small differences, the sources do not settle whether Theocritus spoke of Hermias's memorial (*mnêma*, Aristocles) or tomb (*sêma*, Didymus and Diogenes).[11] Didymus and Diogenes may have found the latter reading in the treatise "On Theocritus." But their versions of v. 2 diverge on whether Aristotle "wrought" or provided the tomb (τεῦξεν) or "erected" it (θῆκεν). As is quite understandable in a text so much "in the air," there is also instability in the deictic language: Aristotle's "this man" becomes "this one" (τόδε, i.e., this tomb) in Aristocles and probably in Didymus, whereas in Diogenes the deictic disappears altogether under the relatively colorless adverb ἅμα ("at once"). Where there is no object in view to which deixis points, substitutions arise easily in this formula-heavy genre, especially when sources quote poetry from memory rather than seeking out and finding the spot in a papyrus roll. The kinds of variation noted here are less likely to result from a scribe miscopying letters than from a performer adapting or slightly misremembering phrases. Such "oral variants" characteristically preserve the meter and general sense of the original in more or less the same words without being resolvable into a clear hierarchy of archetype and copies. The textual transmission of Theocritus's poem thus indicates that it enjoyed a degree of oral performance.

The fictionality of these epitaphs, that is to say their lack of connection to any original source (whether a stone at Delphi or a page of *On Theocritus*), lets them change slightly as they are reused. Partly because his poem has been removed from the historical context that would have limited its reference, Theocritus's meaning is underdetermined at points, notably in his final insult and in the word βορβόρου just before the poem's end. The difficulty turns, indeed, on whether to take βορβόρου as a proper or a common noun, a decision that in turn determines how we date and understand the epigram as a whole. The eminently well-read Plutarch tells us, when he quotes the end of the poem, that *Borborus* was the name of a river in Macedonia (*On Exile* 603C); in that case, the poem would refer to Aristotle's leaving Hermias and "the Platonists" at Assos to take up with Philip and Alexander in 342. But as Michael Flower brings out in an excellent discussion, we are not bound to accept this unconfirmed geographical tidbit. Writing around four centuries after Aristotle, Plutarch may well have been repeating an ad hoc fiction designed to help make sense of the epigram as it aged.[12] Printing lower-case βορβόρου, as I have done, suggests a different context: Aristotle is being mocked for leaving Athens to go to Atarneus in 347, the "outpourings *of slime*" being the debased patronage of Hermias. One point in favor of this reading is that Theocritus's poem becomes a more direct response to Aristotle's if it closes by insulting Hermias and the philosopher together. The connotations of the common noun are consonant with this, since in the vocabulary of the sacred mysteries, to lie in slime or mud was a traditional image for the woeful fate of a non-initiate.[13] The image would be a direct riposte to the pretentiousness of Hermias's philosophizing as Theopompus represented it in his *Letter to Philip*.[14] Page takes a similar view of βορβόρου, but for chronological reasons I do not agree when he adds that the religious connotations of the word hinted at Aristotle's alleged impiety. Theocritus's parodic epitaph would have had most point if it were composed, like its target poem, while the events of the late 340s BCE were still fresh in people's minds; but it appears that the charges against Aristotle surfaced several years later, whether after Alexander's accession in 335 or, more likely, his death in 323.[15] Lower-case βορβόρου puts the parody closer to the death of Hermias in 341 and Aristotle's original. On this interpretation, προχοαῖς, ("outpourings") has a possible *double entendre:* rather than referring to a particular river, it might suggest the hospitality a wandering philosopher requires in images of "pouring out" of toasts and libations.[16] Aristotle abandoned the civilized, Hellenic precincts of Plato (as Theocritus is willing to characterize the Academy for the purposes of this epigram) to revel in the polluted streams of Hermias's hospitality; it is further implied that this hospitality is uncivilized, for βορβόρου chimes with βαρβάρου, "barbarian."

Some interpreters accept "outpourings of slime" here but interpret the insult differently, as intimating that there was sexual impropriety in the relationship between Aristotle and "the eunuch."[17] That charge was certainly floated in the ancient sources (e.g., Diogenes Laertius 5.3), but here I think it would, so to speak, muddy the waters; the basic moral failing that Theocritus imputes to Aristotle in this poem is gluttony, along with the hypocrisy to disguise it with fine language. The word for "belly" in v. 3, slightly indecorous in Greek verse as in English, is a traditional poetic symbol for the body's basic needs that can drive even a hero to undignified acts of self-preservation.[18] In the version of verse 3 recorded in Aristocles and printed by Lloyd-Jones and Parsons, the word helps make a noteworthy phrase: Aristotle left Athens "on account of his unrestrained belly" (διὰ τὴν ἀκρατῆ γαστρὸς φύσιν). The language for lack of restraint (ἀκρατῆ ... φύσιν) comes out of fourth-century philosophical ethics, which debated the nature and causes of being unable to control oneself (ἀκρασία).[19] (It may be significant that the Peripatetic Aristocles is the one who preserves this philosophically inflected reading.)[20] Pairing this high-culture term with the common "belly" makes a phrase that paints Aristotle as *philosophe* and vagabond at once; the deliberately incongruous language exposes the euphemistic rhetoric by which itinerant intellectuals were wont to cloak their "unmentionable" needs in high ethical terms.

Theocritus's little poem thus fits squarely in a satirical tradition that mocked sages who abandoned the cultural centers of Greece for distant courts and hospitality of a not altogether spiritual kind. The theme was struck at the end of the fifth century, when Aristophanes teased the tragic poet Agathon for retiring to "the golden isles" of Macedon and the patronage of Archelaus (*Frogs* 50).[21] Earlier still, the archetypal "intellectual for sale" had been Simonides of Ceos: an avowed consort of tyrants in the late sixth century—for whom he composed songs celebrating the victories that they, like Hermias, won in the games—Simonides was remembered as the first poet to charge money for songs. The life of a wandering intellectual that Aristotle led in the years following Plato's death might appear to critics to have much in common with the ambiguous career of Simonides, who was both counted among the Seven Sages and given the nickname κίμβιξ ("greedy") for the way he capitalized on his wisdom.[22] The charge of excessive appetite can be found laid against the Stagirite already in his lifetime by Cephisodorus: Aristocles reports that Cephisodorus, a "pupil" of Isocrates, criticized Aristotle as self-indulgent and a glutton, as did other of Aristotle's detractors.[23]

Texts and Things: Herodotus on Hermotimus

Theocritus's verse activates a tradition of blame epigrams to paint Aristotle as a hypocrite philosopher enslaved to low desires. The way he inflects this tradition in fourth-century ethical terms suggests that "slime" is not primarily a sexual metaphor, and here we may as well address the delicate question raised by some of our sources: Was Hermias a eunuch or wasn't he? The question is not altogether facetious; trying to give a definite yes-or-no answer is a fair epitome of the historicist's quest for "the truth," even as the desire to gaze upon the *Ding wie es eigentlich gewesen ist* can put the historian in the ridiculous posture of peeking under Hermias's chiton. Theocritus's statement that Hermias was a eunuch is, technically speaking, contemporary evidence, as is the description by Theopompus of Chios.[24] I have noted that Chians were no friends of Hermias, and so even early and corroborated evidence can be disputed. But the fact that Pythias is variously described as Hermias's niece or adopted daughter suggests that her existence had to be squared with some acknowledged reproductive impairment. A different direction is suggested by Mulvaney, who brought up a fascinating parallel for these charges in a story Herodotus tells about Hermotimus of Pedasa, a city a little further down the Ionian coast from Atarneus (*Histories* 8.104–6).[25] Captured in war, Hermotimus was sold to a Chian named Panionius who had him castrated and sold as a slave. Eventually, Hermotimus rose to become the chief of Xerxes' eunuchs and from this position tracked down Panionius in Atarneus and got his revenge. Mulvaney suggests that the nexus slave/eunuch/Atarneus is the "germ" of later slanders against Hermias, whose name is close to Hermotimus and whose life, we may add, was also a rags-to-riches story. We do not have enough evidence to disentangle what, if any, are the connections between the tales, but the phenomenon it points to inspires caution: it is obvious that real facts may become legend in the course of their being selectively recounted and shaped; but it is also true conversely that legends may give rise to historical facts by inspiring legend-like behavior in real historical agents.

Because these epigrams proliferated beyond their immediate contexts, we can no more fix the truth behind them than affix them to an actual stone. The elusiveness of the referents pointed at by these deictic verses is like the undiscoverability of what we can call, taking a euphemism from Freudian linguists, Hermias's "master signified." This elusiveness is partly due to the texts' rhetorical posturing; but we should not ignore the historical forces that are at work to remove us from contact with the past. This can be seen if we consider one final stone from Delphi. Even apart from its prominence as a cultural center of the eastern Mediterranean, Delphi made sense as a place for Aristotle to site his monument to Hermias because of the good connections he enjoyed there. Aristotle had conducted on-site archival research into the victors at Delphi's centuries-old Pythian games. Working with his nephew Callisthenes, he sifted through local records and compiled a Πυθιονικῶν ἀναγραφή, a "List of Pythian Victors."[26] Probably sometime in the 330s, the ruling body at Delphi officially recognized the pair for their labors and erected a stele which still survives bearing an inscription thanking them. We hear from Aelian (14.1) that the honor was later rescinded, and scholars have connected this information with the fact that the stone was discovered in Delphi broken in pieces and at the bottom of a well.[27] If a change in the political winds was the reason that Aristotle's monument was broken, we may see why it fell to the "book" tradition to keep his Delphic epigram alive. In any case, the shattered μνῆμα for Aristotle and Callisthenes provides a tangible and eloquent image of the real danger and violence at the root of these tales, as well as of the processes of propaganda and counter-propaganda that have served as a conduit to bring these realities down to us, even if only in fragments.

The next chapter turns to Aristotle's song for Hermias and the question of its possible performative contexts. It begins with one other extraordinary contemporary document, a prose encomium to Hermias written by Callisthenes of Olynthus. Callisthenes's text, which can be read as if it were designed to complement his uncle's song, has led some scholars to posit that both were first performed in a private ceremony held by Aristotle and a few of Hermias's close friends. Not all the details of this philosophers' rite of remembrance can be accepted with confidence. But even if we cannot be sure of retrieving the "original" context and function of Aristotle's song, comparison with Callisthenes brings out the different meanings that it seems to take on when set in different contexts. Such a perspective will then enable us to say whether the story of the song being put on trial is plausible.

Chapter 4

Performance and Context

We can call Aristotle's hymn an occasional poem in the sense that it was composed to respond to a particular set of circumstances to which its text makes reference. But it may have been occasional in a stronger sense, in having been written to be performed at a specific time and place, for a particular event involving a specific group of people. The idea has been hard to dismiss since Wilamowitz's 1893 work, *Aristoteles und Athen*, in which the great Hellenist mooted the idea that Aristotle wrote the song for a private commemorative ceremony among the Peripatetics. Wilamowitz was struck by the fact that Aristotle barely named the honoree of his song (proper names again) and concluded that the hymn must have been accompanied by a prose encomium giving out more information about Hermias.[1] The suggestion seemed to be confirmed some ten years later when the Didymus papyrus was discovered, for Didymus had included an extract from a prose work in praise of Hermias written by Callisthenes, Aristotle's nephew. D. E. W. Wormell, in a fundamental study of the traditions about Hermias, drew the pieces together: "Aristotle instituted a memorial ceremony in honor of his dead friend, at which the Hymn was sung. It was this service to Hermias's memory which was later used as evidence of impiety by Aristotle's enemies.... There can be no doubt that Callisthenes' *Encomium* was written for this occasion."[2] The inference is attractive, but it is well not to pass over the soft spots in the case. One small detail, though worth pointing out because it touches on the question of genre, is that when Callisthenes' composition is identified as an "encomium," the basis for this is essentially a gap in the papyrus where the work is introduced (in the first line of the quotation below). Scholars quickly proposed that the word ἐγκώμιον would fit the size of the gap and make sense, but other supplements are thinkable. One notable candidate is σύγγραμμα ("composition"), suggested by the first editors of the papyrus and printed by its most recent ones.[3] Filling the lacuna with σύγγραμμα, a general word for prose compositions, would leave open the possibility that Callisthenes, who was a historian as well as a friend of Hermias, composed his account as something other than a ceremonial eulogy. It may have been a history or a biographical essay that was intended to be circulated through written copies (συγγράμματα) rather than performed at a singular event. Moreover, even if we could be sure that Didymus called Callisthenes' text an ἐγκώμιον, this is not of course per se evidence for how Callisthenes' contemporaries would have slotted his work into fourth-century literary categories.

Greek literature of the fourth century BCE is marked by an explosion of new forms of written prose, notably including experiments in prose eulogy.[4] The novelty of prose encomia is made explicit in Isocrates' *Evagoras*, written for a pro-Greek king of Cyprus who died in 374. In the prologue to this work, Isocrates proclaims that his text constitutes a new form of writing that breaks with the tradition of having poets eulogize the noble dead. The tradition had left writers of prose encomia with only figures from myth or the legendary past to celebrate, and so *Evagoras* broke new ground by "encomiazing in prose the excellence (*aretê*) of a man" (8: ἀνδρὸς ἀρετὴν διὰ λόγων ἐγκωμιάζειν) who was not from the distant past but who had just died. The innovativeness of *Evagoras* is highlighted by its artificial stance as a faux-oration, complete with a fictional occasion implied in its opening address to Nicocles, "whom I behold as you honor your father's grave."[5] Isocrates sometimes exaggerates his artistic greatness, but even his detractors allow that his claim about the novelty of prose encomia is tenable. An example from around 360 is Xenophon's celebration of Agesilaus, his friend and a notable Spartan general: the *Agesilaus* was an attempt, as Xenophon put it, to execute "the difficult task of writing a worthy account of his excellence and fame" (1.1: ἀρετῆς τε καὶ δόξης οὐ ῥᾴδιον ἄξιον ἔπαινον γράψαι). Callisthenes was thus working in newly opened fields when he wrote a prose encomium for the recently deceased king of Atarneus. Arnaldo Momigliano notes that Callisthenes' *Hermias* fits beside not only Isocrates' *Evagoras* but also Theopompus's encomia of Philip and Alexander of Macedon. One should perhaps add *The Funeral-feast of Plato* written by Speusippus, the head of the Academy, which has been thought to have had a eulogistic function. The times were also ripe for cross-fertilization, however, and it may be that the *Funeral-feast* was also bound up with the literature recounting symposia in prose (inspired by Socratic *Symposia*, of the sort written by Plato and Xenophon), making for an extra-rich generic mix.[6]

In the background of all this literary experimentation is a persistent ethical norm, which was evidently widely respected by audiences, that the forms of praising men that are appropriate in a given case depend on the status of those praised, and status includes not only greatness of birth or of accomplishment but also whether they are living or dead and whether they belong to the present or the past. The conventions governing "literary" practices in this revolutionary time for prose remain tied to basic religious considerations of what human mortality may claim as its own and what it may aspire to.

Witnesses: Callisthenes' *Hermias*

The extract from Callisthenes that Didymus chose to copy into his text reads very much as if, as Wormell suggests, it was the climax of the piece.[7]

ἀλλὰ γ(ὰρ) κ(αὶ) Καλλισθέν[ης........]τι συν-   Col. 5.64
τάξας περὶ αὐτοῦ π[ολλά τε λέγει ἄλ]λα κ(αὶ) [ταυ-]   65
τί· Οὐ μόνον τοι[οῦτος ἦν ἑκὰς ὢν ἔτι] κιν-
δύνων, ἀλλὰ κ(αὶ) πλησίον κ[αταστὰς ἔθ' ὅ]μοιος
ὢν διετέλει, κ(αὶ) μεγί[στην τότε πίστι]ν ἰ-
δωκε τῆς ἀρετῆς ἐν αὐτ[ῶι τῶι θανάτ]ωι. οἱ
μ(ὲν) γ(ὰρ) βάρβαροι θεωρο(ῦν)τ[ες ἐθαύμαζον
    αὐτοῦ] τὴν   70
ἀνδρείαν. ὁ γ[ο(ῦν)] βασιλ[εὺς οὐδὲν π(αρ') αὐτοῦ
    πυνθ]α-
νόμ(εν)ος ἕτερον ἀλλ' ἢ τοὺς αὐτο(ὺς) λόγο(υς)
    ἀκούων,   6.1
ἀγασθεὶς την ἀνδρείαν κ(αὶ) τ(ὴν) βεβαιότητα τῶν
τρόπ(ων), διενοήθη μ(ὲν) αὐτὸν ὅλως ἀφεῖναι νομίζων
[γ]ενόμ(εν)ον αὐτῶι φίλον πάντων ἔσεσθαι χρησι-
μώτατον· ἀντιπιπτόντων δ(ὲ) Βαγώου κ(αὶ)   5
Μέντορος, διὰ τὸ φθονεῖν κ(αὶ) φοβεῖσθαι μὴ (πρω-)
τεύσηι μᾶλλον ὧδ' αὐτῶν ἀφεθείς, ταύτην μ(ὲν)
πάλι<ν> μετεβάλετο τ[ὴ]ν γνώμην, δικάζων δ(ὲ)
τῶν γιγνομ(έν)ων παρ[' αὐτ]ῶι κακοπαθιῶν ἄμοι-
ρον αὐτὸν ἐποίησε δ[ιὰ τὴν] ἀρετ(ήν)· ἡ μ(ὲν) ο(ὖν)
    τοιαύτη   10

Performance and Context

μετριότης ὑπῆρ[ξε παρ]ὰ τῶν ἐχθρῶν παρα-
δοξ[οτά]τ[η κ(αὶ)] π[ολὺ παρὰ τ]ὸν τῶν βαρβάρων
τρό[πον, ὁ δ' ἤδη] τελ[ευτᾶ]ν μέλλ[ω]ν, φιλι-
.[. . . . .]ον [ἐπικαλ]εσάμ(εν)ος ἄλλ[ο] μ(ὲν)
[οὐδὲν εἶπεν, ἐπ]έσκ[η]ψε δ' α]ὐτῶι πρὸ[ς] τοὺ[ς φ]ί-   15
[λους κ(αὶ) τοὺς ἑ]ταίρο(υς) [ἐπι]στέλλειν, ὡς οὐδ[ὲ]ν
ἀ[(νά)ξιο]ν ε[ἴ]η φιλοσοφία[ς οὐδ' ἄ]σχημον δ(ια)πεπρα-
γμ[(έν)]ος.»

And Callisthenes composed a kind of [. . . . .] about him in which he said a number of things including this: "Not only did he comport himself this way when far from danger, but he remained the same when threatened. And he gave the greatest proof of his *aretê* at the moment of death. Now the barbarians marveled at his courage as they watched him. And the king, getting nothing more out of him than the same responses, was awestruck at his courage and firmness (βεβαιότητα, 6.2) of character and considered letting him off completely, thinking that he would be the most useful of all his friends; but Bagoas and Mentor opposed this course through envy and fear that if released he would become superior to them, and the king changed his mind back. But on account of Hermias's manliness (*aretê*) the king ordered him to be spared the usual tortures. Now such moderateness coming from an enemy was most unexpected, and indeed is contrary to the barbarian character; and when he was about to die he called φιλι[. . . . . .] and asked nothing more than that he send word to his friends and companions (*hetairous*) that he had done nothing unworthy of philosophy or unseemly to the very end.

The extract seems equally suitable for performance as a eulogy and as a piece of artistic prose (a σύγγραμμα) designed to be circulated independently of any ceremony. The alternatives are of course not exclusive, for the scripted remarks could have been subsequently "published" by circulating copies among lettered friends, in the way that Isocrates' "orations" circulated. Jacoby suggests that as a prose work Callisthenes' composition would have been aptly titled "*Hermias* or *On Aretê*," noting that this is the style in which the dialogues of Aristotle were titled.[8] In favor of Wilamowitz's suggestion that Callisthenes' work was intended for a private ceremony is that it resonates so well with Aristotle's hymn: both texts focus on the theme of *aretê*, and both suggest a sharp contrast between Greek and "barbarian" mores; both conclude by praising Hermias and steadfastness. While we may be unable to determine the original genre of Callisthenes' *Hermias*—that is to say, its original performative context—posing the question at least makes clear how closely Greek genre is intertwined with context. This is not simply a pedantic problem of classification, for our answer will determine whether we read Callisthenes' and Aristotle's works as independent compositions or as a diptych, one being designed to be interpreted in light of the other.

We can at least certainly say that the extract from Callisthenes represents another early (he died ca. 327) strand in the battle to define Hermias. As such, it interacts with other accounts that contradict Callisthenes on what exactly Hermias suffered in the end. The basic conflict is that Theopompus (115 *FGrH* F 291) says Hermias "endured brutal outrages to his body and was impaled," whereas Callisthenes says that he was accorded some exemption from Persian torture because of the manly virtue, the *aretê*, he displayed (6.8–10).[9] I cannot sort out what lies behind these Greek reports of Persian barbarity, but it can be revealing to ask on what authority Callisthenes reports Hermias's last words. In reply to those who wonder how an authentic report might have been carried from Persia to Greece,

Jeffrey Rusten suggests that a messenger from Philip could have passed through Artaxerxes' court and brought Hermias's words back. This person's name would then presumably be what is missing in the papyrus after φιλι- in 6.14; of course a number of (proper) names beginning in "Ph" have been suggested to fill the lacuna. But it seems at least equally possible that, as Harding thinks, Callisthenes' report was a "rhetorical fantasy" of a great man's dying words; after all, famous last words were already a popular anecdotal form (such as "I leave lest Athens should sin twice against Philosophy").[10] Herodotus's story of Croesus quoting Solon while on the pyre (*Histories* 1.86-87) and Cyrus's being moved to clemency at this point suggests that the image of the Persian tyrant touched by the spectacle of philosophical suffering was an archetype.[11] Considering that Callisthenes does not "source" his account of Hermias's end, we may identify his audience with the "companions" (6.14) to whom the report is being conveyed from Susa. Whether or not Callisthenes wrote for a particular ceremony, he seems to have written for a particular audience, a restricted group who knew each other and at least indirectly knew Hermias; before such a group the historian felt no need to avow his trustworthiness or to disarm skepticism.

With this scenario in the background, we may further characterize the audience Aristotle aimed at by considering again the functional differences between a lyric (μέλος) and a reciteable verse (ἔπος).[12] As said above, a *song* for Hermias was something quite different from elegiac verses, inscribed or not, and entailed a more restricted audience by its very form. A song is memorizable in a quite different way from stichic or distichic verse: the words of a Greek song were held together— they "scanned" metrically—only by the melody unique to that song; one does not recite μέλη, one sings them. Elegiacs by contrast have a regular, audible rhythm that is perceptible without melody; as in an English verse like iambic pentameter, their rhythm depends only on the normal prosody of the words so that an elegiac couplet can be "read off the page" satisfactorily. It follows further that an elegy can be transmitted by writing it down: it takes only literacy and a little familiarity with verse to "operate" the text. A song, however, has to be heard to be learned. Because the Greeks had not yet developed an adequate musical notation, a tune (μέλος) was not like an epitaph you could leave out in the sun for passersby to read; a potential singer of the song had to hear it from another singer. This means that, simple as its melody may have been, Aristotle's song was bound to a more restricted audience than an epitaph at a Panhellenic sanctuary. A song, moreover, passes most easily within a like-minded group, or among extended groups that are sympathetic enough with one another to sing to each other (at least at first, when it is still a potential performance piece and not yet a precious historical document that is carefully copied out and saved). If this is so, it is understandable that Aristotle felt no need to name Hermias directly in the song, whereas his name was likely to have featured in the title of a prose σύγγραμμα about him.[13] A final respect in which lyric differs from epigram is in its being suitable for singing in unison. Elegiacs were normally recited by individuals, but, as noted, Aristotle's dactylo-epitrites in Doric dialect could be performed by a chorus. This is a main reason that Wilamowitz took the song as a liturgical work, but let us note for now that it was also simple enough in language and rhythm, and presumably in melody, as not to require professional performers to be passed around, something not true of other lyric compositions of the day.

Considerations of form are a main reason not to adopt the antithetical view to such historicizing reconstructions as Wilamowitz's: this would be that the song for Hermias was never intended for an actual ceremony and that the picture it gives of itself as a ritual utterance is a fiction, a poetic stance. The song need not refer to any performative context but works as a self-enclosed composition, giving its listeners the pleasure of being present, vicariously, at a high-toned and solemn commemorative occasion. One could compare Callimachus's collection of so-called "mimetic" hymns, hexameter and elegiac songs that sometimes (esp. *Hymns* 5 and 6) pose as cult hymns, even though scholars have been unable to attach their allusions to ongoing ritual activity to any known rite. Although these literary compositions of the early third century may read as if they were transcripts of what was uttered while the rite unfolded, the purpose of such language is not reference but to invest a poetry modeled on other poetry, especially on the late archaic *Homeric hymns*, with the admired rhetorical quality of "vividness" (*enargeia*).[14] If the song to Hermias were regarded as a "mimetic" cult song, one could see Aristotle once again as a harbinger of Hellenistic poetics, in the same way that his Delphic inscription for Hermias seemed to anticipate the later vogue for fictional epigrams. This cannot be excluded as a possibility. But Aristotle does not seem bent on producing a vivid effect of performance (there are no deictics in his text, for example) and it is notable that Callimachus created his fictional ritual experiences in recitable, and therefore legible meters that can be fully enjoyed in a study; Aristotle's song, in contrast, needs more than words on a page to produce its full effects.

If Callisthenes' *Hermias* may be read either as a performance piece or as a prose text, considerations of form support the hypothesis that Aristotle's song was sung at first within the circle of the Peripatetics and their friends. We may add, if we assume that Aristotle's song was intended for Hermias's intimates, that the group must have been rather small if the ceremony took place in Pella soon after Hermias was killed. But that of course is hardly the end of the story: the song seems to have been reprised by Aristotle and his friends when he returned to Athens in 335; and by the time Demophilus and his cronies get wind of it, the song was allegedly being sung at the common meals (*sussitia*) of the Lyceum.[15] Having gone this far in speculating about the premiere of Aristotle's song, let us turn to the time when it exploded onto the public scene.

Sources: Hermippus's *On Aristotle*

Athenaeus got his account of the trial from others, and to tease out the historical strands that he braids together it is helpful to analyze his account into its basic building blocks. Our passage occurs in the fifteenth and final book of the *Deipnosophistai* as both the party and the work wind down. Athenaeus's speakers break off a lengthy discussion of perfumes (an emolument of the finest symposia) by calling for wine. A hubbub then arises, as some propose to toast the "Good Daimon," others Zeus the Savior, and others still *Hugieia* (Health), and so the savants consult the "testimony of the poets" (692f) about after-dinner toasting. This in turn quickly becomes a learned discussion of the genre of the after-dinner song, the *skolion*. Aristotle's hymn will be brought up at the end of this discussion, and will be pronounced a *skolion*. The term and some of the practices associated with *skolia* can be traced back to the classical age, but it is impossible to reconstruct the full early evolution of the genre. I go into the subject only so far as to understand how some could have applied this label to Aristotle's song.

By the time of Athenaeus, and probably already in the sources he cites on the matter, *skolia* were most easily defined in terms of occasion: they were songs suitable for "social gatherings" (συνουσίαι, 694a), preeminently drinking parties or *symposia*. As performance pieces, *skolia* amounted to stylized graces or after-dinner speeches; their inviolable generic requirement was to project an ethos appropriate to a civilized party. In form, they could be either short, simple quatrains easy to perform or longer, complex compositions calling for some musical skill to carry off. Athenaeus's discussants derive the genre's name from the latter kind of *skolion*, which they understand as the "crooked" (σκόλιον) song, because when it came time to sing the less simple forms not everyone was expected to contribute and the song would follow a "crooked" or zigzagging path around the table (693f-694c). The etymology is highly dubious, but no alternative presents itself: the question was already unsettled when *skolia* were discussed by Aristotle's students Dichaearchus and Aristoxenus.[16] But we can trust that Athenaeus voices a widely accepted ideal when he says that the finest (κάλλιστον) among *skolia* were the ones "containing some advice or wisdom that was helpful in living."[17]

Athenaeus's scholars then exemplify the simple kind of *skolion* by taking turns performing a set of old Athenian drinking songs (694c-695e). (The collection, which is datable on internal grounds to the second quarter of the fifth century BCE, seems to have been known to Aristotle, since one of these *skolia* is quoted as historical evidence in the *Constitution of Athens* [19] that was produced in his school.) The next step in the discussion comes when someone appends a slightly longer but easily singable Cretan song that "people say" is a *skolion* (695f-696a). Once the issue of generically uncertain *skolia* is raised, Democritus of Nicomedia brings up Aristotle's song, which he declares is a kind of *skolion* and not a paean as Aristotle's accusers had alleged (696a-697b):

τούτων λεχθέντων ὁ Δημόκριτος ἔφη· 'ἀλλὰ μὴν καὶ τὸ
ὑπὸ τοῦ πολυμαθεστάτου γραφὲν Ἀριστοτέλους εἰς
Ἑρμείαν τὸν Ἀταρνέα οὐ παιάν ἐστιν, ὡς ὁ τὴν τῆς

ἀσεβείας κατὰ τοῦ φιλοσόφου γραφὴν ἀπενεγκάμενος
Δημόφιλος εἰσέδωκε [Gulick; for εἰς αἴδωτε] παρασκευασθεὶς
ὑπ' Εὐρυμέδοντος, ὡς ἀσεβοῦντος καὶ ᾄδοντος ἐν τοῖς
συσσιτίοις ὁσημέραι εἰς τὸν Ἑρμείαν παιᾶνα. ὅτι δὲ
παιᾶνος οὐδεμίαν ἔμφασιν παρέχει τὸ ᾆσμα, ἀλλὰ τῶν
σκολίων ἕν τι καὶ αὐτὸ εἶδός ἐστιν ἐξ αὐτῆς τῆς λέξεως
φανερὸν ὑμῖν ποιήσω.

At this point in the discussion, Democritus spoke: "But the one [sc. *skolion*] written by the extremely learned Aristotle to Hermias of Atarneus is no paean—as was asserted by Demophilus, when he was stirred up by Eurymedon and brought a charge of impiety against the philosopher on the grounds that he committed impiety by singing the song as a paean to Hermias at the common meals they had each day. But I will demonstrate from its very language that the song has no feature of the paean but is its own kind of *skolion*."

After quoting the song (essentially in the version printed at the head of this book), Democritus goes on to give an analysis of its language with which one is bound to agree (696e):

ἐγὼ μὲν οὐκ οἶδα εἴ τίς τι κατιδεῖν ἐν τούτοις δύναται
παιανικὸν ἰδίωμα, σαφῶς ὁμολογοῦντος τοῦ γεγραφότος
τετελευτηκέναι τὸν Ἑρμείαν δι' ὧν εἴρηκεν 'σᾶς γὰρ
φιλίου μορφᾶς Ἀταρνέος ἔντροφος ἡελίου χήρωσεν
αὐγάς.' οὐκ ἔχει δ' οὐδὲ τὸ παιανικὸν ἐπίρρημα,
καθάπερ ὁ εἰς Λύσανδρον τὸν Σπαρτιάτην γραφεὶς ὄντως
παιάν, ὅν φησι Δοῦρις ἐν τοῖς Σαμίων ἐπιγραφομένοις
Ὥροις ᾄδεσθαι ἐν Σάμῳ. παιὰν δ' ἐστὶν καὶ ὁ εἰς Κρατερὸν
τὸν Μακεδόνα γραφείς, ὃν ἐτεκτήνατο Ἀλεξῖνος ὁ
διαλεκτικός, φησὶν Ἕρμιππος ὁ Καλλιμάχειος ἐν

τῷ πρώτῳ περὶ Ἀριστοτέλους. ᾄδεται δὲ καὶ οὗτος ἐν Δελφοῖς, λυρίζοντός γέ τινος παιδός.

> For my part, I do not know how anyone can see anything specifically paeanic in these verses, since the author concedes that Hermias has died in the expression, "For the sake of your dear shape, Atarneus' nursling left the rays of the sun bereft." And it doesn't even have the paeanic refrain, unlike the song that was composed for Lysander the Spartan, which really is a paean and which Duris in the work entitled *Samian Chronicles* says was sung on Samos. And the song for Craterus of Macedon composed by Alexinus the dialectician is a paean, as Hermippus the Callimachean says in the first book of his *On Aristotle*. It is performed in Delphi with a boy providing accompaniment on the lyre.

This defense of Aristotle makes two assumptions about paeans as a genre. First, it concedes to Aristotle's accusers that a paean addressed to a mortal would, if not ipso facto constituting an act of impiety, at least violate "paeanic idiom" (παιανικὸν ἰδίωμα), that is, would be uncharacteristic of the genre.[18] Second, paeans should have a refrain, that is, some form of the cry "Hail Paean" (*iê Paian*) should be in the text. Aristotle is exculpated on both grounds: he "plainly" admits that Hermias is dead (i.e., this is plainly to be inferred from vv. 15–16) and his song does not have any paeanic refrain.

Now what Athenaeus calls (697a) the paeanic refrain (τὸ παιανικὸν ἐπίρρημα or τὸ παιανικὸν ἐπίφθεγμα) is indeed very common in paean texts, and is taken to be a mark of the genre in handbooks—ancient and modern—that sum up genres in neat recipes.[19] But in point of literary historical fact, not all paeans had a refrain. Athenaeus himself cites a conspicuous exception in this portion of his work when he quotes Ariphron's "paean" to Health entire, which has no refrain (701f); other ancient paeans preserved on papyrus and stone can be found without the refrain.[20] What I suspect is going on here is that the paean-cry could be used like an "amen": in some songs it was integrated into the lyric, while in others it could have been added by the company as an "extra-textual" way of affirming and participating in the prayer, what Athenaeus calls an "added utterance" (*epiphthegma*, 697a).[21] If the question had come up for Aristotle's accusers, they could have exploited this variability to insist that the song was one of those paeans without the paeanic refrain.

Perhaps because he is aware that the refrain is not an infallible litmus test for paeans, Athenaeus goes on to buttress his argument by contrasting Aristotle's song with a number of songs addressed to mortals that are certifiable as paeans because they had the refrain. Here we should take note of the sources Athenaeus cites, for they show that the genre of Aristotle's song had been a matter of dispute for centuries. Athenaeus's list of legitimate paeans to mortals begins with Duris of Samos, who wrote in the later fourth century about a paean the Samians had sung to Lysander, the triumphant Spartan general at the end of the Peloponnesian War.[22] (More on this song below.) The second item is key: Athenaeus cites a paean written by Alexinus of Elis (ca. 339-265) in honor of Craterus of Macedon, probably Craterus the elder, Alexander's general who died in 321.[23] This piece of information Athenaeus attributes to "Hermippus the Callimachean" in the first book of his *On Aristotle*. From the fact that Hermippus mentioned a paean to Craterus in a biography of Aristotle we can infer that the dispute over the genre of the Hermias poem goes back to his day, the later third century. We can further infer that Hermippus was already arguing for a position like that of Athenaeus, for the only reason for him to cite Craterus's paean, complete with its refrain, would be to argue that the absence of a refrain in Aristotle's song precludes it from being a paean. It may be that Hermippus also gave Athenaeus the idea that Aristotle's song was in fact a *skolion*. In that case, Athenaeus's contribution would have been to add to the dossier of actual paeans to mortals examples taken from later works on music, for his list includes a paean quoted by Polemon of Athens, known as a writer of geography in the second century BCE. Athenaeus alludes to other now lost works in which the paean-cry was discussed (cf. 701C); among these, we may do well to recall that Didymus also wrote *On Lyric Poetry*, in which he discussed various kinds of hymns, including paeans.[24]

Hermippus of Smyrna was a scholar and man of letters who made his way to Alexandria and evidently had some association with Callimachus of Cyrene (c. 305–c. 240), one of the great poet-scholars to be found at the library there. Working at the epicenter of ancient literary scholarship, Hermippus contributed to the fledgling genre of biography with portraits of poets and thinkers, including *On Aristotle*. This may have been the earliest biography of the philosopher; it certainly was an influential one. It is often supposed that Hermippus is Athenaeus's prime source for the history of the song,[25] and he is among the authorities cited by Didymus in his discussion of Hermias.[26] Hermippus is also prominent in the *Life of Aristotle* by Diogenes Laertius, though Diogenes probably knew him in extracted form and filled out the story about the trial with material (sometimes contradictory) from Favorinus.[27]

It is worrisome if Hermippus is Athenaeus's sole source, since he has had a spotty reputation for reliability among scholars.[28] His most recent editor, Jan Bollansée, gives a balanced account: he underlines Hermippus's erudition but points out that he appears to have had a weakness for dramatic stories, and that he was drawn to figures like Anaxagoras (1056 *FGrH* F 65) and Socrates (F 67) whose ideas led to their being tried for impiety.[29] Hermippus's appearance on the scene must make us concerned that the story of the trial may contain elements of fiction. That this is certainly the case appears when Athenaeus goes on to quote what is alleged to be Aristotle's actual defense speech (ἀπολογία) from the trial.

Authenticity: "Aristotle's" *Apology*

After cataloging actual paeans to mortals, Athenaeus continues his defense of Aristotle by quoting—possibly depending on Hermippus for this as well—a sentence from a *Defense Speech Against Impiety*, supposedly by the philosopher himself (697A = Aristotle Fr. 645 Rose). Athenaeus adds the proviso "if it is not a forgery" (εἰ μὴ κατέψευσται ὁ λόγος), and we should say this speech was most certainly a forgery: neither Athenaeus nor any source says the charge came to trial, and it seems that if it had, we should have heard much more about the episode. In addition, fictional speeches of famous defendants had been a popular sub-genre of rhetorical prose at least since the 390s when a number of Socratic "Apologies" were produced in the aftermath of that famous trial.[30] Even though Athenaeus is prudent enough to doubt the *Apology of Aristotle*, it is cause for concern that a polemical pseudo-literature may have arisen around these matters early enough to have influenced Hermippus, assuming that he continues to be Athenaeus's guide to the story here. By the same token, even a fake text can supply valuable evidence, and this *Apology* may cast a pre-Hermippan light on the affair and contain one of our earliest references to Aristotle's song.

The sentence Athenaeus quotes from the *Apology* is an elaborate antithesis that one can easily imagine being produced in fourth-century rhetorical schools, perhaps by a novice since it needs a little emendation to come out nicely balanced: "For if I wished to sacrifice to Hermias as if he were an immortal, I would never have prepared a memorial (*mnêma*) for him as if he were a mortal; and if I wanted to attribute an immortal nature to him, I would not have adorned his body with funeral honors" (Fr. 645 Rose: οὐ γὰρ ἄν ποτε Ἑρμείᾳ θύειν ὡς ἀθανάτῳ προαιρούμενος ὡς θνητῷ μνῆμα κατεσκεύαζον καὶ ἀθανατίζειν τὴν φύσιν βουλόμενος ἐπιταφίοις ἂν τιμαῖς ἐκόσμησα τὸ <σῶμα>).[31] The first clause refers to Aristotle's Delphic monument for Hermias (designated a memorial, *mnêma*). The "funeral honors" in the second clause could refer to a commemorative ceremony such as Wilamowitz supposed to be the setting for the hymn, but in any case must include the hymn which was a part of those honors, and which indeed was faulted for wanting to "immortalize" (ἀθανατίζειν) its subject and calling him "immortal" (ἀθάνατον in v. 18). Seeing a reference to the hymn in the second clause gives needed force to the adjective *epitaphiois*: literally, "over the tomb," the epithet counters the charge that the song was a paean by conceding, as Aristotle had in his song, that Hermias was dead. A further implication of the word is to characterize whatever commemorative ceremonies were practiced as no more irregular in substance than Athenian state funerals, at which a funeral oration, an *epitaphios logos*, was customary.

It is notable that this author draws the Delphic monument into the accusations against Aristotle, even though that artifact, in a most respectable shrine and speaking a perfectly conventional verse, had occasioned no charge graver than witlessness. It does, however, furnish the orator with the first half of a pair of balanced antitheses, and this kind of overwrought rhetoric may be the source of Diogenes Laertius's statement, not confirmed by Athenaeus, that both of Aristotle's poems on Hermias were the basis for the charge of impiety.[32] It may be that the pseudo-*Apology* responds to an early stage of anti-Aristotelian propaganda, one that joined his "paean" to other allegedly impious behavior. The Peripatetic Aristocles cites an allegation by Lycon the Pythagorean, whom he dates to Aristotle's generation or the next, that when Aristotle's wife died he "venerated her with the same rite that the Athenians offer Demeter." This bizarre accusation makes a sort of sense—Aristotle immortalizing the daughter as he had the father—and the slur may even have had some basis in fact if, as Wormell suggested, Aristotle staged a grand funeral for his wife, as he is thought to have done for Hermias.[33] Lycon's charge also resonates with the report in Diogenes and Athenaeus that it was an official of Demeter's mysteries, Eurymedon, who was the prime mover of the charge of impiety.[34] We do not hear that Lycon also mentioned the paean to Hermias, but Diogenes quotes a somewhat later source who explicitly links that song to a similar Aristotelian offense against Demeter: "But Aristippus, in the first book of his treatise *On Ancient Luxury*, says that Aristotle was enamored of the concubine of Hermias, and that when Hermias consented to it he married her; so overjoyed was Aristotle that he sacrificed to her in the way the Athenians do to Eleusinian Demeter. And for Hermias he wrote a paean, which is written out below."[35] Diogenes is wrong to attribute *On Ancient Luxury* to Aristippus, an associate of Socrates who would not have lived past around 360. This is too early for Aristippus to have gone into Aristotle's connections with Hermias, and *On Ancient Luxury*, characterized by Düring as "one of the worst products of Hellenistic calumny," is rather to be seen as a piece of anti-philosophical invective forged around 250 BCE. The similarity of both bizarre stories of Aristotle treating his wife like Demeter may indicate a common source, even if pseudo-Aristippus differs from Lycon in making Aristotle venerate his wife while she was alive. If he is garbling (or simply exaggerating) the report in Lycon, his linking of this charge with "the paean to Hermias" may also derive from Lycon, and so the hymn to Hermias will have featured in anti-Aristotelian propaganda from a very early time, that is, from Aristotle's generation or the next.[36]

Let us turn next to the words of the song itself, for the question of whether the poem is by Aristotle or is a fake has yet to be addressed. Hermippus was, as noted, a source for both Didymus and Athenaeus, and if it was he who provided the text of the poem to them, one may ask where he got it. Before Hermippus, the song was mentioned by the pseudo-Aristotelian *Apology* (on the reading given here), and by the pseudo-Aristippan *On Ancient Luxury*, and perhaps before both by Lycon of Iasos. The only modern scholar I know to doubt that the song is Aristotle's is the collector of his fragments, Valentine Rose. Rose judged the poem "frigid and jejune," even if not without elegance, and attributed it to some mediocre talent, "more philosopher than poet," writing between Aristotle and Hermippus.[37] Rose's "frigid" echoes the one ancient source that seems to express doubt about the authorship of the song, though the passage has seemed in real need of emendation. The text also comes from Aristocles (F 2.5 Caesarani = T 58f Düring) as he defends Aristotle from numerous scurrilous attacks, including that of a certain Euboulides. This Euboulides has been identified with a contemporary of Aristotle, Euboulides of Miletus, a Megarian-school philosopher who wrote a book against the Stagirite (cf. DL 2.109). As transmitted in Eusebius, Aristocles wrote:

καὶ Εὐβουλίδης δὲ προδήλως ἐν τῷ κατ' αὐτοῦ βιβλίῳ
ψεύδεται, πρῶτον μὲν ποιήματα ψυχρὰ προσφερόμενος
ὡς γεγραφότων ἄλλων περὶ τοῦ γάμου καὶ τῆς πρὸς
Ἑρμείαν οἰκειότητος αὐτῷ γεγονυίας, ἔπειτα Φιλίππῳ
φάσκων αὐτὸν προσκόψαι καὶ τελευτῶντι Πλάτωνι μὴ
παραγενέσθαι τά τε βιβλία αὐτοῦ διαφθεῖραι.[38]

Euboulides clearly lies in his book against [Aristotle], first in adducing frigid poems about his marriage and his intimacy with Hermias as though others had written them, and then by saying that he was offensive to Philip, that he was not with Plato when he died, and that he corrupted the latter's writings.

This sentence becomes quite significant if we assume that the song for Hermias was among the poems Euboulides cited having to do with the intimacy (οἰκειότητος; cf. οἰκειότατα in Didymus col. 5.63) between Hermias and Aristotle. Citing it as an example of Aristotle's toadying to tyrants would be quite apt, since the song conspicuously mentions their friendship (φιλίας, v. 21). But in that case, what is Aristocles' point about their authenticity? He seems to say that Euboulides' lying or deception (ψεύδεται) consisted first in forging poems, presumably poems that reflected badly on Aristotle's marriage and relationship with Hermias, and then in pretending that they had been composed by others. But it is hard to see that anything turned on the question of whether the damning verses were composed by Euboulides or by some other of Aristotle's detractors. Accordingly, Mulvaney has persuaded many that we should insert a word into the Greek to make it say Euboulides lied in "adducing frigid poems about his marriage and intimacy with Hermias *as if Aristotle had written them* when they were by others" (ποιήματα ψυχρὰ προσφερόμενος ὡς ⟨'Αριστοτέλους⟩, γεγραφότων ἄλλων).[39] On this reading, Aristocles makes a more relevant point in claiming that the hymn was one of numerous forgeries by various hands that were palmed off as Aristotle's by Euboulides. Although a supporter of Aristotle, Aristocles' strategy here is to write off the poem, which he apparently dislikes, as a malicious fiction so that it cannot be used by the opposition as incriminating evidence.

However construed, of course, Aristocles' text is not evidence against Aristotelian authorship of the hymn. In favor of poem being authentically Aristotelian is the fact that it is not the kind of thing a forger would make up. If the poem was forged, it was by someone between Euboulides (who, as Aristotle's contemporary, thus emerges as one of our earliest witnesses to the role of songs in the charge) and Hermippus (for it seems that Hermippus reported Euboulides to Aristocles).[40] If the forger were writing soon after 323, one would expect he would have been more explicitly impious. Moreover, the song contains no reference to any major theme associated with Aristotle's thought or any noted episode from his life. One can contrast in this regard the famous Seventh Letter attributed to Plato, which provides just the sort of "inside" information on Plato's life and methods that would appeal to his ancient readers. If this text, like the equally alluring but more dubious Second Letter, has seemed to some to be too good to be true, Aristotle's hymn by contrast is too idiosyncratic to be fake. Finally, it is far more common to find the ancients devising "just-so" biographical fictions to explain authentic, if difficult lyric texts than making up peculiar and problematic poems around which to spin a fiction.

I therefore take the lyric as Aristotle's, which is not to say that the story of the trial is completely reliable. On the assumption that a real song by Aristotle made its way to later scholars, we must still be concerned by the fact that ancient critics often made up special historical contexts that could explain peculiarities in old texts. Wehrli, for example, thinks that the story of the impiety trial and the defense speech were an invention superposed on a historically more plausible tradition to account for Aristotle's removal to Chalcis in 323.[41] But precedent supports belief in the dramatic story, even if it be somewhat embellished in our sources. After all, Socrates was actually tried (and executed) on charges that included impiety. And in his case, too, a pseudo-literature arose early: Plato's reference in his *Apology* (19C) to Aristophanes' *Clouds* shows that in such literature, intertextual squabbling could begin quite soon after the event. The historicity of that trial is made harder to know, but is not put in doubt by the fact that a fictional literature grew up around it.

Nor were Socrates and Aristotle the only philosophers harassed at Athens with charges of impiety. A number of high-profile impiety trials are attested in the later fourth century that make sense as attempts to bring down influential figures, including philosophers, who were thought to be too pro-Macedonian. Aristotle's associate Theophrastus was charged with impiety in 319, and though he was acquitted, a speech alleging to be his *Apology* emerged from the case, possibly in time to provide the model for the pseudo-Aristotelian *Apology*.[42] Perhaps the only secure time for philosophers of Aristotle's stripe in Athens was between 317 and 307, when the Macedonian regency imposed Demetrius of Phaleron on the city, a man of philosophical culture and in fact a student of both Aristotle and Theophrastus. We are told that when Demetrius was later forced to leave the city, he found refuge with a successor of Alexander's, Ptolemy I, in Egypt; the result would have been that this student of Aristotle played a key role in conceiving the great Alexandrian library that would be realized under Ptolemy II.[43] Demetrius's comparatively benign rule for philosophers came to an end in 307 when he was deposed and the city "liberated" by a new Demetrius, a disgruntled Macedonian warlord surnamed the Besieger (*Poliorcetes*). There ensued another upsurge of anti-Macedonian sentiment from which another document in the war on philosophers emerged, this one from the prosecutors' side. Almost immediately upon the Besieger's arrival, philosophers and other teachers found themselves attacked in a law proposed by a certain Sophocles of Sounion. Sophocles' law made it a capital crime for "philosophers" or "sophists" to open a school without a license from the city's council; the pressure was great enough that Theophrastus and a number of other philosophers left Athens.[44] One year later, the law was overthrown when Philon, identified as a pupil of Aristotle (Athenaeus 610f), charged that Sophocles' law was illegal. He was opposed by Demochares, a nephew of Demosthenes who had taken part in the prosecution of Theophrastus for impiety. Demochares' "Against the Philosophers," according to Aristocles, reviled Aristotle particularly among philosophers.[45] Like later, literary slanderers, Demochares pretended to have incriminating documents from Aristotle's own hands, in this case letters from which he charged that the philosopher had betrayed not only Olynthus and Athens to Macedon but his own hometown of Stagira as well. The episode suggests that if an animus against Aristotle persisted among some Athenians as late as 306, when he had been dead for more than 15 years, it is entirely possible that he and his songs could have drawn hostile scrutiny in 323, when Alexander had just died and resistance to Macedonian hegemony seemed feasible. This little part of the story at least had a happy ending: Demochares' side was defeated; Sophocles had to pay a fine; Theophrastus and the other philosophers returned to the city, from which they would not be expelled again until Justinian.

Chapter 5

Genres of Poetry

The previous chapter has argued that Aristotle's song to Hermias is not an ancient forgery and that it was mentioned early in the denunciations of the philosopher that sprang up in 323. If these source-critical arguments make the story of the trial more plausible, they also raise questions about the literary culture of the time. For the allegation that Aristotle's song was impious turned on a question of genre: whether it was a paean, a species of hymn, or a kind of song appropriate to mortals ("whether it was a paean, a species of hymn, or a kind of song appropriate to mortals").[1] But when one considers how simply the idea that the song was a paean is dismissed in Athenaeus, one wonders what Aristotle's antagonists had in mind. Is it credible that they expected a jury of several hundred Athenians, chosen at random from the citizen body, to follow, as if they were savants in Athenaeus, arguments about whether the song was a paean or a *skolion*? Would a popular jury feel so much outrage at a generic misstep as to expose the defendant to capital punishment? The story of the song at trial thus requires that we consider questions of a literary historical nature, specifically what sort of definitions of paeans were on offer and how far public interest in such matters reached. I propose to show in this chapter that it is quite credible that a charge of criminal paean-singing could have been circulated against Aristotle at the time and that such behavior could be felt to deserve severe penalties. But to see this we have to nuance our understanding of literary genres in fourth-century BCE Greece with religious and political considerations.

Ultimately, I pursue genre to identify features of Aristotle's text that audiences found salient and significant. The goal is not to fix, once and for all, the true generic identity of the poem, but to specify how Aristotle evoked and played with contemporary ideas about different kinds of song. In this way, genre will bring to light a central dynamic of the lyric, which gives every sign of beginning as a hymn but seems as it proceeds to lose sight of its initial hymnic object and to veer off into other business. A detailed consideration of the hymn's formal properties must await the next chapter. The first step in characterizing the genre of Aristotle's song will be to consider how the Greeks broke down the category we call lyric poetry (λυρική, a Hellenistic term), but which they called songs (μέλη, ἀοιδαί), into kinds or genres. The history of lyric classification is a complex area of ancient criticism that could use more study, but it cannot be left out of account; it is obvious that we cannot rely on Athenaeus, who wrote almost half a millennium after the fact, to understand how a paean was recognized when Aristotle was accused. But neither, as will be seen, can we settle on a single "right" way to define genres in the 320s, for the question was usually negotiable and the concepts were still evolving. I will focus on how such terms as hymn (ὕμνος), paean (παιάν), *skolion*, and *enkômion* were defined, contrasting early classical usage with the Hellenistic age when the vocabulary Athenaeus uses was developed. In this history, political and religious notions will not be absent, which will help us see that more than literary issues could be involved in taxonomies of song, and why those issues mattered to the people at large.

Lyric Genres from Plato to Alexandria

To ask what genre a lyric poem belongs to can seem fussy and academic, especially from a Romantic perspective that tends to equate lyric poetry with poetry itself. But in Greek literary culture it is fair to say that a song without a genre, without a putative context and social function, was inconceivable. In the performative culture of the classical period, song was for social life, and different kinds of songs were recognized as suitable for different events. Because such "rules" as there were flowed from social contexts, it is important to think of genres not as recipes that had to be followed to the letter but as sets of expectations that might be adapted and re-negotiated for particular occasions. Again, Romantic criticism tends to envision genre as a constraint on poetic originality, but a classical perspective would feel that an exclusive focus on the poet's creativity overlooks the audience's legitimate expectation that performers address appropriate topics and express felicitous sentiments in suitable language. A good θρῆνος, or funeral lament, for example, was essentially something that everyone attending the ceremony would agree had been a suitable thing to say; a very good one might be remembered and referred to or re-performed on later occasions. If you were to assemble enough of the latter kind, you would have materials from which to deduce general rules for what a dirge-writer ought to aim at to succeed; this kind of genre-theorizing was exactly what was going on in institutions of higher study in fourth century Greece.

In the decades between Aristotle's lectures on the art of poetry, usually dated to around mid-century, and the founding of the Alexandrian Museum in the early third century, Greek scholars settled on a vocabulary for defining poetry and its kinds that is still widely used in Western criticism.[2] This obscure period of literary history seems to have continued a tendency that can be seen in fifth-century criticism to favor formal definitions of genre over the more socially based terminology and practice of the early classical and archaic periods. An example is the word *paean* itself, a very old name for a kind of song. The genre term *paean* derives from a cult song in honor of the pre-Homeric healing god *Paiêôn*. A song of supplication or thanksgiving to this god was called a paean, a metonymy doubtless supported by the song's use of the god's name as a refrain. Paean kept this sense even as *Paiêôn* came to be displaced by Apollo. A social conception of a paean would consider the god to which the song is addressed and the circumstances in which *Paiêôn*/Apollo might be invoked; a more formal approach might focus on the refrain "Hail Paean!," or the absence thereof. Conceptions of genre that entailed specifiable properties were especially useful when one wanted to categorize, and therefore be able to retrieve from library shelves, songs that had come down independently, without being embedded in a dramatic text, for example, or in an anthology of verse. The utility of formalist reductions is evident in the success they have enjoyed, but we must be wary about attributing them to Aristotle's accusers. To sketch how the main lyric kinds were recognized in his day, I will begin with songs in praise of mortals, starting with the early classical period and the epinicians of Pindar.

A seminal study of the evolution of Greek genre terms by A. E. Harvey showed that in the fifth and fourth centuries the genre that we and Hellenistic scholars call epinician or "victory-song" (*epinikion*) would have normally been included under the broad term *enkômion* or "revel-song," with its implication of "praise of mortal achievement."[3] Only twice in nearly sixty epinicans do Pindar and Bacchylides refer to their compositions as "songs upon a victory" (*epinikia*); a far more common self-description is as a "revel-song" (*engkômios* [sc. *melos*], or simply *kômos*), picturing them as sung by a band of young men on a carouse.[4] This terminology is far from proof that Pindar's songs were actually performed by young male choristers: any poem's references to its own performance may be metaphorical or fictitious; we cannot tell because—unlike the case with Aristotle—we lack reliable early evidence for the how epinician was performed. indeed, we are so lacking in evidence that scholars differ about such a fundamental question as whether Pindar's odes were choral or solo pieces. Nonetheless, the prominence of *kômos* is significant because it shows Pindar submitting his song—however it was actually performed—for social acceptance under the same terms accorded to a *kômos*: this form of public celebration was long sanctioned for a man of outstanding achievement; one who had, for example, won Panhellenic victory was entitled, in return for his efforts, to noisy public acclaim led by those near and dear to him, and so epinicians often pose as exclamations of the victor's boisterous male age-mates. It was presumably unobjectionable to refer to a Pindaric epinician as a "victory song," as he himself does once, but not very informative, and indeed almost tautologous in context. (The redundancy is like calling an anthem sung on July 14th a "14th of July song.") By contrast, to call an epinician an *enkômion* implied that it was a measured and socially appropriate recognition of mortal success and—since the *kômos* was more public than a dinner party—contrasted this form of praise with that found, for example, in sympotic *skolia*, which could also make praise of a mortal their theme. This sense of *enkômion*, not altogether rigid to begin with, is loosening already in the fourth century when we find the word used for any kind of formal eulogy for a great man, whether in verse or prose.[5] In his *Rhetoric*, Aristotle tried to impose some precision in terminology when he recognized a broad category of speech in praise of humans, "whether by poets or prose writers" (2.11,1388b21), and subdivided it: he would use *enkômion* for praise of an individual's deeds in particular circumstances, and *epainos* ("approval") for praise of general personal qualities as manifested in deeds (1.9, 1367b26-29).[6] But the Alexandrian editors of Pindar's considerable poetic output found themselves with enough victory songs to fill four books, and so it seems they decided to put songs having to do (mostly) with victory celebration into their own (newly titled) class, *epinicia*; they resupplied the depleted corpus of Pindar's *enkômia* by taking in certain convivial songs that would have been called *skolia* in their day.[7]

Harvey's study shows that, for similar reasons, most of the terminology for lyric genres used in the age of Alexandrian scholarship either did not exist or had different meanings at the time when the poets wrote. Plato stands out in the transition between the two worlds because he rejected both the looseness of archaic classifications and the pragmatism of later literary systems. His ideal of generic purity, derived from his metaphysics and theology, was the first to demand that every Greek song have a single, uncompromisable generic identity. The idea that songs must belong to one genre or another and that no song should be mixed is first explicitly articulated in his attack on "modern" musicians (i.e., poets of the last decades of the fifth century and the first of the fourth) for mixing genres. In a well-known passage in *Laws* (700A-E), Plato fantasizes that in the good old days people regarded prayers to the gods as a distinct kind (*eidos*) of song and kept them apart from anything having to do with songs for mortals. He illustrates by citing traditional hymnic forms: songs for the gods include the dithyramb, Dionysus's cult song, and paeans, defined as songs for Apollo. (Plato's clarity is purchased at the cost of some reductivism, since, as noted, paeans are found addressed to Apollo's sister Artemis and to other gods in the fifth century.)[8] Plato assigns such songs to the larger category he calls "hymns" (ὕμνοι), which is the first attestation of this word for "song" in the restricted sense "song for a god." Though *humnos* was an old word for any kind of song, in his day hymns were often enough so designated as to make his restriction of the word's meaning plausible. To the class of hymns Plato opposes all songs for mortals, which he exemplifies by a genre inextricably connected to mortality, the dirge. When Plato goes on to complain that modern poets go so far as to mix dirges (θρῆνοι) with hymns (ὕμνοι), he is anticipating, in theoretical and highly ideological terms, the essence of the charge against Aristotle's song, which is that it was at once a lament and a *paean* for Hermias: "in their enthusiasm and excessively given over to pleasure, they blend dirges with hymns, and paeans with dithyrambs ... utterly confounding everything."[9] Plato's view points up the formalism and its theological component that underlies Eurymedon's charge.

Aristotle basically agreed with Plato on these matters, and his own work in poetics and rhetoric was in line with the general trend toward making genre terms more formalistic and prescriptive. Generic classification was fundamental to his attempt to put the study of poetry on a properly "technical" basis in the *Poetics* or "*art* of poetry" (*poiêtikê*). Students who attended his lectures learned to define a tragedy, for example, without reference to its context—for example, as the kind of play one could expect at the Dionysian festivals—but as a distinctive form of musico-poetic composition exhibiting a set of formal and thematic qualities that were laid out in chapter 6 of the published notes. Aristotle seems not to have gone very deeply into lyric genres in his *Poetics*, which in its surviving form focuses on tragedy and epic. But we can infer how he would have classified his song from Hermias from the general analysis of kinds of poetry that begins the work: in formal terms (in terms of its "media"), a lyric or a song is a kind of artistic representation (μίμησις) that is distinctive from other forms of *mimêsis* in being composed of melody (μέλος), language (λόγος), and rhythm all blended together. Such "songs" (literally, "tunes," μέλη, a part-for-whole designation for words set to music) are exemplified in the *Poetics* through two popular kinds, the dithyramb and the kitharodic nome (1447a14 ff.); the pair is probably meant to suggest that the class of lyric song could be further sub-divided according to the criterion of "objects of imitation" that Aristotle will set out in chapter 2: while dithyrambs were for Dionysus, nomes were usually for Apollo.

This basic division of song-types following cult recalls Plato's in *Laws*, and the history of poetry Aristotle gives in the fourth chapter of *Poetics* shows that he also subscribed to the idea that songs to the gods belonged to a separate category from songs for mortals.[10] Having raised the question of how poetry and its main genres arose, Aristotle reasons that poetry must derive from natural human appetites and aptitudes. Where his evolutionary account will differ from Plato's story of a fall is in referring generic distinctions to inherent human capacities, not to transcendent religious laws. Aristotle then speculates—for we are talking about the deep past here—that two basic genres arose when serious kinds of people "naturally" represented the actions of worthy types, while innately vulgar poets represented people of a baser sort, "the latter composing blame (songs), the former ὕμνοι and ἐγκώμια."[11] Subdividing serious poetry into hymns and encomia compendiously accepts Plato's distinction between songs for gods and mortals. Beyond this, Aristotle has little to say about specific lyric genres such as the paean.[12] Such questions he seems to have left to his students, like Dichaearchus, who discussed the nature of paeans and sympotic song, and another associate, the musical expert Aristoxenus, who considered the etymology of *skolia* and debated which songs deserved to be so designated.[13]

The evolving Greek conceptions of lyric genre also underwent pressure from institutions, notably the Alexandrian library, founded by a successor to Alexander possibly on the advice of one of Aristotle's students. This was the world's largest collection of books (i.e., papyrus rolls), and its sheer size must have encouraged multiplying literary categories and making them more precise. Large personal libraries had existed earlier: Aristotle kept his voluminous lecture notes and published works, and bought works from others; Athenaeus says his collection of books was remarkable, even if he is not likely to have been, as Strabo said, "the first man we know to have had a library."[14] But at Alexandria, scholars were confronted with literary texts on an unprecedented scale and so needed more ramified and "objective" taxonomies. For master-genres like epic and tragedy, it was usually no problem to fit a given text in its appropriate pigeonhole, but sorting old occasional songs into formal classes could be tricky, and the schemes for classifying lyric appear to have developed in a rather ad hoc manner. How librarians classified songs depended a great deal on how much of a given author's work was available and what information came down along with it, as a few "classic" lyric poets may show.

The evidence for how Sappho's poetry was organized in Alexandria contains gaps, but it seems that only one of the nine (or eight) book rolls preserving her songs was unified by a social occasion, the wedding songs (*epithalamia*). The rest were grouped primarily according to meter, an expedient that was made possible by the fact that very many of the songs Sappho composed for her circle favored a limited number of short stanzaic or distichic forms that were repeated from song to song.[15] The editors' formalism was encouraged by the fact that the social functions her songs had filled in archaic times had become little understood. In contrast, Bacchylides' songs in various meters were organized according to occasion: one book of *epinikia*, then of dithyrambs, paeans, hymns, processional songs (*prosodia*), songs for girls' choirs (*partheneia*), dance songs (*hyporchemes*), erotica, and *enkômia*. We know how the lyric corpus of Pindar was organized in more detail: scholars used the same occasion-based system as for Bacchylides, with the difference noted above that Pindar's erotic poems were included among the class of *enkômia*. Further classificatory refinements were wanted for Pindar's *epinikia*, which survived in sufficient quantity to require four books. Each of these was dedicated to a single festival where the victory was won (a method possibly devised by Callimachus); within each book, songs were arranged according to a complex logic that took into account the prestige of the contest and the number of victories of the winner.[16] Still, some texts remained hard to pin down: an ancient introduction to a song now cataloged as Pindar's second Pythian ode records that, "Some say it is not an epinician; Timaeus calls it a sacrifice-song (θυσιαστική); Callimachus a Nemean, Ammonius and Callistratus an Olympian, some (such as Apollonius the eidographer) a Pythian, and others a Panathenaic" (II 31.10–14 Drachmann). Classes of lyric poems continued to multiply thereafter, for there is no end to the taxonomic drive, as Barthes describes it, "trying to hold within a necessarily more and more discriminating network the 'manners of speaking,' i.e., trying to master the unmasterable."[17] By the fifth century CE, Proclus's *Chrestomathy* could list 28 genres (*eidê*) of lyric poetry, broken down into four main categories: songs to gods, songs for humans, songs to both, and occasional songs addressing neither gods nor mortals particularly.[18] Here, at last, *epinikia* recover their old place beside *enkômia*, and together with *skolia* make up the super-category of "songs for human beings." It is noteworthy that, almost a millennium after Plato, the basic terminological distinction between songs for gods and songs for mortals is preserved, even as the system has become very elaborate.[19]

It was at Alexandria that Hermippus researched his biographies in the later third century. He is called "the Callimachean" by Athenaeus, though this need not mean that he worked directly with the scholar-poet. He could nonetheless have imbibed a great deal of Callimachus's literary system by perusing his "Tables" or *Pinakes*, the 120 book-rolls he had composed as a guide "to those distinguished in all branches of learning and to what they have written" in the library.[20] Hermippus at all events seems to have defined paeans in the same way as Callimachus, to judge from a scrap of papyrus from Oxyrhynchus in Egypt that records a dispute over genre at Alexandria. The papyrus concerns a poem called *Cassandra*, probably by Bacchylides.[21] According to the note, Callimachus had classed the poem as a paean, whereas Aristarchus of Samothrace, head of the Library in the mid-second century BCE, argued that the poem was a dithyramb. The papyrus gives the grounds for each scholar's choice, but there is, once again, a gap—the gods of papyri seem to enjoy teasing genre-critics—just where the decisive word occurred: on the reading proposed by Edgar Lobel, the papyrus's first editor, Callimachus called *Cassandra* a paean because it had a version of the paeanic *refrain* (reading *epithegma*), whereas Aristarchus argued that the prominence of *myth* in the poem made *Cassandra* a dithyramb; he held against Callimachus that the paeanic refrain could be found in other kinds of poems besides paeans.[22] Athenaeus, who it will be recalled was relying on "Hermippus the Callimachean," pointed to the lack of refrain in Aristotle's song as proof that it was not a paean.

This, then, was the trend in academic reflection into which Demophilus intruded in 323. Although Plato could give voice to the reactionary's fantasy that literary kinds should be restored in line with ancient religious traditions, most of those dealing with literature took a more pragmatic and empirical approach to lyric classification. All this time, of course, songs continued to grace cults, social events, and musical competitions throughout the Greek world, and so the connection between generic forms and social occasion was not forgotten; it was philosophers and librarians who had most reason to prefer neat, formalistic rather than performance-based definitions of genres. Such an approach would be happy to have a shibboleth that identified all paeans (and only paeans) as paeans, despite a certain amount of messiness in actual practice. But in the 320s all these terms were being revised: Plato had offered a severely rigorous definition of *humnoi* as songs for gods; the category of *enkômia* was still accepting new entrants; *skolia* were easier to define by their context than by form, and how to recognize a paean was to remain for centuries a debatable question. The fact that lyric genres were being reconceived in the later fourth century as new approaches encroached on traditional conceptions allows us to see how the genre of Aristotle's song could be a matter of dispute among sophisticated readers; but we still have to consider why a larger public should have cared.

Impious Song: The Paean to Lysander

Werner Jaeger's justly influential study of Aristotle presented his song as a defiant affirmation of loyalty to Hermias in the face of a hostile world: "While the nationalist party at Athens, led by Demosthenes, was blackening the character of the deceased, while public opinion was dubious about him in Hellas and feeling ran very high throughout the land against Philip and his partisans, Aristotle sent out into the world this poem, in which he declared himself passionately on the side of the dead man."[23] To say Aristotle sent his song "out into the world" suggests publication of some sort, but the story of the trial implies that the song was not widely known outside the Lyceum: if it were circulating widely, it would have been widely used (for why concern oneself with it except to sing it?); if it were widely used, it would have been hard to smear as pernicious. The only poem Aristotle "published" on the Hermias affair was the Delphic epigram. A short song like the Hermias hymn was likely to have circulated especially by word of mouth, with the result that it remained mainly within the circles of Aristotle's friends until Demophilus and Eurymedon got wind of it. Its relatively restricted circulation would have made it all the more shocking if it were presented as sensational evidence leaked from the inner sanctum of a dangerous cabal.

In quoting the song, Aristotle's accusers would doubtless have fixed on verse 18, which says that the Muses will make Hermias "immortal." Here the ostensibly hymnic form of the song (detailed more fully in the next chapter) is joined with an explicit declaration that its subject is beyond mortality. But to say that one's commemorative act has made the deceased immortal was one of the oldest topoi of consolatory eloquence. We can find in such classic exemplars as Simonides' *thrênoi* and Pericles' funeral oration the idea that the dead will never die so long as we remember them.[24] In themselves, the words of this verse are not excessive, and the charge against Aristotle therefore necessarily turned on the question of genre. Jan Bolansée (2001, 81) has judged that "it is not hard to see how an Athenian jury could quite easily have been (mis)led to believe" that Aristotle's poem was a paean. One question that scholars seem not to have addressed is why anyone should have cared.

Is it credible that the anti-Macedonian agitators could have counted on the public to get riled up over such a point?

Generic expectations are in practice rather fluid at any time, and it is hard to imagine even the litigation-loving Athenians being eager to enforce literary definitions that were being rethought and in any case were difficult to apply. However, in the political context of Aristotle's later years, it is plausible that a broad public would have been concerned over such allegations as Athenaeus reports. For the issue of whether one is praising a god or a mortal in song resonated with powerful political currents that had been set in motion by the rise of Macedon. Alexander and his father Philip before him showed the Greeks new forms of absolute power in which, in the words of Momigliano, "the traditional notion of hero lost in importance in comparison with that of divine man." Greek cities had long offered signal honors (sometimes in the form of hero cult) to eminent benefactors, but the self-presentation of Macedonian monarchs augmented a trend "toward blurring the distinction between man and god."[25] Philip II was accused of wanting to be taken for a god, and when Greek cities later offered Alexander honor as a god, this made sense of "an otherwise incomprehensible intrusion of authority into their world."[26] From the time of his crossing into Asia in 334 (possibly passing Atarneus on his way), Alexander's representations of himself underwent a marked elevation. His family had traced its lineage through Heracles, but this gave him a Heracles-like mixed paternity that was heroic, not divine. It was thus a major step up when he began to represent himself as a direct son of Zeus and to accept divine worship as "Ammon Ra" in Egypt in 331.[27] There also seems to have been an attempt to introduce into Alexander's court the practice of *proskunesis*, the ritual obeisance (or debasement, as the Greeks thought of it) that was *de rigueur* at the Persian court. Among those resisting it was Callisthenes, and his quarrel with Alexander over this practice is said to have played a part in his downfall and death.[28]

After his return from the east in 325, a number of Greek cities inferred that Alexander would be pleased to be offered divine cult.[29] Demades, an Athenian politician, was prosecuted and fined for having proposed to make Alexander "the thirteenth Olympian."[30] Alexander's death in 323 made any such request moot, but its shock was such as not to be forgotten. In the end, though, Athens was not to hold out against the new trend toward treating the eminent living like gods: in 291 BCE when Demetrius the Besieger had replaced Macedonian tyranny with his own, the Athenians greeted his arrival in the city with incense, garlands, and choruses singing paeans and other cult songs, including one hymn that hailed him as "a god we see present before us."[31]

Back at the end of the fifth century, to sing a paean to a mortal was a major innovation and a shocking act of obsequiousness. The traditional way that Greeks honored the very great was by offering them cult as heroes after they died. In exceptional cases, hero cult was offered to living benefactors, such as victorious athletes in the great games.[32] But the paean was already associated in Homer with Apollo and the healing god *Paieôn*: its purpose was to thank the god for a victory or to pray for release from ills. The first mortal to have a paean written to him that Greek historians knew about was the Spartan general Lysander at the end of the Peloponnesian war. In the wake of his stunning defeat of Athens at Aegospotami in 405—for which Lysander had a commemorative monument erected at Delphi— the rulers of Samos (who had been put in place by Lysander) gave him extraordinary honors: they rechristened one of their old festivals "the Lysandreia," erected an altar in his honor "as to a god," and sang paeans to him. This is reported to us by Duris, the fourth-century historian from Samos who is cited by Athenaeus for this unusual paean. In an extract cited by Plutarch, Duris names Lysander as the first Greek to receive divine worship while alive, and records the beginning of one paean (867 *PMG* = Pai. 35 Käppel):³³

> Τὸν Ἑλλάδος ἀγαθέας
> στραταγὸν ἀπ' εὐρυχόρου
> Σπάρτας ὑμνήσομεν, ὦ,
> ἰὴ Παιάν.

> Let us hymn the Leader
> of sacred Hellas,
> from wide-way'd Sparta,
> Hail Paian!

The verse is little more than a chant—a triumphal cry at the defeat of an enemy harking back to one of the oldest attested uses of paeans as thanksgiving hymns for military victory. The use of the verb "hymn" need have no generic implication beyond its old, general meaning "let us sing."³⁴ Nor is there anything suspicious in the epithets: both are traditional, with an ancestry in epic. They are almost banal, except that the placing of ἀγαθέας ("sacred" in the sense of under divine protection) may invite an auditor to consider if it is a transferred epithet, in which case the idea of a "sacred general" presents itself before being rejected as violating common usage, not to mention traditional piety.

If paeans to mortals could acknowledge new forms of political power, we can see why an alleged hymn to a friend of the self-aggrandizing Macedonian monarchy could raise the hackles of the Athenian public. We cannot be sure what exactly may have been on the indictment drawn up by Eurymedon and Demophilus, but there is nothing implausible in Athenaeus's general scenario for the 320s.³⁵ In such a political context, Aristotle's old song could have been dredged up as incriminating evidence, even if only to fan prejudice against Macedonian sympathizers.

(The defense speeches of Socrates by Xenophon and Plato show that his idiosyncratic habit of referring to his *daimôn*, something like an inner voice urging virtue, was brought up against him and exaggerated into a sign that he was manufacturing new gods.) A political figure's lyric poetry had figured in another proxy trial about Macedonian politics around 346, when Aeschines saw some of his personal love poems read out in court by opponents who claimed his "little verses" revealed him as lewd and hypocritical.[36] Ian Rutherford points to a slightly later speech by Aeschines to show that a person's way with a paean could be exploited in political fights. Demosthenes had attempted to smear Aeschines by telling a jury that he had had the effrontery to sing a paean when being entertained at an ambassadorial dinner by Philip of Macedon, which was a detestable piece of obsequiousness given Philip's recent aggression against Phocis.[37] Aeschines seems somewhat anxious in his defense, not exactly admitting that he sang the paean but insisting that even if he had, it was directed to a god and that he had, as an ambassador, only done the ritually correct thing, and that (multiplying excuses) Athens had not in any case been directly harmed by the fall of Phocis: "If—with my country safe and my fellow citizens come to no harm—if I did join in with the other ambassadors in singing the paean, so that the god was honored while the Athenians lost no face, I was being pious rather than unjust, and it is just that the charge against me should fail" (163: εἰ δὲ ὀρθῆς ἡ μῖν τῆς πατρίδος οὔσης, καὶ τῶν πολιτῶν κοινῇ μηδὲν ἀτυχούντων, συνῇδον μετὰ τῶν ἄλλων πρέσβεων τὸν παιᾶνα, ἡνίκα ὁ θεὸς μὲν ἐτιμᾶτο, Ἀθηναῖοι δὲ μηδὲν ἡδόξουν, εὐσέβουν, ἀλλ' οὐκ ἠδίκουν, καὶ δικαίως ἄν σῳζοίμην). Rutherford is right, I think, to infer from this text that even at the time Aristotle composed his song, the way a person engaged in paean-singing could be taken as an index of his piety and basic decency. Plato's *Laws* connected the collapse of traditional distinctions among song-classes with political instability, and Aristotle's "paean" could well have struck listeners as a sign that this known Macedonian sympathizer was willing to praise a tyrant as if he were addressing a god.

Paean, Hymn, *Skolion*?

We come then to the question of whether Aristotle's accusers were right: Was the song a paean or some other kind of hymn or something else? Ancient references support all three possibilities. Hermippus, as we have seen, seems to have taken it as a *skolion*; according to a probable restoration, Didymus called it a paean (col. 6.19: ὁ γραφεὶς ἐπ' αὐτῶ[ι Παι]άν); Athenaeus introduces it as a "song" or "lyric poem" (ᾆσμα), and argues that it belongs in a category of its own, being a unique kind of *skolion*.[38] Diogenes Laertius takes it, I think, as a hymn, for this is the title under which he quotes the song (5.6.10; cf. 5.5.10); he calls it a paean when he first refers to it (5.4.1), but the term may be taken over from pseudo-Aristippus, whose attacks on Aristotle Diogenes is at that point retelling.[39]

Modern scholars on the whole have agreed that it cannot be a paean, but differ about what it might be. Wilamowitz concluded that it belonged to the class of ritual religious hymns, but he found the lack of refrain decisive against taking it as a paean; he would not take it as a *thrênos* because the taking up of the deceased into the circle of heroes was too pronounced.[40] Richard Reitzenstein also denied that the song could be a paean—in his case because he held all paeans were choral, whereas Aristotle's song would have been a monody if, as reported, it was sung at meals in the Lyceum. Reitzenstein's conclusion was similar to that of Athenaeus: Aristotle's song was "a free development" of the *skolion* that incorporated some features of the contemporary paean; his book argued that mixing of genres was typical of mid-fourth century *skolia* when the older sort (as exemplified by Athenaeus's Attic collection) were on their way out and there was a tendency for the *skolion* to merge with the paean.[41] Conversely, H. W. Smyth assumed Aristotle's song was a choral piece, but he could not accept a song directed to an abstraction as a genuine paean. Neither could he see it as a conventional lament, which he expected (on a view now discarded) to be in elegiacs; he presented it as religious hymn influenced by the style of the fourth-century dithyramb, which was somewhat less extravagant than the "new" dithyramb of the late fifth century.[42] Other scholars see a mixture of two genres in the poem: C. M. Bowra makes it a paean blended with a *thrênos*, part of a secularizing trend in the history of Apollo's song; Plato would have agreed and deplored the development. Jaeger calls it a "hymn to Areta" but understands it as "primarily a tribute to Hermias," a view shared by a number of scholars.[43] More recently, some have recognized in the song elements of epinician, suggesting an attempt by Aristotle to transmute Hermias's death into a triumph.[44] Such a range of views may tempt one to throw up one's hands with A. E. Harvey: "If even in those days people could not always tell a paean when they saw one, we cannot expect to discover a reliable criterion ourselves"; of paeans he expostulated impatiently "there seem, indeed, to have been practically no rules at all."[45]

These scholars do not consider the possibility of a song's adopting a new genre when introduced into new contexts. This clearly happened to Aristotle's song if there is any basis to the allegation that it was sung at the common meals of the Lyceum. The idea that poems should be consistently and unambiguously one genre or another, or even a mixture of clearly definable genres, is useful in attaching labels to boxes of song-books but not necessarily related to the ways they work in performance.

The Platonic assumption that the generic identity of songs could not be compromised neglects the power of context to reshape a song's meaning. In reading song texts, one has less need for inflexible generic rules than for a "situation generics" in which a song is what a performer can persuade a given audience to call it on a particular occasion. Such a perspective suggests that the genre of Aristotle's song was up for renegotiation when it was performed in new places. If it were, as Wilamowitz imagined, intoned by all at a memorial ceremony for Hermias, it was a sort of philosophers' hymn. But those who learned the song for that occasion could carry it away and sing it, for example, at drinking parties. There it could function as a paean if it were sung by the company among the preliminary libations or at the party's close, at both of which points a group paean was customary; libation paeans were conventionally directed to Zeus and the heroes, both of whom are well celebrated in the lyric.[46] The fact that paeans were "required" at the beginnings and ends of symposia as well as on a great many other occasions meant that there was always a demand for songs that could do the job. Their popularity is implicit in Plato's reference to the poet Tynichus, a "one-hit wonder" who achieved a single musical success, "the paean that is on everyone's lips" (*Ion* 534D = 707 *PMG*). Finally, the short song was suitable for performance as a solo piece after the libation paeans, as a contribution to the evening's drinking songs in which a *skolion* was wanted. In this case, the allusion to "sleep with its soft beams" in the offing becomes pregnant.[47]

Thus, whatever its "original" genre, Aristotle's song could have functioned as a hymn or a sympotic paean, and, once it passed outside the circle of those who used it in a ritual way, could become a *skolion* simply by being performed after the inaugural rituals. In entering new contexts, the speech act scripted in the text would change: what a hymn prays to be accomplished becomes in a *skolion* a generalizing statement offering "wise advice" about living, as Athenaeus characterized the genre. One can extend this line of analysis and say that the song changed genre yet again when it entered the pages of the *Deipnosophists*. To be sure, Athenaeus, with his essentially Alexandrian view of genre, holds that the song falls in the category of *skolia*; but when he quotes it along with a number of other paeans in the closing pages of the work, the song reverts in effect to being a paean as part of the textual "ceremonies" by which he brings his long sympotic book to a close.

The best modern approaches to Greek lyric genres avoid Procrustean classifications, and indeed a recent study by Anna Santoni holds that Aristotle deliberately combined elements of ritual song, encomium, and sympotic *skolion* to make the song adaptable to different contexts.[48] In a similar vein, Renehan judges it an "experimental" poem.[49] There is something unsatisfying, however, about the extreme position that comes into view—holding that the genre of Aristotle's poem was whatever occasion and context held it to be. One problem is that such a perspective gives us no answer to the question of what kind of song he composed. The question might be thought too "intentionalist," a futile attempt to look into the philosopher's mind, but some answer to it is necessary if we are to have a view on the legitimacy of the condemnation of the poem by the prosecution.[50] More generally, it is wrong in my view to conceive genres as so fluid in action that they can never provide any "push-back," so to speak, limiting their song's adaptability. Boundaries between one kind of song and another were doubtless negotiable in practice, but the situation could not have been completely up for grabs—someone who attempted to recite the *Iliad* as a *skolion*, for example, would have been accounted a boorish symposiast (as Aristophanes' *Peace* 1265 ff. shows), and a poet proffering *skolia* is likely to have been drubbed at a competition in epic rhapsody. If any song could be used for any occasion at all, the concept of genre becomes vacuous. Finally, giving generic expectations some sort of traction is not only necessary to stave off interpretative chaos; the putative stability of generic form is also a resource by which poets can make songs more resonant, giving them the opportunity to evoke and exploit the social, political, and religious values packed into conceptions of genre, and to extend them by "crossing" one genre with another. Only if performers and audiences agree to endow conceptions of genre with normative force can genres arouse and satisfy expectations, or toy with expectations after having evoked them through significant forms. Robert Frost once said he did not write "free verse" because it seemed to him like playing tennis with the net down. This is a playful but fair analogy for the constraints—at once arbitrary and enabling—that a conventional genre can provide. I submit that Aristotle's poem was made to be something, not everything, and I do not see it as a catchall in the way Santoni suggests. If it was an experiment, as Renehan concludes in his valuable discussion, it is legitimate to ask just what Aristotle was trying to prove.

Whatever we decide is the best way to categorize Aristotle's song, this study of Greek lyric genres has suggested that they had a paradoxical role. Genre must have acted as an anchor, a drag on free motion; and yet it was an anchor that could be moved and set down in new places. In a culture that had at once numerous performance venues and deeply seated expectations about propriety, genre had to be at once changeable and authoritative. The genre of Aristotle's song might shift as it moved into new situations, but in those situations it had to continue to provide some restraint, limiting and stabilizing meaning before releasing it to move again.

Chapter 6

Kinds of Hymn

Let us turn now from reception to "internal" evidence, that is, to the explicit formal indications the text gives of affiliation with other recognized kinds of song. On this basis, Aristotle's song for Hermias appears as a hymn, and indeed seems very like a fourth century paean, as his accusers charged. Of all Greek songs to have survived, the closest to Aristotle's is a song quoted in the *Deipnosophists* and called a *paian* (701f).[1] It was composed by Ariphron of Sicyon, whose date is unknown, and is addressed to *Hugieia,* Health personified (813 *PMG* = Pai. 34 Käppel). Like Aristotle, Ariphron opens with an invocation to a deified abstraction, pronounces an epithet, and gives an extended argument – complete with priamel – for her worth.

Hymnic Form: Ariphron's Paean to Health

Ὑγίεια βροτοῖσι πρεσβίστα μακάρων, μετὰ σεῦ
ναίοιμι τὸ λειπόμενον βιοτᾶς, σὺ δέ μοι πρόφρων ξυνείης.
εἰ γάρ τις ἢ πλούτου χάρις ἢ τεκέων

ἢ τᾶς ἰσοδαίμονος ἀνθρώποις βασιληίδος ἀρχᾶς ἢ πόθων
οὓς κρυφίοις Ἀφροδίτας ἕρκεσιν θηρεύομεν,   5
ἢ εἴ τις ἄλλα θεόθεν ἀνθρώποισι τέρψις ἢ πόνων
ἀμπνοὰ πέφανται,
μετὰ σεῖο, μάκαιρ' Ὑγίεια,
τέθαλε καὶ λάμπει Χαρίτων ὀάροις·
σέθεν δὲ χωρὶς οὔτις εὐδαίμων ἔφυ.   10

Health, the first of blessed gods for mortals, with you
may I dwell for the rest of my lifetime, and may you be
    gracious to me;
for if there is any delight in riches, or in children,
or in the royal power that makes man's fortune match the
    gods', or in the longings
we hunt down with Aphrodite's secret snares,   5
or if any other heaven-sent delight for mortals or respite
from toils has been revealed,
it is because of you, blessed Health,
that it flowers and shines in the talk of the Graces;
apart from you is no man happy.   10

Lucian refers to this lyric as "that extremely well known song on everyone's lips," and the number of inscribed copies that survive confirms it was widely popular.[2] For this reason people have tended to assume that Aristotle is the debtor, but as we do not know the date of Ariphron, we cannot determine whether Aristotle is imitating him or the reverse. Some direct contact seems in either case undeniable: resemblances between the two songs extend beyond the merely generic and include meter (both employ dactylo-epitrites with an anapestic lead-in), themes, and a number of specific phrases (for hunting, being "like" divinity, toiling, and longing). The main difference is that Ariphron places a petition immediately after the invocation, before proceeding into his argument ("for," v. 3).³

There is no reason to think that either Aristotle or Ariphron was doing something shocking in addressing a hymn to an abstraction. A song in praise of Virtue would have been no more unconventional than the song composed to *Kairos*, Opportunity, by the fifth-century litterateur Ion of Chios (742 *PMG*) or a short anonymous hymn of the same type to *Tukhê*, Chance (1019 *PMG*).⁴ Greek mythopoetic thought drew no clear line between divinities and personified abstractions: a passage like Hesiod's extended description of *Phêmê* or "Rumor" in the *Works and Days* can be read as praise of a minor deity, as a vivid description of a social process, or even as an allegory. One distinction historians of religion sometimes make is that full-fledged divinities, unlike abstractions, were the object of actual cult. This may be useful if it is borne in mind that the line between them was not impermeable: in fourth-century Athens there was an altar in the city center to Rumor.⁵

Returning to Ariphron's hymn, the epithet πρεσβίστα in his invocation stands out in its form (the usual superlative of this ancient adjective of unknown etymology is πρεσβύτατος) and perhaps in its meanings, which suggest that his poem, though popular, sounded some "modern" and even ironic notes. My rendition, "first of gods" combines two notions the word can project, "very venerable" and, because age was associated with honor, "eldest."⁶ Although Health was not the first born of the gods in any standard account, the implication that she is "very old" (a possible nuance of the superlative) is appropriate in two ways. One is obvious and conventional: Health is a very ancient divinity and so venerable.⁷ However, the lack of support in traditional theogonies for making this (rather new) divinity so early may encourage us to take the epithet anthropologically, suggesting she was one of the "earliest" divinities to be granted cult. This would be in line with an idea found among Aristotle's enlightened contemporaries that religion began with elemental goods being deified by primitive people. The sophist Prodicus, for example, had taught that Demeter was nothing more than a personification of early man's appreciation of the importance of bread, as Dionysus was of wine. Health is obviously a primary good of the same sort, and since health, like bread, is necessary for the race's survival, it can be reasonably affirmed that she was among the first divinities to be venerated. This double implication of the epithet, traditional and innovative, is signaled in the pre-posed word "for mortals" (v. 1): this at once strikes a note of piety (mortals cannot hope to live forever, but may pray for health at least) and of anthropological awareness (venerating abstractions is what human beings do). It did nothing to curtail the popularity of the song that its opening phrase, "first among the blessed gods as far as mortals are concerned," expressed a sophisticated, humanizing attitude in religiously unobjectionable terms. In their study of Greek hymns, Furley and Bremer associate the songs to Health and Virtue as "Philosophical hymns," anticipating the Hellenistic trend away from the gruesome myths of the Olympians.[8]

The witty inventiveness of Ariphron (which Aristotle shared) is played out in prose in the after-dinner speeches in Plato's *Symposium* in honor of Eros, passion personified. Although Hesiod had assigned Eros an early place in Greek cosmogony (*Theogony* 120), he played a minor role as a mythological figure and seems not to have been the object of cult before Hellenistic times. Plato's first speaker, Phaedrus, champions Eros as a god, and complains "we have numerous hymns and *paeans* composed by poets to the other gods, but for Eros we have not even an encomium" (*Symp.* 177A–B). Phaedrus's prose performance has much in common with Ariphron's hymn: he begins by proving that Eros is among the "oldest" gods with mythological evidence that includes *Theogony* 120 to affirm that "it is agreed on all sides that Eros is among the oldest gods" (οὕτω πολλαχόθεν ὁμολογεῖται ὁ Ἔρως ἐν τοῖς πρεσβύτατος εἶναι); "being very old," he continues "Eros is also the cause of the greatest boons to us" (πρεσβύτατος δὲ ὢν μεγίστων ἀγαθῶν ἡμῖν αἴτιός ἐστιν, 178A–C).[9] It is all (Socrates' speech excepted) sophistical fun: later the exquisite Agathon politely takes the opposite view and argues for Eros as the youngest of the gods (195C). In this move Agathon seems to have had a predecessor in Ion's hymn to *Kairos* mentioned above (742 *PMG*), which saluted Opportunity as the "youngest" of the immortals, presumably because *kairos* in the sense of the "right" moment to strike is always arising "now."

Turning back to Ariphron's song, we observe its body is mostly priamel, listing aspects of human life that are better when accompanied by health (vv. 3–7). The elements are not ranked in any obvious way, but four "or's" clearly punctuate the series before the period closes with a return to Health in v. 8 (the vocative absent since vv. 1–2). The extended list varies the hymnic topos of listing the god's many cult locales: Ariphron begins with (a) wealth, which also comes first in Aristotle's priamel ("gold," v. 7),[10] and then names (b) having children, (c) royal power, and (d) Aphrodite. This can be closely correlated with Aristotle's tripartite priamel comparing Virtue to (a) gold, (b + c) noble ancestry,[11] and (d) the sensual pleasure of sleep, perhaps not unconnected with sex.[12]

Ariphron concludes (vv. 8–10) on a complex and self-reflecting note (as we will see Aristotle doing). Having shown how many human activities "flourish" (*thallein*) with Health, he adds that she is also the precondition for their being discussed in "graceful conversation." This nice old, partly obscure word for "conversation" (*oaroi*) is suited to cap the priamel because it could also be a stylized way of referring to poetry (as in Pindar

Nemean 7.69).[13] The implication is that performing the song itself is an expression of the kind of happiness Heath makes possible. The connection between Health and poetry would be especially vivid if the song were performed as a sympotic paean, making it at once a prayer of thanks and an instance of the goods for which the group is thankful. In such a case, the paeanic function of the song could have been signaled by the company's adding "hail Paian" at the end. Given the brevity and simplicity of Ariphron's song, we should also consider the possibility that in sympotic contexts, the same song, with no *paian* added, could have functioned as a solo piece, one of many *skolia* praising the joys of health. Sympotic songs often represent themselves as a form of gracious speech, and Ariphron's song contains in its *oarois* an allusion to such stylized talk – high-minded, pious but enlightened reflections on human life and the good. In such a context, Ariphron's would have been a wise and popular choice, and the performance would have confirmed the song's assertion that "Every happy thing depends on Health."[14]

If Ariphron shows what a paean could look like in the fourth century, one can see that William D. Furley and Jan Maarten Bremer had good reason to include Aristotle's song in their collection of Greek hymns. They recognize that the final purpose of the song seems to be to honor a mortal, but remark with justice that Aristotle "wanted his poem to sound like a hymn" (1.265). It is hard, however, to go further and try to decide, as is often done, whether either song was a "religious" hymn for actual cult or a "literary" composition executed in hymnic style.[15] One can conceive of situations in which Aristotle's or Ariphron's song could be used as part of a ceremony appealing to a god; but by virtue of being arguments for praise, both texts also constitute coherent and forceful statements of practical ethics suited for other occasions. We will consider in the following chapter on ethos how Aristotle's song might have played as a form of intellectual debate; at present, it is enough to have troubled the Platonic idea of genres fixed at a song's birth by pointing to the possibility that the "hymns" of Ariphron and Aristotle could have had a second career in schools or dining halls.[16] The idea of hymns being reused as other kinds of songs is not often entertained by literary scholars, and so may be worth supporting by an earlier example in which cult song-forms are adapted to other ends. It comes from the first half of the fifth century and from an author no one would accuse of impiety.

Hymnic Flexibility: Pindar's Fourteenth Olympic Ode

As extensive as are the resemblances between Ariphron's paean and Aristotle's song, they do not prove that the latter is a paean as well. For it was a long established lyric practice to borrow the modes and style of hymns and incorporate them into other kinds of song. Pindar often put a hymnic "façade," as he put it (*Ol.* 6.4), in front of his epinician odes; indeed, a number of these hymnic proems are, like Aristotle's, addressed to personified abstractions such as Fortune or Peace.[17] One of Pindar's shorter epinicians is especially worth reading in relation to Aristotle's song, since its first stanza resembles the philosopher's hymn in several respects. The ode repays study as an example of a song's projecting the context of its own performance, and also as suggesting how it too might have been adapted for re-performance.

The ode we call *Olympian* 14 celebrates the crown won at Olympia by Asopichos of Orchomenos in 488. Orchomenos was a major city in the central Greek region of Boeotia and was known as the site of a very ancient cult to the Graces. Pindar accordingly seems to anchor his occasional poem by invoking these Graces in hymnic fashion:[18]

Καφισίων ὑδάτων
λαχοῖσαι, αἵτε ναίετε καλλίπωλον ἕδραν,
ὦ λιπαρᾶς ἀοίδιμοι βασίλειαι
Χάριτες Ὀρχομενοῦ, παλαιγόνων Μινυᾶν ἐπίσκοποι,
κλῦτ,' ἐπεὶ εὔχομαι· σὺν γὰρ ὔμμιν τὰ τερπνὰ καὶ   5
τὰ γλυκέ' ἄνεται πάντα βροτοῖς,
εἰ σοφός, εἰ καλός, εἴ τις ἀγλαὸς ἀνήρ.
οὐδὲ γὰρ θεοὶ σεμνᾶν Χαρίτων ἄτερ
κοιρανέοισιν χοροὺς οὔτε δαῖτας· ἀλλὰ πάντων ταμίαι
ἔργων ἐν οὐρανῷ, χρυσότοξον θέμεναι παρὰ   10
Πύθιον Ἀπόλλωνα θρόνους,
ἀέναον σέβοντι πατρὸς Ὀλυμπίοιο τιμάν.

πότνι' Ἀγλαΐα
φιλησίμολπέ τ' Εὐφροσύνα, θεῶν κρατίστου
παῖδες, ἐπακοοῖτε νῦν, Θαλία τε   15
ἐρασίμολπε, ἰδοῖσα τόνδε κῶμον ἐπ' εὐμενεῖ τύχᾳ
κοῦφα βιβῶντα· Λυδῷ γὰρ Ἀσώπιχον τρόπῳ
ἔν τε μελέταις ἀείδων ἔμολον,
οὕνεκ' Ὀλυμπιόνικος ἁ Μινυεία
σεῦ ἕκατι. μελανοτειχέα νῦν δόμον   20
Φερσεφόνας ἔλθ', Ἀχοῖ, πατρὶ κλυτὰν φέροισ' ἀγγελίαν,
Κλεόδαμον ὄφρ' ἰδοῖσ,' υἱὸν εἴπῃς ὅτι οἱ νέαν
κόλποις παρ' εὐδόξοις Πίσας
ἐστεφάνωσε κυδίμων ἀέθλων πτεροῖσι χαίταν.

By Cephisus' waters,
Your lot to dwell in a place of fine horses,
O, celebrated in song, royal
   Graces of splendid Orchomenos, who oversee the ancient
      clan of Minyans,

hear me as I pray. For it is with you that all that is
    pleasant 5
and sweet arises for mortals –
whether someone is skilled in art, or is fair, or gleams with
    success.
Not even the gods do without the august Graces
in arranging a dance or feast; they are the stewards
of all that is done in Heaven, and setting their thrones
    beside 10
the one with the golden bow, Pythian Apollo,
in reverence they make the honor of their Olympian father
    flow forever.

Lady Aglaia
and Euphrosuna fond of song, the greatest god's
children, be our witnesses now, Thalia, too, 15
lover of song, as you behold our band of high stepping
    revelers
at this happy event: for to sing of Asopichos have we come,
well rehearsed in the Lydian mode,
because the city of the Minyans has won at Olympia –
with thanks to you. And now, to the dark hall 20
of Persephone, Echo, bring the resounding message
to his father, and tell Cleodamus when you see him
that his young son, in the famous glens of Pisa,
with wings of glorious conquest crowned his hair.

It is common in Pindaric epinicians that the specifics of the victory being celebrated are not given immediately; here we are well into the second stanza before we hear details of the victory – the name of the victor, his parentage, home city, and the venue (vv. 17–23). Only after this stanza has sounded, in fact, is it clear that that what began as a hymn is a victory ode. The two-stanza song seems to evolve from one genre into another.

Because of the way particulars are withheld, the first stanza holds together as a self-contained song for no particular occasion. It can "play" as hymn to the Graces, a general song of praise without a petition. The opening epithet-phrases invoke and localize the Graces, calling them to the Cephisus in Orchomenos, one of two famous rivers by that name. The body of the hymn then praises them by adducing arguments ("for," v. 5) to show how extensive is their domain: a priamel lists three spheres of human excellence with which the Graces are intimately involved – wisdom (which includes poetry), physical beauty, and success (which includes athletics) all come about "with the Graces."[19] The priamel is capped by turning to their role among the gods: surely, the Graces are "stewards" of divine felicity, for it is unthinkable that the dances and feasts of Olympus should lack graciousness.[20] As a hymn, the first stanza offers no myth, in the sense that no traditional story is alluded to; but there is mythologizing in the image of the Graces setting up their thrones beside Apollo's. This snapshot, executed in the third person rather than in the "you-style" more common in the hymn, encapsulates a common plot in archaic hexameter hymns in which one of Zeus's children, such as Hermes or Apollo, is shown making his way to Olympus and claiming an honorable place among the great gods. With this image Pindar grants Panhellenic importance to a proud ancient cult of Thebes.

Taken by itself, the first stanza of *Olympian* 14 has numerous similarities to Aristotle's "hymn" (and to Ariphron's as well). Formally, both contain an opening invocation, a priamel, and an argument. When Pindar caps his praise of the Graces by moving from occasions of mortal felicity (v. 6) to those on Olympus (v. 8), he makes the same swerving move as Aristotle, though in the opposite direction. The end of Pindar's first stanza also recalls Aristotle in that both leave us with the picture of a maidenly group of Zeus's daughters perpetuating their father's honor (with σέβοντι of 12, cf. Aristotle's σέβας αὔξουσαι, v. 20). Pindar manages to impart a sense of closure to the stanza with the evocative adjective "ever-flowing" (*aenaon* – given emphasis by its separation from the noun it modifies in v. 12): the metaphor returns us to the river waters in the opening line, while the religious charge in "ever-flowing" concludes the mini-hymn on an image of eternal festivity.[21]

Through this combination of ring-composition and imagistic poise, Pindar's first stanza achieves such closure that it is not hard to imagine it being sung separately as a one-verse song about the size of Aristotle's. By placing in the second stanza the details about Asopichos and his victory, Pindar has made the first more generally relevant, all the more so by including no specific request. At Orchomenos this mini-song could be used in a number of contexts. Feasts followed athletic victories, and such occasions would welcome a pious *skolion* (cf. βροτοῖς, v. 6), an acknowledgment that festivity and song are divine gifts, and a reminder that these pleasures derive from properly conducted prototypes on Olympus (vv. 8–9). Symposia would also have afforded an opportunity to replay the song as an epichoric paean: an address to one of the most ancient cults of the Graces may perhaps seem not easily convertible into Apollo's song – though he is notably prominent (v. 11). The opening libations of symposia, however, called for songs addressed to various divinities, and this stanza could be suitably performed while wine was poured to the gods and the group prayed. Zeus in particular was regularly invoked in sympotic prayers, and in such a context Pindar's closing image of honor "flowing" to Zeus would coincide with the libations poured out in Thebes. The first stanza of this epinician, a prayer-song celebrating graciousness, would be a perfect "grace" to begin a civilized feast.[22]

My speculation about possible re-uses of part of a Pindaric ode ought to be balanced by restating that in this case, as usual, we know nothing about the performance of the song that does not come from the song.[23] But even on that limited evidence, we can say that the song envisions its own repetition outside of its premiere. Let's put the two stanzas back together and focus on Pindar's most striking literary conceit, the invocation of Echo at the end. It is worth noting that Echo in some accounts was the daughter of the river Cephisus, and so may be apostrophized here as a figure of local cult. Be that as it may, invoking Echo raises the possibility that the song's message will be heard by other audiences beside the one awaiting the chorus at a Theban shrine. In summing up for Echo the information to be relayed to the victor's dead father (vv. 22–24), Pindar incorporates into his song its first echo, so to speak. In addition, the rhetoric of these closing verses conflates Asopichos's dedication of his crown to the Graces with his original crowning at Olympia and so makes the "present" performance of the song a follow-up to an earlier, original rite. Even at its putative premiere before the Theban Graces, then, the song posed as a sort of reenactment, and appropriately so since all human occasions for enjoying wisdom, beauty, and glory are reflections of the divine festivity that the Graces superintend in the hymn. Pindar's song – in many respects tied closely to a particular Theban cult and locale – thus closes by making the act it professes to accompany a ritual repetition of a gesture already performed, and one whose substance is to be preserved into the future. The figure of Echo reinforces this conceit, authorizing future repetitions of the song, even past the barrier of death. Crossing this final barrier opens the possibility for the song to convey its message to an entirely different set of listeners, including readers who were not present at the Graces' shrine on that happy occasion.

It remains of course possible that all my suggestions are off or wrong and are based on a misreading of statements in Pindar that ought to be taken at a symbolic level. But to read what presents itself as Theban cult song as a context-less fantasy is to turn it into an artistic phantasmagoria one has difficulty imagining being of interest to, far less being commissioned by anyone, least of all by Greek aristocrats anxious to advertise the excellence of their families and cities. My own response to this predicament is that the danger in attempting to conceive a song's contexts is not so much that we may write a historical novel as that we may write a bad one, forgoing vital detail by not pressing the poem for all the evidence it gives about its situation in the world. To change the analogy, reading Greek lyric with no thought for performative context is like regarding Greek sculptures as pure white objects, forgetting the vivid colors and jewels with which they were once bedecked but which time and pilferage have stripped away. In some Greek lyric texts, as sometimes in sculpture, residual flecks of color remind us of the fuller range of their effects in situ. Such a reminder is the way that *Olympian* 14 *represents itself* as a processional, sung by a troop of revelers celebrating Asopichos by Cephisus's waters, for I repeat that the picture a song gives of its own performance qualifies it significantly, even if the scenario was never actually played out.

The declared destination of this high-stepping band of singers (κῶμον, v. 16) is the shrine of the Graces, where they hope – the hymn turns out to have a formal petition after all (v. 15) – to be received. The deictic in v. 16 referring to "these" revelers/performers is the moment when the song most concretely ties itself to a context and event, which prompts further speculation about possible cult performance. Crown-bearing processions were a common form of Greek religious celebration, and if such were the first context of Pindar's song, the final image would take on extra point: the song ostensibly describes the victor bearing his wreath through the streets of Orchomenos, but it ends by making the bestowing of the votive at a Boeotian shrine coincide with the crowning ceremony at Olympia. The result is that the "this" in "this chorus" is a little destabilized, reenacting a past celebration and beckoning to a re-performance in the future. This motile stance is supported by the song's metrical scheme. Matching stanzas rather than triads supports the self-description as a processional hymn performed on the way to the shrine. Triads are best performed by dancing so as to lend visual reinforcement to the song's complex metrical articulation into "turn, counter-turn, and stand"; but the isometric, end-stopped stanzas of this song can be repeated without breaking the rhythm of the procession. Ending on an echoing note also allows one to make a repeating loop of the song, as it must have been sung again and again while the parade went down the streets of Orchomenos. Wherever else it was carried, Pindar's song let his patrons bring their Pan-Hellenic glory back home in resounding fashion.

Pindar's "hymn to the Graces," then, may support the hypothesis that Ariphron's and Aristotle's hymns were re-performable pieces, and that they may contain reflections on their possible reuse in the future, for good hymns were reused. To conclude this consideration of lyric genres, we should contrast the one other most important form for Greek hymns, though prosodically very different, the recited dactylic hexameter. The short example I select will afford a convenient opportunity to notice two hexameter lines from other hymns Aristotle wrote. More importantly, comparing sung and recited hymns will show that, although the Greek poetic tradition developed an array of distinct musical modes and distributed these among different contexts and occasions, Greek poets delighted in translating the themes of one idiom into another, in other words, in adapting the same kind of speech to different performative styles. The result is to see the extraordinary degree of integration among the entire poetic tradition, which can make individual poems richer and more intelligible.

Hymns in Hexameters: "Homer" and Aristotle

To begin, let us return to Ariphron's epithet πρέσβιστος, which we remarked was used in a way that did and did not rely on its possible sense of "oldest." Surprisingly for a word that can be used loosely as "very venerable," *presbistos* is not widespread as a laudatory epithet before Ariphron, and his use was subtle enough that later readers had to explain why it was appropriate to health.[24] One other instance of *presbistos* in the sense of "eldest" is worth a look because it occurs in a hexameter hymn that shows that certain hymnic topoi we have met in lyric remain recognizable when executed in the meter and dialect of heroic epic. There are also, unsurprisingly, differences entailed by specifics of each performative mode, notably in this case a different strategy to attain closure.

Hymns in recited hexameters are attested from the archaic age, and are mainly known from an ancient anthology attributed to Homer but containing works from all periods.[25] One of its shorter items may have been composed later than Aristotle, though the language is so traditional it is hard to be sure. It shows in any case how hymnic form persists across different metrical modes:

Γαῖαν παμμήτειραν ἀείσομαι ἠϋθέμεθλον
πρεσβίστην, ἣ φέρβει ἐπὶ χθονὶ πάνθ' ὁπόσ' ἐστίν·
ἠμὲν ὅσα χθόνα δῖαν ἐπέρχεται ἠδ' ὅσα πόντον

ἠδ' ὅσα πωτῶνται, τάδε φέρβεται ἐκ σέθεν ὄλβου.
ἐκ σέο δ' εὔπαιδές τε καὶ εὔκαρποι τελέθουσι   5
πότνια, σεῦ δ' ἔχεται δοῦναι βίον ἠδ' ἀφελέσθαι
θνητοῖς ἀνθρώποισιν· ὁ δ' ὄλβιος ὅν κε σὺ θυμῷ
πρόφρων τιμήσῃς· τῷ τ' ἄφθονα πάντα πάρεστι.
βρίθει μέν σφιν ἄρουρα φερέσβιος, ἠδὲ κατ' ἀγροὺς
κτήνεσιν εὐθηνεῖ, οἶκος δ' ἐμπίπλαται ἐσθλῶν·   10
αὐτοὶ δ' εὐνομίῃσι πόλιν κάτα καλλιγύναικα
κοιρανέουσ,' ὄλβος δὲ πολὺς καὶ πλοῦτος ὀπηδεῖ·
παῖδες δ' εὐφροσύνῃ νεοθηλέϊ κυδιόωσι,
παρθενικαί τε χοροῖς φερεσανθέσιν εὔφρονι θυμῷ
παίζουσαι σκαίρουσι κατ' ἄνθεα μαλθακὰ ποίης,   15
οὕς κε σὺ τιμήσῃς σεμνὴ θεὰ ἄφθονε δαῖμον.
Χαῖρε θεῶν μήτηρ, ἄλοχ' Οὐρανοῦ ἀστερόεντος,
πρόφρων δ' ἀντ' ᾠδῆς βίοτον θυμήρε' ὄπαζε·
αὐτὰρ ἐγὼ καὶ σεῖο καὶ ἄλλης μνήσομ' ἀοιδῆς.

Earth all-mother I shall sing, she with a firm foundation,
the eldest, who nourishes all things on earth:
whatever passes over the divine land or over the sea,
and whatever flies, these are nourished from your bounty.
You cause people to be blessed with children and
    fertility,   5
Mistress, yours is the giving of sustenance and its
    taking away
for mortal men: happy is he whom you graciously
honor: for him all stands ready in abundance.
His life-nurturing plough-land is laden, and in his fields
flocks and herds flower, his house is filled with good
    things.   10
Men like this are lawful leaders in a city of fair women,
and prosperity and wealth attend them.
Their boys rejoice in youthful happiness,

in flower-bearing choruses their young girls with glad hearts
play and sport among the grass soft with flowers –   15
such are those you honor, reverend goddess, boundless divinity.
Rejoice, Mother of gods, wife of starry Heaven,
and kindly in exchange for my song grant heart-cheering sustenance;
and I shall call you to mind and another song.

Among the usual hymnic elements present here – invocation, praise focusing on the scope of the divinity's power, petition – the description of Earth's blessings are particularly developed; the effect is, in Bowra's words, a "vivid document of the aristocratic life."[26] For our purposes, more informative may be the close, which is typical of hexameter hymns but not what we have seen in Aristotle or Ariphron (or Pindar). This hymn signals that the end is coming by the stereotyped cry "Rejoice" (*khaire*, in v. 17), a vocable found at the close of many hexameter hymns. This is followed by a formulaic final line that is repeated a dozen times in the corpus.[27] Stereotyped language is emphatic here because closure needs to be marked more strongly by diction in hexameters, which, metrically, can be added to *ad lib.*; in a song, closure is at least in part signaled by music – the melody gives shape to each stanza, and melodic ends of repeated stanzas reinforce the end of the whole.

Conventional as this hymn is, each of the opening epithets has something to arrest attention. Most immediately striking is ἠϋθέμεθλον, which is found only here in Greek literature. Apparently coined for this song, "having a solid foundation" is appropriate for Earth qua earth, as in Hesiod's anthropomorphic "broad-breasted Earth" (Γαῖ' εὐρύστερνος, *Theogony* 117). But θέμεθλα were also the foundations of temples, and so the epithet evokes the hymnic topos of praising a god's haunts or places where his shrines were established. Earth is the seat of all holy places and so offers a fine point of departure for the poet's praise. More complex is παμμήτειραν "all-mother."[28] Saying that Earth was the "mother of all" is not new (e.g., Hesiod, *Works and Days* 563, γῆ πάντων μήτηρ; cf. Pindar, *Ol.* 7.38, Aeschylus, *Libation Bearers* 128). But the epithet παμμήτειρα is oddly formed in its second element, differing from the synonymous and more regular compound παμμήτωρ, which is applied to earth in the *Prometheus* (90: παμμῆτόρ τε γῆ). The second element of παμμήτειραν is possibly reflecting a fine point of Homeric scholarship in Alexandria, which wondered whether in *Iliad* 14.259 Night is called the "mother" (μήτειρα) or "subduer" (δμήτειρα) of gods and men. It is a complex and not fully known story, but Earth clearly has the pedigree to claim this old epithet.[29] So too with πρεσβίστα: Mother Earth is certainly "very venerable," but there is point in activating its other sense and naming as "oldest" of the gods the Earth, who springs up in Hesiod's *Theogony* immediately after Chaos, the primal void.[30]

The epithet shared by Ariphron and the "Homeric" hymn is also found in the opening of a hexameter hymn written by Aristotle. Surveying the books written by the philosopher, Diogenes mentions one in hexameters (ἔπη) and quotes the opening line from what must have been the first poem in the collection: "Pure one among the gods, eldest, far-darter" (Ἁγνὲ θεῶν πρέσβισθ' ἑκατηβόλε, DL 5.27 = Fr. 671 Rose). The first epithet suggests, and the third clinches Artemis as the likely addressee: ἁγνός, "pure" both as "undefiled" and as "chaste," is an epithet of a variety of gods in early poetry, most often of the virgin Artemis, though Demeter bears the epithet in Hesiod;[31] Artemis is clearly pointed to by ἑκατηβόλε (an ancient epithet which I render by an old convention as "far-darter" because its true etymology was not clear); the epithet ἑκατηβόλος is exclusive to Apollo in Homer and Hesiod, and preeminently associated with him thereafter. But the form is potentially feminine and is so applicable to his sister Artemis, to whom the word is applied in a *Homeric Hymn* (9.6). Reinforcing this relation suggests that Aristotle's is a hexameter paean invoking the god of paeans as well as his sister. As there is no tradition or plausible reason to call Artemis "eldest," *presbiste* here might be rendered "very venerable," unless what followed was a sophisticated hexameter hymn of the sort Callimachus wrote, justifying the word's other sense in a syncretizing or even allegorizing fashion.

Of course, if we had more of the poem we might find that it was an ordinary enough hymn, and the same uncertainly would be involved in thinking about another recitable hymn that Aristotle composed, this time in elegiacs. The same list in Diogenes also records a book of elegiac poems (ἐλεγεῖα, no. 146) and quotes the opening phrase of what sounds like a hymn to Artemis: "O Daughter of a mother with fair children" (καλλιτέκνου μητρὸς θύγατερ, Fr. 672 Rose = 672 *IEG*). It is hard to say much about these scraps of recitable hymns because they are heavily formulaic; without a context to resonate against, the traditional language conveys little that is particular. The lyric hymns we have seen, in contrast, seem to devise ways to import something of their performative contexts into their rhetoric, either because they were composed for specific festival events or because they wish to pose as such. One other way to provide poems with contexts, of course, was for readers to tell stories about how they were composed, and the difference this can make can be illustrated by a paean said to have been composed by Socrates. Diogenes, allowing that there has been some question as to its authenticity, quotes the opening line of what he calls a paean by Socrates (DL 2.42 =[2] *IEG*): "Delian Apollo, rejoice, and Artemis, glorious children both" (Δῆλι' Ἄπολλον χαῖρε, καὶ Ἄρτεμι, παῖδε κλεεινώ). A suggestive context for such a poem can be found in a well-known passage of Plato's *Phaedo*, in which Socrates says he has been inspired by a dream to take up composing verse while awaiting execution in prison (60C–61B). Among Socrates' poetic activity, Plato mentions putting Aesop's tales into verse and composing a "prelude" for Apollo (60D: ἐντείνας τοὺς τοῦ Αἰσώπου λόγους καὶ τὸ εἰς τὸν Ἀπόλλω προοίμιον καὶ ἄλλοι τινές). The poem cited by Diogenes could have been composed as, or forged to represent, the Apolline prelude. Its genre cannot be pinned down; Diogenes calls it a "paean," presumably because Apollo and his sister are featured. The paeans we have seen are in lyric meter for musical accompaniment, but either because he is in prison or because his musical education did not advance that far, Socrates does not avail himself of a lyre but resorts to a recitable meter to give his song formal integrity. At a festival for Delian Apollo, however, hexameters on a suitable theme could be set to a lyre and be performed as a kitharodic "prelude" or overture to the god's celebration. As always, occasion can powerfully influence meaning, and the context Plato suggests for a text such as Diogenes cites would make it richly ironic: it is fitting that, even in prison, Socrates should have done his pious best to compose a paean or proem to greet the god whose festival is underway while the *Phaedo* plays out. This is also, of course, the same festival at the conclusion of which Socrates is scheduled to die (*Phaedo* 58A–C).[32]

Such scanty fragments can perhaps best serve to remind us of the range of forms that hymns could take and yet remain recognizable as hymns. They also indicate some ways in which Greek poems were enriched by tying themselves, or by being tied by readers, to specific and highly charged social events. It seems that lyric hymns designed to be repeated in the future were more apt than recitable poetry to import something of their informing context with them into different performative situations.

This means that, for readers, Greek lyric genre may be defined as the frame of expectations that social context ordains, even when that context is to be found only in the rhetoric of the poem. With this in mind, we return to Aristotle's song, this time in its rhetorical aspect.

Chapter 7

Ethos

Having examined the formal means by which Aristotle positioned his song as a kind of hymn, I turn to the ethos of the piece. This aspect of Greek poetry is hard to discern solely through verbal analysis but would have meant a great deal to ancient audiences. I have noted that most Greek lyric texts read more like scripts for giving a speech than records of private meditations. As such, they project a persona that is "ethical" in the Greek sense of the word, that displays the speaker's character (*êthos*) and values by declaring, as Aristotle would put it in his ethical treatises, what is to be pursued and what avoided in life. As a mode of rhetorical analysis, ethos considers a song as a performance of "self," a metrically and otherwise stylized version of what a person of a certain sort might say in a certain situation. From this perspective, a strong ethical strand emerges in Aristotle's song, one that blends his hymnic argument with another discursive mode.

To bring out this dimension of Aristotle's text, I will adduce two earlier lyrics that on first glance may seem neither much like it nor like each other, a five-stanza song by Sappho and a quatrain by an anonymous Athenian symposiast. Although these songs are very different from Aristotle's on their surface, fundamental to them all is the way they take up and address a popular and often-discussed topic: What is the most important thing to pursue in life? What deserves to be called the "finest" (*kalliston*) thing? The ethical stands of these different kinds of song will be illuminated less by Aristotle's philosophical ethics than by his remarks in the *Rhetoric* on how to praise and what to praise. Rhetorical ethos is expressed most obviously in what speakers choose to praise and the reasons they give for it, but almost every word of Aristotle's song has ethical force when one appreciates that it is arguing for a vision of what is *kalliston*. A lyric by Sappho in the same vein will bring out most clearly the rules of the game they both were playing. But first it will be useful to exemplify the genre through a short *skolion* mentioned by Plato.

Ethos in Debate: An Attic *Skolion* and a Poem by Sappho

If the opening of Aristotle's poem suggests a hymn is under way, the second line complicates things when he declares Virtue "the finest" (*kalliston*) thing to hunt down in life. Piling up complimentary epithets is common in hymns, but predicating a superlative would have been heard by Greek audiences as a moral proposition that they were invited to accept or dispute. Such a declaration functioned as an opening gambit, inviting members of the audience to take the floor in their turn and discourse—in whatever poetic or prose form was appropriate in that context—upon their view of the "best" or "finest" (*kalliston, ariston*) thing in life. Speakers can be found striking this note in virtually every kind of Greek poem, and in prose texts as well, so that we are not dealing with a literary genre but with a genre of discourse, a traditional concatenation of themes, rhetorical forms, and rules for transforming them that had been developed in different performative modes to suit different groups and occasions. It was a widely adaptable form of civilized entertainment, of "employing one's leisure time in a noble way" as Aristotle would put it.[1] We find out from Plato that a favored space for such performances was the symposium. His Socrates gives a capsule description of the form in a debate about moral education with a sophist: "I assume that you have heard at symposia men singing this *skolion* in which they count off as they sing, 'Health is best,' and 'second is being fair, but third,' as the poet of the *skolion* says, 'is wealth won without trickery.'"[2] The reference is to a famous verse that is quoted by Athenaeus among the Attic *skolia*, but Plato's contextualization lets us see that it has a slightly more than playful purpose:[3]

Ὑγιαίνειν μὲν ἄριστον ἀνδρὶ θνατῷ,
δεύτερον δὲ φυὰν καλὸν γενέσθαι,
τρίτον δὲ πλουτεῖν ἀδόλως,
εἶτα τέταρτον ἡβᾶν μετὰ τῶν φίλων.

Health is best for a mortal man,
and second is to be born fair;
third is to grow wealthy without trickery
and fourth is youthful sport among friends.

The simple song is lighthearted, but strikes an ethical posture from the end of the first line: the addition of "for a mortal man" indicates the singer will not aim at some impossible perfection but will content himself with those goods a mortal can hope to attain (what was called at the time "the human good," *to anthrôpinon agathon*). The choice shows a symposiast who keeps a sense of human limits without losing an appreciation for pleasure. Health, as we saw, was praised by Ariphron in religious terms as "most venerable for morals." The *skolion* shows that choosing to praise health could have a political dimension as well: the singer gives first place to a good that is in principle available to all, not the desirable but less widely distributed goods of inborn beauty or wealth. The final verse can also be seen as achieving closure by a bit of self-reference, as in Ariphron's paean. In the company of friends, "being young together" (*hêban*) is virtually synonymous with sympotic activity. (The marriage of Heracles upon his ascent to Olympus to *Hêbê*, "youth, youthful vigor," symbolizes not only perpetual youth but also the enjoyment of perpetual felicity.) The symposiast thus closes with the implication that another candidate for the finest thing to do in life is to sing this song among friends. This wittiness and the mild irony may be why in part the verse was sometimes ascribed to "wise" Simonides (651 *PMG*; cf. 579 *PMG*).

Aristotle, we recall, also began by declaring that *Areta* was *kalliston*, and ranked her above fine birth, wealth, and pleasure. Both verses defend an ethical position. This is the reason that Socrates adduces the Attic *skolion* in his debate with a sophist, and for this reason too Aristotle quotes it in his *Rhetoric* as the kind of thing an orator should say to project his values.[4] The game of striking an ethical attitude in verse was played in various musical modes, as in this elegiac couplet from Theognis (255–256):

Κάλλιστον τὸ δικαιότατον· λῶιστον δ' ὑγιαίνειν·
πρᾶγμα δὲ τερπνότατον, τοῦ τις ἐρᾶι, τὸ τυχεῖν

What is finest [*kalliston*] is what is most just; health is most
  to be desired;
but the most pleasing thing is to get hold of what one
  loves.

Difference within the requirements of form is prized in this competitive game, and Theognis's catch offers us a slightly different, justice-centered ethics along with an off-beat focus on ranking superlative adjectives as much as goods. Another aspect of this verse worth remarking is that the elegiac couplet, as noted, is legible in the sense that it could be learned right out of a songbook, and indeed the poetry collection that went under Theognis's name appears to have been such a collection of easy sympotic pieces. Neither the lyric *skolion* nor the songs of Ariphron and Aristotle are legible in the same way. (In *Gorgias*, Plato assumes that his interlocutor knows the skolion from *having heard* it: 451E: οἴομαι γάρ σε ἀκηκοέναι.) Thus it was an elegiac version of the sentiment that was chosen to be inscribed on Leto's shrine in Delos for passersby to read. We know this fact from Aristotle, who quotes and discusses its wisdom in the beginning of the *Eudemian* and the *Nicomachean Ethics*.[5] One may say that the *kalliston* game takes on new life when such verse is quoted in these treatises, as it does in Plato's dialogue, though its rules are reformulated to suit the new mode of discourse that came to be called philosophy.

This game, really a pretext for descanting on a moralizing theme in a suitable register, was already refined in Lesbos around 600 BCE when Sappho gave the following elaborate reply. It has come down to us on a papyrus with four of its five stanzas relatively clear:[6]

οἱ μὲν ἱππήων στρότον οἱ δὲ πέσδων
οἱ δὲ νάων φαῖσ' ἐπὶ γᾶν μέλαιναν
ἔμμεναι κάλλιστον, ἔγω δὲ κῆν' ὄτ-
    τω τις ἔραται·

πάγχυ δ' εὔμαρες σύνετον πόησαι   5
πάντι τοῦτ', ἀ γὰρ πόλυ περσκέθοισα

κάλλος ἀνθρώπων Ἑλένα τὸν ἄνδρα
   τὸν πανάριστον

καλλίποισ' ἔβα 'ς Τροΐαν πλέοισα
κωὐδὲ παῖδος οὐδὲ φίλων τοκήων   10
πάμπαν ἐμνάσθη, ἀλλὰ παράγαγ' αὔταν
   [...]σαν

[2 lines illegible]
..]με νῦν Ἀνακτορίας ὀνέμναι–   15
   σ' οὐ] παρεοίσας,

τᾶς κε βολλοίμαν ἔρατόν τε βᾶμα
κἀμάρυχμα λάμπρον ἴδην προσώπω
ἢ τὰ Λύδων ἄρματα κἀν ὄπλοισι
   πεσδομάχεντας.   20

Some say an array of cavalry, others foot soldiers,
and others say ships are, in this wide world,
the finest [*kalliston*] sight to behold. But I say it is
   whoever one loves.

It is easy to make this clear to all: 5
for that one – who surpassed
all other mortals in beauty – Helen abandoned
   her most excellent husband

and sailed off to Troy,
without a thought for child   10
or her own parents. But she was swept
   away [sc. by passion]

[2 lines illegible]
And when I think of Anactoria,
   no longer with us here,   16

> I would rather look on her lovely step
> and the bright glance of her face
> than Lydian chariots
>   and soldiers in panoply.   20

Sappho opens with a priamel naming three forms of military splendor as candidates for the "finest" sight to be found on earth. She then, like Aristotle, caps the tricolon with a strong shift that presents us with the spectacle of Anactoria dancing. (So I think we should understand *bama*, "footstep," in v. 17.) Like Aristotle too, Sappho goes on to argue her case from mythology.[7] Perhaps most strikingly, both poems turn at the end from myth to mortal. If Aristotle shifted from *muthos* to *logos* in moving from heroic figures to a friend, Sappho makes an equally broad jump in turning from war to love. Her poem is a version—elaborate, refined, and with an ethos that is open to oriental luxury – of the *kalliston* game played by the *skolion*. Indeed, the conclusion of Sappho's argument, though worked out with exquisite control of tone and pace, is not dissimilar from the Theognidean entry in the game: "the most desirable thing is to get what one loves" (256).

Putting Aristotle's song against these formally disparate texts shows that all exhibit the same deep structure, so to speak. In the background is a grammar that organizes the range of conceivable ethical postures and provides the elements by which these can be transposed and presented intelligibly. The form is finally determined by the kind of speech that is appropriate to the occasion and the attitudes and abilities of the group.[8] Whether one recited a familiar elegiac sentiment conned from a songbook, or tossed off a four-line *skolion* from the good old days in Attica, or exhibited real virtuosity by singing a full five-stanza song in Lesbian dialect, one put familiar themes in play within recognizable transformations, so too, inevitably, when one raised one's voice in Doric hymnic style to perform Aristotle's song. It is noteworthy that this deep structure can emerge in quite concrete details of the text: these can range from the conjunctive "for" as a signal that the argument is beginning (Ariphron v. 3, Sappho v. 6, Aristotle v. 17) to the trick of closing a priamel with a categorical twist and the predilection for ending the song on a self-reflective note.

In Sappho, however, we are pulled back from general moralizing by Anactoria, which Sappho's scholars have conjectured must be the name of a beloved former member of her group. She is the Hermias of her poem: as a proper name, "Anactoria" would seem to focus this brilliant exercise in traditional form on a specific person in a specific place and time. And yet Anactoria is all but unknown to us outside of Sappho; the few brief ancient references to her may well be based on later attempts to understand this passage. Indeed, Page raised the possibility that the name is a shell and that Anactoria is a pseudonym for one of Sappho's pupils whose real name was Anagora.[9] We cannot tell. In favor of Page's suggestion, however, we may observe that pseudonymity was intrinsic to later instantiations of Sapphic love poetry, such as the odes Catullus addressed to Lesbia, "the woman from Lesbos." Within Sappho's text, the function of "Anactoria" may be regarded as purely rhetorical, what Elroy Bundy in his classic analysis of praise poetry termed a "concrete name cap" to close a priamel.[10] In a similar way, more recent perspectives from structural anthropology would identify Anactoria as a name for some archetypal role that many Lesbian girls, whatever their actual names, took on: she is the girl who has graduated from the choral group and gone away (e.g., found a good marriage). This happens to every debutante in every season, and there is no possibility or need to look for a specific Anactoria "outside" the text.

If there was an Anactoria, even under another name, we would say that from our perspective she has moved further than Hermias along a path that leads from historical particularity toward a kind of literary *katasterismos*, becoming a purely textual effect. The comparatively greater obscurity that a historical Anactoria has suffered, however, is not simply due to her belonging to an earlier, less well-documented age than Hermias, for she is already moving in this direction within Sappho's song: her epiphany in the poem, which is to say the moment when the image of her dancing is superposed on the visions previously evoked, arrives with the qualifying phrase, "who is not present" (v. 16). For all her elusiveness and playfulness, Sappho does not pretend her words can conjure the loved girl to the occasion of the song. Much as with Hermias, absence is not denied.

Ethos in Protreptic: Aristotle's Hymn to Hermias, vv. 1–8

Considered in this light, the opening words of the song for Hermias take on extra weight: ἀρετά πολύμοχθε is not only a hymnic invocation but also Aristotle's answer to the question of what is most choiceworthy in life (*kalliston*, v. 2). The answer is not virtue per se, but the kind of excellence that can only be achieved through toil (μόχθος). Aristotle thereby commits himself to a well-established set of ethical beliefs. That *aretê* was worth pursuing despite the toil it entailed is taught in Hesiod's *Works and Days*: with personification verging on allegory, the archaic poet declares that Baseness or Misery (*Kakia*) is easy to attain, for it dwells nearby and the road thereto is smooth; but "the gods have put sweat before Virtue," who dwells at the end of a long, steep road that is painful going at first, though wonderful upon arrival (287–292). This passage was much reprised in Greek discussions of excellence, including a paraphrase in lyric form by Simonides: "there is a story that Virtue dwells amid rocks difficult to reach," he sang in the sixth century, "and is only beheld by those whose hearts have felt the sting of sweat" (579 *PMG*). To choose to praise "Virtue of much toil," then, was hardly breaking new ground; but a song in her honor may have been a novelty: it seems that no one had previously addressed a hymn to Virtue personified, and one may suppose this was part of Aristotle's inspiration.[11] If this were not distinctive enough, he has animated conventional hymnic topics with the discourse of popular ethical debate. The double game continues as the poet pursues two discursive agendas at once. In this light, let us go through the beginning of the song again and observe its shifting ethical stances.

The end of the first verse inserts a qualification for Aristotle's assertion by specifying that it is valid "for the race of mortals" (γένει βροτείῳ: the stance is almost too insistently pious, for the mention of βίῳ in v. 2 is nearly pleonastic). The dative can be construed with ἀρετά πολύμοχθε in two ways: if we take it with ἀρετά, virtue is the best thing we mortals can strive for, though if we were gods we might have different priorities; taken with πολύμοχθε, the expression implies that virtue is absolutely desirable, though it is our sad lot as mortals that it only comes with much toil. The key word πολύμοχθε thus wavers in tone, depending on whether the speaker adopts the perspective of a mortal or of a god who might pity mortals.[12]

The metaphor in v. 2, θήραμα, "quarry," is conventional, almost banal, but suggests something about the target audience: this is hunting not as a necessity to get the basics of life – one can eat acorns for that – but as sport or avocation, a civilizing art that, notionally at any rate, tames land for agriculture and prepares young men for leadership and war. An audience so addressed is very much like the audiences wooed by sophists and other teachers of advanced education in the classical age. They developed a rich prose literature of protreptic in order to convert young men at the turning point of adulthood to the path of Excellence as they defined it. In such discourses, the hunting metaphor appealed to young men who had the freedom to choose their occupations and who, we may add, had the talent, training, and leisure to enjoy songs that deliberated in stylized form about the finest object in life.[13] The social significance of Aristotle's metaphor can be seen in a prose essay written not very much earlier, Xenophon's "On Training Hounds" (*Kunegetika*). This manual on hunting commends the pursuit to noble youths as a preparation for leadership in civic life, and it concludes with an impassioned attack on the amorality and uselessness of sophistic education of the day. In the fifth century, the sophist Prodicus had created a prose discourse in praise of *aretê*, which Xenophon esteemed enough to copy into his *Memorabilia* (2.1.21–34 = Prodicus 84 B 2 DK). Prodicus anticipated Aristotle by developing the personification of Virtue in Hesiod and "wise" Simonides into a prose drama: he pairs *Aretê* with *Kakia* (Baseness), as Hesiod had, but represents them as two female figures accosting young Heracles "at the crossroads" of his life. The personified figures, each arrayed as one might expect, speak in turns for and against the worth of a life of virtuous toil. These protreptic passages suggest that Aristotle's discourse could have had a similar role if it were reprised in sympotic contexts. For in the course of "being young together" over wine and song, as the anonymous skoliast put it, old men were wont to give advice about life to the young.

The similarity in ethos between Aristotle's song to *Areta* and Prodicus's *Heracles at the Crossroads* does not mean that we should reduce the lyric to a recruiting anthem for the Lyceum. But in considering its meanings, it is well to bear in mind that one of the most active and culturally significant branches of fourth-century literature was protreptic (in which I would include swathes from early Plato).[14] Protreptic discourses are ethical in a double way, not only in projecting the persona of a trustworthy and well-intentioned speaker but also in aiming to transform the character of the addressee. In adopting the protreptic mode, a poet aspired to induce a particular *pathos* in his audience; a protreptic poem offers the possibility of shaping its audience on repeated hearings, forming in them a habit of taking pleasure in the proper praise of excellent actions.[15] This was, in Aristotle's view, the noblest function of poetry, including song, in the education of the young.[16]

Such a context gives more force to the "toil" in Aristotle's keynote epithet. In sense, μόχθος is not far from πόνους, which occurs just below at 5. Both words are formulaic in the epinician vocabulary that praises an athlete for expending effort (and money) to demonstrate *aretê* in the games and win glory for his city.[17] They name the "pain" in the American protreptic adage, "no pain, no gain." The underlying ethic is articulated in Aristotle's section on praise in the *Rhetoric* (1.9, 1366a23–68a37) in which he says that virtue is particularly praiseworthy when it comes not from birth or chance but as the result of effort. In an epinician perspective, "toil" makes virtue more admirable; what epinician praises, protreptic commends as the means to the goal.

Some readers would take a further step and adduce Aristotle's philosophic books to argue that his poem expresses his particular conception of "the good." Jaeger, for example, took Aristotle's *Areta* with her "fair shape" (*morphê*, v. 3) as a correction of Plato's metaphysical conception of "the form" (*eidos*) of excellence.[18] But this seems an approach that is easily overdone. The discourse genre in which Aristotle participates encourages the expression of attitudes that are intelligible and acceptable to the group. Convivial song is not a medium for debating metaphysical systems, and Aristotle's song was bound to have a short afterlife if it rattled sensibilities or overturned ideas that had been expressed on the subject for centuries. The after-dinner performer may be a philosopher, but one does not behave only as a philosopher.

With his ethical proposition fully if somewhat enigmatically stated in the first two verses, Aristotle reasserts hymnic style with a series of second-person pronominal forms in v. 3 and following, initiating what Norden identified as the "you-style" characteristic of a great many ancient hymns.[19] With these apostrophes *Areta* undergoes, figuratively, a reverse metamorphosis: the quarry turns from a wild animal to an addressable maiden. The grammar becomes a little tense when the physical form of Virtue is broached: there is anastrophe of the preposition and hyperbaton of the vocative in v. 3, σᾶς πέρι, παρθένε, μορφᾶς. Language becomes a bit jumpy when Virtue makes her epiphany.[20]

As a maiden, *Areta* is both beautiful and elusive – all men desire her but she is not easily possessed; this Virtue is more erotized than the prudent, temperate counselor of Prodicus. When in vv. 6–7 she casts a fruit before the mind's eye, the imagery may suggest a scenario like the Atalanta story, in which the speedy maid was outraced by a cunning suitor who distracted her by throwing apples of Aphrodite in her way.[21] But the epithet that follows immediately changes the picture: calling the fruit of *Areta* "immortal-like" (καρπὸν ἰσαθάνατον) moves us away from Atalanta and toward the apples of immortality that grew in the garden of the Hesperides at the edge of the world: seizing these apples was among the first of Heracles' labors and a prototype of any hero's quest for immortal glory. The compound epithet that I translate as "immortal-like" (ἰσαθάνατον) seems to be Aristotle's deliberately awkward invention, and such compounds are among the stylistic features that make critics call this poem dithyrambic. Wilamowitz divined that such a word must have underlain the banal epithet "immortal" transmitted in the sources known at the time (Athenaeus has τ' ἀθάνατον, Diogenes εἰς ἀθάνατον), and his suggestion was confirmed when the Didymus papyrus appeared. The key semantic difference is that, while ἰσαθάνατον may evoke the idea of literal "immortality" (as does ἀθάνατον), such "equal-" compounds imply that Virtue's reward is not actually deathless but only "equal to" immortality in its extraordinary worth.[22] Hence it seems that Aristotle coined this new word precisely not to destroy the sober ethos he was projecting. The thought-arresting combination "immortal-like fruit" creates an oxymoronic conjunction of permanence and seasonal change that suits the dominant theme of the poem, and the novel epithet shows that Aristotle was willing to strain poetic diction so as not to trespass on the mortal/immortal divide that kept hymns and encomia distinct.

Even so, the Prince of Critics got in trouble because of the way he phrased his theme. The flashpoints can be identified by comparing one final poetic protreptic with a quite extraordinary ethos. When a deified Heracles descends from Olympus near the end of Sophocles' *Philoctetes*, he delivers a speech on *aretê* that is, upon analysis, virtually a synonym of Aristotle's song. Although many texts in the tragic corpus treat the themes of excellence, its price, and reward, none so closely resembles Aristotle's song as these spoken verses. What makes Sophocles' text particularly revealing to set beside Aristotle's is that the tragic poet, in striving to formulate the promise of posthumous glory in a vivid new way, exhibits two moments of verbal excess (see underlined notes on p. 127 last line and p. 128 2nd from last line) that are similar to the controversial spots in Aristotle's song: Sophocles uses the word *athanaton* in a disconcerting way, and he ends with an apothegm that, on its face, sounds impious. More generally, Sophocles' gambit of putting this traditional theme in the mouth of an Olympian highlights the strong connection between the message and the ethos of the speaker.

Ethos in Epiphany: Immortal Virtue in Sophocles' *Philoctetes*

Produced in 409, *Philoctetes* is centrally concerned with heroic suffering and its reward.[23] The suffering is Philoctetes', cast ashore by the Greek army on its way to Troy because of a noisome and excruciating wound; the reward is the prospect of glory to be won if he rejoins the expedition and takes his destined part in the fall of Troy. Our passage comes from the play's conclusion, which suddenly and radically reverses the plot: up to v. 1409, Philoctetes appears determined to nurse his bitterness against the Greek army and go back home to his father. As he is about to depart, abandoning any prospect of heroism for himself and for his newly won ally, Achilles' noble young son Neoptolemos, a godlike figure, appears over the stage and in a *coup de théâtre* changes Philoctetes' mind. Heracles, now made an Olympian and privy to Zeus's great designs, persuades his protégé to go to Troy, where he will find a cure for his ills and play a glorious part in the fall of the city. Omitting a brief aside to Neoptolemos, the climactic speech (1409–1471) runs as follows:[24]

Μήπω γε, πρὶν ἂν τῶν ἡμετέρων
ἀΐῃς μύθων, παῖ Ποίαντος· 1410
φάσκειν δ' αὐδὴν τὴν Ἡρακλέους
ἀκοῇ τε κλύειν λεύσσειν τ' ὄψιν.
τὴν σὴν δ' ἥκω χάριν οὐρανίας
ἕδρας προλιπών, 1415
τὰ Διός τε φράσων βουλεύματά σοι,
κατερητύσων θ' ὁδὸν ἣν στέλλῃ·
σὺ δ' ἐμῶν μύθων ἐπάκουσον.
καὶ πρῶτα μέν σοι τὰς ἐμὰς λέξω τύχας,
ὅσους πονήσας καὶ διεξελθὼν πόνους
<u>ἀθάνατον ἀρετὴν ἔσχον</u>, ὡς πάρεσθ' ὁρᾶν. 1420

καὶ σοί, σάφ' ἴσθι, τοῦτ' ὀφείλεται παθεῖν,
ἐκ τῶν πόνων τῶνδ' εὐκλεᾶ θέσθαι βίον.
ἐλθὼν δὲ σὺν τῷδ' ἀνδρὶ πρὸς τὸ Τρωϊκὸν
πόλισμα, πρῶτον μὲν νόσου παύσῃ λυγρᾶς,
ἀρετῇ τε πρῶτος ἐκκριθεὶς στρατεύματος,   1425
Πάριν μέν, ὃς τῶνδ' αἴτιος κακῶν ἔφυ,
τόξοισι τοῖς ἐμοῖσι νοσφιεῖς βίου,
πέρσεις τε Τροῖαν, σκῦλά τ' ἐς μέλαθρα σὰ
πέμψεις, ἀριστεῖ' ἐκλαβὼν στρατεύματος,
Ποίαντι πατρὶ πρὸς πάτρας Οἴτης πλάκα.   1430
ἃ δ' ἂν λάβῃς σὺ σκῦλα τοῦδε τοῦ στρατοῦ
τόξων ἐμῶν μνημεῖα πρὸς πυρὰν ἐμὴν
κόμιζε.
. . . . .
         Ἐγὼ δ' Ἀσκληπιὸν
παυστῆρα πέμψω σῆς νόσου πρὸς Ἴλιον.
τό δεύτερον γὰρ τοῖς ἐμοῖς αὐτὴν χρεὼν
τόξοις ἁλῶναι. Τοῦτο δ' ἐννοεῖθ', ὅταν   1440
πορθῆτε γαῖαν, εὐσεβεῖν τὰ πρὸς θεούς·
ὡς τἄλλα πάντα δεύτερ' ἡγεῖται πατὴρ
Ζεύς· <u>ἡ γὰρ εὐσέβεια συνθνῄσκει βροτοῖς</u>,   1443
κἂν ζῶσι κἂν θάνωσιν, οὐκ ἀπόλλυται.

Not yet, not before you hear our
speech, son of Poias;
conceive that this is the voice of Heracles
that you hear, and the one you see here is he.
For your sake I have come down from my heavenly seat
in order to reveal Zeus' plans to you   1415
and to check you from your intended course.
Hear then what I say:
First I shall tell you of my own fortunes,
How after toiling through many labors

I won immortal aretê, as is plain for you to see. 1420
For you too, be assured, the same is in store,
to make your life right glorious (*eu-klea*) after these travails.
When you go with this man here to the city
of the Trojans, you will first off find relief from this painful disease,
and then be judged foremost of all the army in *aretê*; 1425
Paris, the cause of all these ills,
with my bow you will absent from life,[25]
and you will sack Troy, and booty back to your halls
you will send, taking the top prizes for military valor,
back to Poias your father by Mt Oeta's plateau. 1430
And whatever booty you get from these troops,
carry off to my pyre to make a memorial offering
for my bow.
. . . . .
   For my part, I will send Asclepius 1437
to Troy to be the healer of your sickness.
For once again by my bow she must be
captured. And know this, when 1440
you come to sack the land, keep a pious respect for the gods' things;
for father Zeus considers everything else of less import.
For piety dies along with mortals 1443
and whether they live or die is not destroyed.

Opening anapests (1409–1417) inform the audience that the figure appearing is none other than Heracles, whom Philoctetes had last seen when agonies drove him to immolate himself on Mount Oeta. For his tendance on that occasion, Philoctetes has inherited the bow that Heracles used in an earlier capture of Troy and that is destined to be present when she is conquered again. Sophocles exploits these and other mythological connections that Heracles has with Philoctetes to compose a unique kind of exhortation. If Heracles was usually, as in Prodicus, on the receiving side of advice, Sophocles allows him to play the role of the one who commends *aretê* to a young comrade. It is also ironic that this Heracles, like Aristotle, can find no better example of the rewards of toilsome virtue than the myth of Heracles.

The divine Heracles, like the singer of Aristotle's hymn, speaks of *aretê*, its price, and its immortal reward, and ends with a tribute to piety (*eusebeia* 1441, cf. *sebas* in Aristotle v. 20). But at two points – underlined above – Sophocles' language is so unusual that scholars have been unsure of what he is saying. The first comes early on when Heracles says that as a reward for his labors he has won "immortal excellence, as you can plainly see" (1420). "Immortal" (*athanaton*) is an unusual epithet for *aretê*, perhaps because *aretê* is so closely associated with mortal excellence; but the phrase is easy enough to make sense of if we interpret *aretê* as a cause-for-effect metonymy meaning "glory."[26] Heracles' phrase thus condenses the common topos that *aretê* leads to renown and the greatest *aretê* to glory that never dies.[27] Understanding the phrase as "immortal glory" makes the reward Heracles won not much different from what he promises Philoctetes just below, that the latter's toils will make his life glorious (*eu-klea*).[28]

The problem with this construal of *athanaton aretên* is that it is not clear how Heracles' "immortal glory" is, as the rest of the line indicates, something visible. Accordingly, Richard Jebb extended the phrase still further, taking it as "the glory of [Heracles'] becoming immortal," the unique reward he won for his uniquely toilsome labors. Heracles' immortalization could easily have been made visible, either by costume, as Jebb suggests, or from the fact of his appearing in the way gods usually did, from an elevated platform (*theologeion*) or a cranelike suspension device over the stage. (It was Aristotle's ἀπὸ μηχανῆς in *Poetics* 1454b2 that gave such forced plot-resolutions as that in *Philoctetes* the name *deus ex machina*.) On this view, *athanaton aretên* is a riddle; the expression, like the hero's fate, is unprecedented.[29] It follows that we must contrast this form of immortalization with that promised Philoctetes, survival after death through commemorative speech (εὐ-κλεᾶ) being a pale reflection of the apotheosis that Heracles obtained.

Both "immortal glory" and "the glory of immortalization" are tenable construals of *athanaton aretên*, and it may be that Sophocles has made both available because "immortal excellence" means different things to Heracles and to his human auditors: mortals undertake extraordinary efforts in hopes of a glory that does not die, but Heracles has found out that Herculean efforts lead to an even greater reward. Pointing to a gap between Heracles' perspective from Olympus and what mortals are permitted to hope for is a subtle but unambiguous signal in his promise to send Asclepius to cure Philoctetes (1437). This contrasts sharply, though for no immediately apparent reason, with a promise made by Neoptolemos not much earlier in the play, that if Philoctetes came to Troy he would be cured by Machaon, the son of Asclepius (1333). Relying on the legend that Asclepius was brought back from death and made an Olympian at the urging of Apollo, Sophocles has Heracles "up the ante" on Neoptolemos: whereas the best hope of remedy a merely heroic person can promise is a descendent of Asclepius, the immortalized hero enjoys access to the healing god-man himself. The gap between the epigone and the immortal healer, like that between the two meanings of *athanaton aretên*, is that between human and divine. It is surely relevant that the main reason that Zeus first struck down Asclepius was that he had in one way or another attempted to close this gap by "healing" death.[30] As in Aristotle's poem, Sophocles wants a strong new statement of excellence's survival, and like him has used the epithet *athanaton* in a way that raises difficulty.

Allowing for a special double ethos in this speech may help with another puzzling expression near its end – Heracles' injunction to the young warriors not to lose a pious respect for the divine in victory. This warning evokes the story told in epic that after the fall of Troy, Neoptolemos impiously killed old king Priam as he was huddled at Apollo's altar in supplication. Within the dramatic frame, piety (*sebas*) and its link to Zeus provide Heracles with closure on a high note, as they do for Aristotle. The hero expands on this, however, with a puzzling final thought: "Zeus regards all other matters as secondary; for the sense of reverence [*eusebeia*] dies along with mortals and whether they live or die is not destroyed" (1443–1444).

The adage seems scandalous on its face, and it has needed a change only of two or three letters to convert the manuscripts' "for . . . surely piety dies" into its opposite: "for piety does *not* die together with mortals, but whether they live or die it is not destroyed."[31] On this reading, printed in most modern editions, "piety" must be taken as "the reputation for doing pious acts" (a metonymy analogous to the use of *aretê* at 1420). Heracles thus adds to the prospect of Philoctetes' "glorious life" (1422) the additional incentive of being celebrated after death for piety.[32] A problem with this view, which its proponents admit, is that the emended text is a banality. Nor is it clear why, apart from the reference to an extra-dramatic event, Heracles should stress piety among the virtues, rather than courage, or indeed steadfast friendship. The alternative is to take the manuscript reading as another strong figuration for living on after death, along lines proposed by Wilamowitz: piety "dies with men" not in the sense of perishing away but of accompanying them in the afterlife.[33] Though there is much that must be given up when the body dies, piety is the one excellence that, even when we are dead, does not pass from us.³⁴

On the manuscript reading, Heracles would be giving a new perspective on the usual sentiment one hears, for example, in Euripides that "*aretê*, even if one dies, is not destroyed, but lives when the body is no more" (ἀρετὴ δὲ κἂν θάνῃ τις οὐκ ἀπόλλυται, / ζῇ δ' οὐκέτ' ὄντος σώματος, Fr. 734.1–2 *TrGF*). The mortal Olympian initiates us into the mystery that, among the virtues, there is something unique about piety and the way it survives death. (Its uniqueness is reinforced by the almost outrageous apothegm.) In support of his gnome, Heracles can cite no less an authority than Zeus, who cherishes piety above all other forms of excellence.³⁵ As an Olympian, Heracles can tell us how the greatest god answers the "What is best?" question. From the other side, *aretê* and piety are said to bring greater rewards than we can imagine.

Quite unlike Aristotle, Sophocles enjoyed a reputation in his time as especially pious, and so in refurbishing the ancient exhortation to virtue he seems to have been free to utter an almost impious paradox with impunity.³⁶ His language in this speech also differ's from Aristotle's in being striking at points but without resorting to the attention-getting epithets of dithyramb, for Heracles is a solemn speechmaker, not a singer. The dramatist's primary creative move in this speech is to invigorate the protreptic to virtue by composing one that a man-god might give, and so the fact that the speech is spoken in epiphany turns out to be crucial. At the same time, this is an eminently performable stretch of iambics on a standard theme, and its general conventionality makes it suitable to be recited as a stirring discourse on its own; we know that in Aristotle's era an ability to recite speeches (*rhêseis*) from tragedy was considered a social accomplishment.³⁷ In its context as part of *Philoctetes*, however, the unique ethos of the speech is more apparent. Taking advantage of his medium, of the power of spectacle over narrative, Sophocles can bring Heracles before our eyes, so that we see him and not just hear him speak or hear about him, as we might from an epic rhapsode or mythologist. We register the strong language that crops up in the speech in light of its unique speaker, whose status is reinforced, "as you can see," by the dramatist's resources.

The interdependence of ethos, genre, and context to be seen in this speech suggests a final general formulation for the subtle ways in which, when we read a poem removed from its original setting, the context from which its words first emerged is a hovering presence behind the words themselves. Epiphanies in Greek poetry often allow for an ineliminable ambiguity about what actually occurs: songs bidding a god to come usually request a literal apparition, but often suggest that the arrival of the divine will be noticeable only as a general enhancement of the scene, a scene that may remain unchanged in other respects.[38] The ambiguities of presence and absence in Greek representations of epiphany seem to me to provide a good way for thinking about how contexts may appear in texts. In theory and often pragmatically, words in a text refer only back and forth to each other, but they can in the aggregate evoke an "outside" world, an external presence to which they point and where they will be received. In this "outside" where the text is bodily performed, words find their "things" and ethical exhortation finds its end in the soul of a hearer. But as with a divine epiphany, the presence of this outside world cannot be pressed too hard. Like a prayer, a poetic text calls forth an external presence, even if only through a single proper noun or demonstrative adjective; but the power that is invited to appear will always remain somewhat less solid than the audible or visible poem itself. All that is needed for a successful poetic epiphany is that the scene of its utterance be enhanced, even if only by the addition of the hymn itself. Conceived in magical terms, a prayer aims to constrain a god to appear on a scene; conceived as song, an effective hymn changes the scene first of all by entering it, and then by bringing some other reality or context, however glancingly, into view.

Chapter 8

Reading

My final approach to Aristotle's text examines its metaphorical and figurative language in light of similar turns of phrase to be found in the Greek poetic tradition. I consider this to read the poetry in the poet, for I hold with Aristotle that the poet's native gifts are to be sought on the level of language. By figurative language I mean the kinds of things that the *Poetics* says make language distinctive: "archaic words (*glôssai*), metaphors, unusual forms, and all deviations from ordinary usage"; in particular, an ability to manage metaphors well is a sign of the born poet, for the crucial skill of "divining resemblances" is one that cannot be taught.[1] I would blend Aristotle's essentially rhetorical approach to poetic language with the practice of Harold Bloom, who shows that these devices must be considered not inertly, as merely ornamental variations, but as purposeful deviations, "swerves" as Bloom would say, from earlier poetic expressions; moreover, these earlier texts were themselves swerves, so that the tradition passes down not only memorable turns of phrase but patterns of evasion. Bloom teaches us to analyze figurative language not simply as the lexical difference between two statements but as an active interaction between two energetic systems. It allows us to read not only Aristotle the poet but Aristotle the reader of poetry.

An attempt to read Greek lyric in this light should begin by acknowledging that we have lost so many poetic texts—to say nothing of the innumerable songs that went unrecorded—that we cannot be sure we possess what Bloom would call the most important "precursor" texts for Aristotle. Nevertheless, looking at Aristotle's tropes in this dynamic way, as far as the evidence allows, is the best way to bring the song into focus as a particular poetic utterance, and to bring out the unexpected and illuminating connections it has with earlier texts that appear to be concerned with other matters.

Troping: πολύμοχθος in Euripides and Bacchylides

In poetry at once traditional and competitive, engaged with a range of generic expectations and aiming to make a unique statement on a common theme, the identity of the poem as poem lies in its tropes, in how convention is "turned" on this occasion from the literal to the figurative. Aristotle shows a distinctive use of language almost immediately, in the epithet πολύμοχθος. We have examined the word as a cue to the song's ethos, but it also bears notice as an element of *logos,* of Aristotle's diction in response to the poetic tradition. The epithet is not an odd word in itself, and indeed compound epithets with "much-" as the first element are very common in hymnic proems. But Aristotle seems to indulge in a slight catachresis, since the usual meaning of the word, "suffering many toils," does not make sense applied to Virtue. Wilamowitz characterized Aristotle's epithet as "venturesome" (*kühn*), the first of several expressions in the poem he called "dithyrambic." In this he relied on Aristotle's own insight that dithyrambic poetry had a special liking for long, compound epithets, even to the point of courting obscurity.² Using such an epithet as a term of praise in a hymnic address thus challenged listeners, especially since, as far as we can tell, no one had ever applied that word to Virtue. Hence Aristotle's opening phrase sounded less like a hymnic formula ritually intoned than like a kenning, propounding a new concept in language demanding to be clarified. A closer look at the word's semantics brings out some of the puzzles it posed. The adjective's second element implies a verb, "to toil" (μοχθέω), and verbal elements in compounds can have an active or passive sense. The Euripidean scholar Donald Mastronarde has noted that πολύμοχθος most often bears what he calls a quasi-passive sense, "implicated in" or "experiencing many toils." "Much labouring" is the first definition given in the dictionary (*LSJ* s.v.). In ἀρετά πολύμοχθε γένει βροτείῳ, this meaning would only be appropriate as a transferred epithet belonging to the following "humankind"; saying that humanity is immersed in toil would be an unexceptionable instance of the usual view Greek poetry takes on life, for "no one is without toil" (ἄμοχθος γὰρ οὐδείς, Soph. Fr. 410.1 Radt). But there is no removing πολύμοχθε, the vocative, from ἀρετά: an invoked deity requires a title, and "generation" has its own epithet anyway. Mastronarde thus attributes to the word here a quasi-active sense, "occasioning many toils"; for this active sense, two precedents can be cited from Euripides, a lyricist whom Aristotle admired.³

The first comes at the beginning of a choral ode that has much in common with Aristotle's opening: "O Ares [who provides] much toil, why do you deal with blood and death, out of tune with the feasts of Dionysus?" (*Phoenician Women* 784–5: ὦ πολύμοχθος Ἄρης, τί ποθ' αἵματι / καὶ θανάτῳ κατέχῃ Βρομίου παράμουσος ἑορταῖς). This invocation to an abstraction, essentially war personified, resembles Aristotle's opening in rhetorical posture, in rhythm (Euripides' dactyls have the same "time signature" as Aristotle's anapestic opening), and in giving an active meaning to πολύμοχθος. The fact that Euripides' epithet is decidedly negative shows what a swerve was needed to apply πολύμοχθος to *Areta*: even turning the voice of the word into the quasi-active does not convert it into a term of praise.

A second Euripidean use of "active" πολύμοχθος as causing toil is closer in tone to Aristotle. A speech lamenting the unpredictability of human life begins (645a *TrGF* = Fr. 916 Nauck):

ὦ πολύμοχθος βιοτὴ θνητοῖς,
ὡς ἐπὶ παντὶ σφαλερὰ κεῖσαι,
καὶ τὰ μὲν αὔξεις, τὰ δ' ἀποφθινύθεις·
κοὐκ ἔστιν ὅρος κείμενος οὐδεὶς
εἰς ὅντινα χρὴ κέλσαι θνητοῖς,   5
πλὴν ὅταν ἔλθῃ κρυερὰ Διόθεν
θανάτου πεμφθεῖσα τελευτή.

O life of much toil for mortals
how you are unstable at every point,
and some things you make grow, others you make wither;
and there is no clear boundary stone set up
to which mortals know they must steer,   5
except for the miserable, Zeus-sent
culmination that is death.

As in the address to Ares, the vocative epithet has active voice, but πολύμοχθος here differs in having adversative force, not simply invoking the god who causes toil but setting up what follows: life engenders many troubles for mortals, but especially in being unreliable. Bundy would call this use of πολμοχθος a "summary foil" to highlight the truly dreadful thing about life, its insecurity. So in Aristotle, Virtue is associated with toil, but immediately declared the finest things for mortals to seek. This second Euripidean use of the word, then, is closer to Aristotle's than the prayer to Ares in the way it puts weight on the epithet and exploits one of its possible senses as a springboard for what follows.

But there is one aspect of Aristotle's πολύμοχθος that neither precedent captures, that is, its surprise, its force as a rhetorical provocation. Our lexicographical analysis can go further if we consider not just the shades of meaning this word can be shown to bear but also its roles in discourse genres. From this perspective, Aristotle's use of πολύμοχθος is most closely paralleled in the literature of protreptic where, as noted, words like μόχθος named the painful price one pays for true excellence. With this admonitory flavor, Aristotle's πολύμοχθος easily becomes "only to be acquired through many toils," a conventional laudation in line with conventional notions of *aretê*, as voiced by Euripides: "who is glorious without toil?" (Fr. 240.2 Nauck: τίς δ' ἄμοχθος εὐκλεής). The closest precedent I find for this nuance in the epithet is in an author Aristotle may not have read, and in a slightly different "toil" compound, ἐπί–μοχθος. But unlike the other parallels, this text applies ἐπίμοχθος to ἀρετά, and this is but one of a number of points in which it resembles Aristotle's song. Here is a little peroration on excellence from the conclusion to Bacchylides' first epinician Ode (1.178–84 Maehler):

ὄντινα κουφόταται
θυμὸν δονέουσι μέριμναι,
ὅσσον ἂν ζώηι †χρόνον, τόνδ' ἔλαχαν† τι-   180
μάν. ἀρετὰ δ' ἐπίμοχθος
μέν, τ]ελευταθεῖσα δ' ὀρθῶς

ἀνδρὶ κ]αὶ εὖ τε θάνηι λεί-
π[ει πολυ]ζήλωτον εὐκλείας ἄ[γαλ]μα.

> Whoever's heart is stirred
> by flighty ambitions,
> may yet, for as long as he lives,   180
> win honor [*tima*]. But excellence [*areta*] is attended by toil,
> yet when brought to its perfect end
> provides for a man even after death
> the much-envied monument of glorifying speech.

The key point of contact between Bacchylides and Aristotle is *areta* (vv. 181/1), around which congregate positively construed "toil" (*mokhthos*, 181/1), the choiceworthy (with *poluzêlôton* v. 184, cf. *zalotos* in 4), fame (vv. 184/17), and some kind of survival after death (vv. 183/16). Like Aristotle's "of much toil," Bacchylides' "attended by toil" (ἐπίμοχθος) is adversative: *tima*, "respect" or "honor," can be acquired by people of small ambition, but *areta* inescapably involves effort. Beyond this dictional affinity, both songs move toward a similar end, concluding with a complex conceit describing posthumous glory as the ultimate reward of *areta*. In Bacchylides, *areta* is said to give rise to celebratory speech (εὐ-κλείας in v. 184), as in Heracles' promise of a glorious life to Neoptolemos in *Philoctetes* (εὐκλεᾶ βίον, *Phil.* 1422). Bacchylides adds the promise that this fame will last after death in the same way as an ἄγαλμα, a monument or temple dedication.[4] Something of the same promise, as we will see, is implicit in Aristotle's assertion that Hermias will be "celebrated in song" for his "steadfast" friendship (βέβαιος, v. 21), an apt adjective to describe a statue or a monument. On the whole, it is as if Aristotle has taken the ἀρετὰ ἐπίμοχθος with which Bacchylides winds down his epinician and modified it slightly to make an opening for his own song, creating a space he fills in with Hermias before coming to the same Bacchylidean close.

Now the name Bacchylides is never found in Aristotle's writings, and it would be rash to assume that he is alluding to or even reacting to this specific text. It is possible that another poet, Aristotle's beloved Euripides, for example, mediated such language to him. For these texts draw on a tradition of moralizing lyric that offered composers a set of recognizable rhetorical postures along with a traditional set of themes and lexical items in which to execute them. It is because of this integrated tradition that Aristotle, resembling a poet he may not have directly known, opens his speech with an emphatic "toil" and closes it by figuratively describing posthumous fame. This same traditional nexus, I suggest, can be dimly discerned in the Euripidean discourse above on the many "toils" in life (Fr. 916). Though its tenor is blame instead of praise, the theme of immortal glory is quietly present: when Euripides' speaker says that Life makes everything "wax" (αὔξεις) and "wither away" (ἀπο-φθινύεις, v. 3), he means to stress the breadth of her power, polar expressions being traditional in this mode of speech. (So a good king makes "the crooked straight and the rough places plain.") But the pair of vegetal metaphors also has connections with the very ancient poetic theme of immortal glory, or to use the Homeric trope, of "glory that does not wither" (κλέος ἄ-φθιτον). In portraying Life as controlling what waxes and withers, Euripides invests her with power over his own aspirations to poetic fame. We shall see below that Aristotle drew from this same deep reservoir of imagery when he selected the other word from that verbal pair to say the Muses will make Hermias "wax" or grow (αὐξάνειν) into immortality. Before we come to this, the concluding figuration of Aristotle's poem, let us take a look at the myths in between.

Mythologizing: Hymn to Hermias, vv. 9–16

Forms of the second-person pronoun acoustically mark off Aristotle's mythic section proving the excellence of *Areta*. The two pairs of heroic exempla followed by Hermias are articulated by forms of "you" (9, 12, 13), and the entire excursus is enfolded by a pair of "your's," with the one at v. 15 (σᾶς δ' ἕνεκεν φιλίου μορφᾶς) echoing that in anastrophe at v. 3 (σᾶς πέρι, παρθένε, μορφᾶς). Through these audible cues, the mythic section is sealed off as a coherent block of argument. Heracles leads off the myths as befits a son of Zeus, a paternity emphasized in v. 9. One may suspect that Aristotle had in addition political and philosophical reasons for beginning with this figure: Heracles was something like a patron saint for the house of Macedon, and his labors were used by philosophers to symbolize philosophy as a heroic quest.[5] In the company of Achilles and Ajax, however, Heracles is fully intelligible as a figure from popular ethics embodying excellence attained by toil.[6] A comedy about education produced in 423 showed an aspiring sophist being trained to play the "What is best?" game: when set the challenge "Of the children of Zeus, which do you think had the most excellent [*ariston*] soul, and endured the most toils?," the student, a traditionalist, reveals his conservatism by declaring "No man was better than Heracles" (Aristophanes *Clouds* 1047 ff.).

For all these reasons, Heracles is perfectly expectable in this context, but things become more resonant with the addition of Castor and Pollux: Heracles, of course, ultimately ascended to Olympus after his labors, and these other sons of Zeus also achieved immortality of a kind in taking turns, one dwelling in Hades while the other was on earth. Both Heracles and the Dioskouroi were used as paradigms for achieving immortality in the secret initiatory religions that go under the name of

"Orphism," and their apotheosis entered Alexander's propaganda as precedents for the king's divinity.[7] In Aristotle, then, the first two examples are at least intimations of immortality, though it should be said that he remains mute about anyone's being divinized: Heracles and the Dioskouroi exemplify toiling for Virtue (11), not dying for and being resurrected by her. There is no doubt that the next pair, Achilles and Ajax, die, even in periphrasis (14). Yet Achilles' fate is also potentially ambiguous: his death in battle is presupposed by Homer and other early epic, but elsewhere the tradition hints that his goddess mother Thetis secured for him a special status in the afterlife. The story that she transported him to the Isles of the Blessed is a mythic paradigm in an Attic *skolion* in praise of Harmodius (894 *PMG*), the young tyrant-slayer of the end of the sixth century who was honored by many in Athens as a martyr who ushered in the democracy. The *skolion* asserts that Harmodius never died but dwells in the Isles of the Blest, along with Achilles and Diomedes. The sequence from Heracles to the Dioskouroi to Achilles thus might give a listener a hint that heroes somehow overcome death, or at least prepare us for the award of some form of immortality to Hermias; but the last hero named—solid, stubborn, suicidal Ajax—remains to insist on the fact of death. What joins him to Achilles is not immortalization but the fact that both were venerated posthumously with heroic cult.[8]

At this point Hermias enters, marked as the culmination of the argument by the ring-composition that seals the mythic section. As with Sappho's Anactoria, Hermias's first appearance in the poem can be thought of as his epiphany, as the reappearance of the longed-for one, insofar as language can bring him back. Aristotle marks the epiphanic moment with a not-immediately-legible expression, the kenning "Atarneus' nursling," thereby making him arrive suddenly and invisibly, as the hearer's solution to a riddle. Evasive language also marks the mention of his death, which comes in periphrastically but heroically: "depriving the rays of the sun of his presence" (ἀελίου χήρωσεν αὐγάς, 16) is a strong twist (which some have found awkward) on a series of epic expressions for life as "looking upon the light of the sun" and for death as "leaving the sun's rays."[9] Periphrasis is always welcome in mentioning death, a word which was not exactly taboo in speeches over the grave but which could readily be given up when an ennobling alternative was available.[10]

There is no doubt that Hermias dies in Aristotle's song. The speaker never takes leave of his senses and closes not with his hero's deification but with the perfectly traditional idea of his immortalization in memory. Indeed, the first allusion to immortality in the poem—the aforementioned epithet *isathanaton* for the fruit that Virtue casts before the mind's eye (v. 7)—is decidedly qualified: despite having a root sense that can mean "*equal to* immortal," the exaggeration amounts to equivocation, precisely implying that "equal to" is *not* "the same as" immortal. I have identified the closest thing to a *causus belli* in the poem as v. 18, where Aristotle comes out with the simple, unambiguous *athanaton*, "immortal," modifying Hermias.[11] But in the grammar-plot of that sentence, *athanaton* is not an attribute bestowed by the speaker but one that will be bestowed on Hermias in the future, and by goddesses who, like Sophocles' immortalized Heracles, can be presumed to know what they are talking about. For his part, Aristotle offers Hermias only the conventional promise that his name and exploits will be repeated in song. I cite but one earlier example of the convention, from Homer, who also seems to know the trick of referring to his poem as it approaches its end. In the underworld scene from the last book of the *Odyssey*, a deceased Agamemnon predicts that Penelope's excellence will be rewarded by the gods, "and so the glory of her *aretê* will never die, and the gods will contrive for her a song among mankind, a gracious song for prudent Penelope" (24.196–8: τῷ οἱ κλέος οὔ ποτ' ὀλεῖται / ἧς ἀρετῆς, τεύξουσι δ' ἐπιχθονίοισιν ἀοιδὴν / ἀθάνατοι χαρίεσσαν ἐχέφρονι Πηνελοπείῃ). The word translated "gracious" (χαρίεσσαν) is often understood as "pleasing," suggesting that the song of a faithful wife, reunited with her husband after many trials, will give pleasure; so it doubtless does in the form of the *Odyssey* itself. But Agamemnon sees this song as a reward for Penelope, and so it is "gracious" because enduring glory is how the gods reciprocate (extending χάρις for χάρις) her devotion to *aretê*. Clearly, Hermias fits into the Homeric model of fame. The venerable pedigree of Aristotle's promise of fame is signaled in v. 17 by the word ἀοίδιμος, "celebrated in song," a word that occurs just once in Homer in a memorable scene from the *Iliad*. Referring to itself with a directness unparalleled in the rest of the poem, the *Iliad* shows Helen complaining that her sad fate will be ἀοίδιμος, a subject of song in the future (*Iliad* 6.358). Helen's prediction is, needless to say, fulfilled in the very work that reports it, and the trick of ironic self-reference accompanies the word when Aristotle takes it over. Like Homer, he manages to make the promise of songs to come for Hermias come true in the course of singing about them. The intricate way in which he does so, however, repays a closer look at the way fame is spread in the finale.

Immortalizing: Hymn to Hermias, vv. 17–21

In shaping an ending for his poem, Aristotle took up a very old pattern for closing a Greek lyric, a reflection on fame that was also a self-reflective allusion to the poem's future re-performances. The two ideas were connected by the fact that the word for fame, κλέος, meant "what people hear," and much of what people heard about the past they heard in song and verse.[12] A striking archaic example may be quoted from Ibycus in the sixth century BCE.[13] An itinerant poet who frequented courts and symposia, Ibycus addressed one longish ode of uncertain genre to Polycrates, tyrant of Samos and one of the most influential patrons of the arts in his day. The last three verses of the poem (quoted below) suggest that it was an *enkômion*, a praise song directed at a living person.[14] But we must be tentative since we do not know what form *enkômia* were expected to have in the sixth century, and Ibycus seems to be toying with whatever form he has chosen as his point of departure. The beginning of the poem is missing, but the 48 verses that survive are almost completely taken up with summarizing the Trojan War, including a mini-catalog of Greeks in which Achilles and Ajax are paired as the foremost spear-fighters (vv. 32–34 *PMGF*). Closing the penultimate triad with this item, Ibycus leads off the final one by identifying a certain Cyanippus as "the fairest" (κάλλιστος, 36) of the Greeks; it seems he had such a lovely "form" (μορφάν, 45) as to outshine even Troilus, a Trojan youth celebrated for his beauty. Having set up, as it were, a beauty contest for the fairest young man at Troy, Ibycus breaks off his myth and turns to Polycrates in the "here and now": he concludes by promising the prince "unwithering" glory alongside Cyanippus and Troilus:

τοῖς μὲν πέδα κάλλεος αἰὲν
καὶ σύ, Πολύκρατες, κλέος ἄφθιτον ἑξεῖς
ὡς κὰτ ἀοιδὰν καὶ ἐμὸν κλέος.

These will have a share in beauty forever,
and you too, Polycrates, will have a glory that does not wither,
so far as song assures, so far as is assured by my glory.

Ibycus's narrative shift from the martial to the erotic recalls, in a general way, Sappho's poem on Anactoria, and the shift in the quoted lines from *muthos* to *logos* is familiar from both Sappho and Aristotle. As in Aristotle, a final conceit about the fame conferred by poetry caps a mythologizing core. What is most pertinent about this text, however, is that it finds closure by turning the age-old topos of the glory conferred by song on itself. Ibycus concludes not with a general promise that Polycrates will be celebrated in song but with the assertion that his future fame will take the form of repetitions of this very song; Polycrates' hope for future remembrance and Ibycus's quest for poetic glory are jestingly identified: the patron's beauty will be dateless as long as the singer's song is heard. In a similar way, Aristotle's prediction that Hermias will be "sung of" alongside heroes (*aoidimos*) will have been fulfilled any time his ode, with its mythological core, is sung. What is distinctive about Aristotle's development of this conceit is that his hopes for his song's being repeated through time are expressed in the figure of a song endlessly sung by the Muses; as we will see more fully below, this connection is reinforced by making their song a sort of echo of his. At present we may parallel this closing move by adding Ariphron's hymn to Health and the suggestion near its end, on my interpretation, of re-performances in future "conversations" (*oarois*). It seems that the end of praise songs—we have also considered the flourish about *kleos* ending Bacchylides' first epinician—was felt to be a place where thinking about *kleos* and its ironies was appropriate. The trick was not forgotten, and can be seen closing many a Renaissance sonnet: "So long as men can breathe, or eyes can see, / So long lives this, and this gives life to thee."[15]

The fact that Aristotle is executing a traditional conceit in its expected *sedes* allows him some complexity in developing the figuration of fame; indeed it demands that he be ingenious in expression to make the song new.[16] So let us press closely the logic of the sentence, curious though it may seem at points.

Here again is the last movement of the song, after Hermias has "died" in the poem:

> τοιγὰρ ἀοίδιμος ἔργοις,
>   ἀθάνατόν τε μιν αὐξήσουσι Μοῦσαι,
> Μναμοσύνας θύγατρες, Δι-
>   ὸς ξενίου σέβας αὔξου-   20
> σαι φιλίας τε γέρας βεβαίου.

> Hence he will be a subject of song because of his exploits,
>   and the Muses will grow him into immortality,
> those daughters of Memory,
>   making reverence for Zeus grow,   20
> god of guest-friends, and the rewards of steadfast friendship.

A logical particle (τοιγάρ, cf. γάρ in Ariphron) articulates a break: Hermias, having crowned the list of Virtue's devotees, becomes the subject of a new discourse about the rewards she bestows. The Muses will create songs about Hermias because his "exploits" (ἔργοις in v. 17) in pursuit of *Areta* are on a par with the legendary exploits (ἔργα, v. 10) of Heracles and the other heroes. Applying to Hermias the Homeric word ἀοίδιμος (v. 17) was enough to promise enduring poetic glory; but Aristotle adds that Hermias will thereby become "undying" (ἀ-θάνατος), a strongly affirmative swerve from fame's traditional epithets like "unwithering" (ἄ-φθιτος), which might be expected in this context. Still, this bold predicate is only bestowed in prospect: "undying" is proleptic and Hermias's immortality is only an anticipated result of the Muses' assiduous singing.

The Muses are introduced as the daughters of Memory (*Mnamosuna*); this too is quite traditional, but also susceptible of an anthropological interpretation to the effect that Hermias's immortality will consist in this song's being remembered, that is, re-performed. Aristotle is not obtruding a philosophical doctrine, but uses the Muses as a figure for a human faculty in order to express himself in words that an "enlightened" sort of person could sing. In the background here must hover the role of the goddess Memory in Greek religious beliefs concerning the afterlife. Although these ideas tend to be submerged in our literary texts, recent years have seen the recovery from tombs throughout Greece of small gold tablets and other inscribed tokens that carry instructions for securing a happy existence in the underworld. In many of these texts, and in the mystery initiations they point to, *Mnamosuna* was a powerful goddess who had to be entreated to ensure the continued personal identity and status of the deceased.[17] In the context of predicting Hermias's immortality, mentioning the daughters of Memory could not have failed to touch on widely held spiritual hopes. But Aristotle's Muses are also, as the run of the sentence quickly reminds us, daughters of Zeus; the father's name places *Mnamosuna* in the poetic tradition of Homer and Hesiod, thereby affirming the Olympian order in which great men are immortalized through song, not through secret initiations or cult. In fact, with the mention of Zeus's name, the Muses' song glorifying Hermias morphs in the final verses into an act of reverence for their father—it is Zeus that they venerate. This is also quite appropriate, for in the canonical picture of the Muses in Hesiod's *Theogony*, they do nothing so much as "delight the mind of their father with song" (*Theog.* 36–37; cf. 11, 40–41, 47–48, 68–71).

Taking things quite literally, however, this song-within-a-song makes the genre of Aristotle's hymn shift a final time: in describing the song the Muses will sing as an act of reverence for Zeus *xenios* (vv. 19–20), Aristotle quotes the keynote epithet they will give him, in effect echoing their song in advance. But so potent is the venerable epithet *xenios* that Aristotle's song to Virtue undergoes influence, as Harold Bloom might put it, from the Muses' future song, in which praise of Hermias will be transmogrified into a hymn to Zeus. In heaven, Hermias will change from the *dedicatee* of the song to Virtue and become an *example* in the Muses' song: the suggestion is that the firm friendship he showed will be the story (the *muthos*) they tell to exemplify the rewards in store for those who honor the god of guest-friends. Aristotle's own song for Hermias does not entirely disappear as it is sublimated into a hymn to the god of guest friendship, for a self-reinforcing irony remains: the heavenly hymn of the Muses will only be heard on earth to the extent that Aristotle's hymn of praise, predicting that hymn, is performed.

In this way, Aristotle's close entangles an encomium for Hermias with a hymn to Zeus. This overlapping of songs is brought out by repeating the verb αὐξάνειν in 18 and 20 to describe both song-acts. Some have found the repetition awkward, and Wilamowitz suggested that the first (v. 18) be changed. But both should be kept, as the Didymus papyrus confirms. The most general sense of αὐξάνειν is to "make increase" (cognate with English "augment"), but relevant here is the verb's special vegetal sense, to "foster" or "make grow." (Its Indo-European root is the source of "to wax.")[18] The verb had been used with this sense in connection with *areta* in earlier songs of praise: "Virtue when praised grows like a tree" declared a praise poet sometimes thought to be Bacchylides (Fr. dub. 56 Maehler: ἀρετὰ γὰρ ἐπαινεομένα δένδρον ὣς ἀέξεται); and Pindar expressed the idea with a typical increase in density, "Virtue springs up like a tree freshly bedewed when it is raised among just and wise men to the watery heavens" (*Nemean* 8.40–42: ἀΐσσει δ' ἀρετά, χλωραῖς ἐέρσαις / ὡς ὅτε δένδρεον, <ἐν> σοφοῖς ἀνδρῶν ἀερθεῖσ' ἐν δικαίοις τε πρὸς ὑγρόν αἰθέρα). When Octavian became the first emperor of Rome, he exploited this same root to rename himself "Augustus" as a fostering tutelary spirit rather than tyrant over his people.

Activating the vegetal sense of αὐξάνειν well suits the context of v. 18, for, as noted above, the metaphor of growing or fostering is traditionally associated with enduring glory. Again, Pindar says "The Pierian daughters of Zeus [i.e., the Muses] cause glory to increase far and wide" (*Ol.* 10.95: τρέφοντι δ' εὐρὺ κλέος / κόραι Πιερίδες Διός) and Bacchylides says much the same: "The gleam of *areta* does not die out for men along with their bodies but a Muse makes it increase" (3.90–92: Ἀρετᾶ[ς γε μ]ὲν οὐ μινύθει / βροτῶν ἅμα ϛ[ώμ]ατι φέγγος, ἀλλὰ / Μοῦσά νιν τρ[έφει.]). I have noted that vegetal tropes run very deep in the traditional vocabulary of glorification, as in the epic phrase κλέος ἄφθιτον, glory that does not "wither away" (ἀπο-φθίνειν). The same complex of ideas sustains Aristotle's nearly oxymoronic phrase "immortal-like fruit" (καρπὸν ἰσαθάνατον) in v. 7.[19] In this sphere, αὐξάνειν functions as the opposite of φθίνειν (as in Euripides Fr. 645a.3, quoted above) and so it is very neatly used in v. 18 to depict the Muses' "fostering" of Hermias by using song to prevent his falling into oblivion. Up to Aristotle's time, αὐξάνειν is not commonly found in connection with the bestowing of κλέος, and so its use here may be a slightly fresh variant for such expected (and tired) verbs as "glorify" (κλείω) or "celebrate" (ὑμνέω).[20] Wilamowitz's proposal to change the first to αὐδήσουσαι, "voicing," could claim as a merit that it would be a fresh turn on traditional language while remaining traditional in expressing the often acknowledged truth that the glory (κλέος) bestowed by song is not abstract but depends on the name of the honorand being "heard," being voiced in repeated oral performances. (In this respect it surpasses Bergk's ἀσκοῦσαι, "making, adorning," or Crusius's ἄζουσαι, "venerating.") Yet I fear Wilamowitz may have been overimproving Aristotle. Repetition or near-repetition is not something the song tries to avoid; rather, it seems to resort to repetition consciously for emphasis and connection.[21]

In "augmenting" Hermias's excellence, then, the Muses will "keep him growing" until he becomes immortal in song. The same verb can be repeated in v. 20 (σέβας αὔξουσαι) because by the same act they will "make increase" the respect owed to Zeus *xenios*. Keeping the second instance of αὐξνειν, we may note that it had a further range of meanings quite different from the ones above but relevant here. In rhetorical contexts αὐξάνειν (and its noun αὔξησις) had the technical sense of "amplifying" or "magnifying" a subject through a discourse of praise.[22] Aristotle's recommendations for rhetorical *auxêsis* appear in his discussion of prose encomium in *Rhetoric* 1.9 (esp. 1368a): praise "amplifies" its subjects through examples (*paradeigmata*), comparisons (*parabola*), and rhetorical arguments (*enthumêmata*).[23] Aristotle takes his own advice in framing his praise of Hermias: the *paradeigmata* of his song are Heracles and the heroes, the priamel supplies flattering *parabola*, and the whole is a rhetorical argument ("therefore," 17). This recipe for praise is followed not only by Aristotle's song but within it, in the song the Muses sing for Zeus. As suggested, their praise would be rhetorically strong if they found examples of devotees of Zeus *xenios*, an obvious possibility being Hermias of Atarneus, who had found a reward (*geras*, 21) for being firm in friendship. If in Aristotle's song Hermias is an example of the desirability of *Areta*, his story will figure in the Muses' song to show the greatness of their father. The repetition of αὐξάνειν underscores the doubleness, or echo-effect, with which the song is invested at the end.

A doubling or echo-effect need not lead to confusion, and the lurking charge of impiety compels us to be clear that Aristotle does not collapse the distinction between god and mortal. The twin objects of the second αὐξάνειν are sharply contrasted in a way that strikes again the note of piety in the song's opening. The Muses' singing will keep alive the worship (*sebas*) of Zeus *xenios* and the reward (*geras*) that Hermias is owed for his friendship toward Aristotle and all things Greek (vv. 20–21). The direct objects, formally and phonetically parallel (both are neuter s-stems with preposed genitives), are strongly antithetical: whereas a *geras*, "reward," is what a hero gets (it is often used of booty as a reward or prize of honor, sometimes of last honors), *sebas* belongs to gods. (So the name "Augustus" was translated back into Greek as *Sebastos*.[24]) The chime makes more prominent the different prospects open to gods and men—as Pindar put it, the vast difference in power that separates them (*Nemean* 6.1–7). Provided that the crucial gap between mortal and immortal is not forgotten, the two songs tend to converge, for one can praise Hermias and honor the divine mandate to hospitality at the same time.

There is, then, nothing impious in a song that acknowledges the limits of mortality and the sovereignty of Zeus. Aristotle today would not be accused of impiety, though some would not like it that in the end he takes a secular, humanistic attitude toward the nature of human excellence and the prospects of life after death. The sequence of noun phrases beginning with the appearance of the Muses in v. 18 creates a steady diminuendo away from myth back to reality: the Muses first appear as the daughters of Zeus and Memory, as they do in Hesiod; then they seem to personify an awe-inspired respect for *xenia*; lastly, what is in view is the stableness of firm friendship. What will ultimately keep Hermias's example alive is a combination of the power of memory, veneration for basic social principles, and loyalty among friends, especially those who may embody their friendship in sharing and handing on old songs. In the more poetic terms of Harold Bloom, this pious poem is not Romantic; it is not a lie against time. I find it a courageous poem, one that discovers within hard limits a reason to praise, a confidence to affirm that praise is worthwhile, and a hope that praise of the good will last through time and may even reach the one praised.

The ultimate law the text obeys is not one of literary genre, but the ancient religious and ethical ideal of *do ut des*, let good be repaid with good.

Aristotle's reference to future glory is not merely a pretty final conceit but the real end of his poem (or his prayer). As long as people sing this song, which commends in words what Hermias commended in action, the devotee of virtue will have left behind something lasting, something with a power to influence the character of people in the future, a paradoxical "monument" or "reminder" composed of speech, as Bacchylides put it. Aristotle's sense of commemoration is not the old magical one of intoning the deceased's name to bring the shade near, of the name as a metonym for the person. This may explain why he conspicuously declines to fulfill one of the oldest functions of commemorative verse and flat-out name his friend.[25] His vision of the function of song is a more humanistic and philosophical one of providing an example to remind the living of the rewards that friendship brings and to encourage the preservation of this value with promises that stop just short of being incredible. The excellence that Hermias's life displayed is reciprocated in the praise his steadfast friends bestow on him, and, as the last chapter will show, repeating this praise will sustain the community of his survivors.

Chapter 9

Endurance

A book devoted to reading and re-reading a single lyric from many angles might end by trying to tie everything together neatly. But the previous chapter has argued that Aristotle placed Hermias's immortalization in an endless series of musical re-performances, and so it would be wrong to impose any reading of this text as its complete or final one. I therefore propose by way of conclusion to connect some episodes in the later career of Aristotle's song with its principal theme, showing how the survival of its words in fact depended on the friendship it celebrates.

Much is packed into Aristotle's final words of praise of Hermias's "steadfast" (βέβαιος) friendship. The same virtue is cited by Callisthenes when he praises Hermias's courage and steadfast character (τὴν ἀνδρείαν καὶ τὴν βεβαιότητα τῶν τρόπων, col. 6.2). In part, this emphasis can be understood in light of Aristotle's ethical writings, especially his discussion in *Nicomachean Ethics* of friendship as a form of virtue, as a mutually shared enjoyment at the exercise of high human capacities. Scholars have thought of Hermias in connection with Aristotle's discussion of how friendships are possible with those who are outstanding in wisdom or political power.[1] With each contributing his proper part, such men can have the best kind of friendship, that based on the excellence of each partner, rather than their usefulness or the pleasure they afford (*NE* 8.6). As in Aristotle's relationship with Hermias, we may understand, virtuous friendships are proof against slander, and they last (*NE* 8.6, 1158b8–9: ἀδιάβλητον καὶ μόνιμον); friendships based on utility or pleasure are less enduring (1158b4: ἧττόν . . . μένουσιν). The steadfastness of Hermias's friendship, therefore, is reciprocated by Aristotle's steadfastness in coming to his aid even after death. In this way, the word *bebaios* takes on a second referent and suggests the lastingness of Aristotle's tribute to Hermias, his song as "stable" monument. In what follows I will argue that the last word of the song is not only ethical praise but also alludes to the afterlife of the song, in line with the assertion of Plato that the products or "offspring" of spiritual friendship are "more steadfast, finer, and more immortal" than physical progeny (*Symposium* 209C: φιλίαν βεβαιοτέραν, ἅτε καλλιόνων καὶ ἀθανατωτέρων παίδων κεκοινωνηκότες).

Literally, *bebaios* denotes standing firmly, immovably in space; it is a good word to describe a monument or a border-marker, any hard and hardy object like a statue or a stele planted to stay fixed in the ground. In praise discourse, *bebaios* is frequently extended metaphorically to time, referring to "enduring" virtue and memory. With such a resonance, the metaphor at the end of Aristotle's poem takes on something like its function at the end of Bacchylides' ode quoted above: the virtuous man's reward after death—to be celebrated in song and have glory— is the best possible monument (ἄγαλμα) he can leave behind. Bacchylides' *agalma*, literally an "object of delight," commonly denotes objects dedicated in sanctuaries, often commemorative objects inscribed with a message to posterity. (The cenotaph or statue for Hermias in Delphi would be an example.) I suggest that Aristotle's closing phrase glances at this traditional idea of spreading glory through both a solid monument and a lasting oral report: like Bacchylides and many other praise poets, Aristotle wants his winged words to have the heft and durability of stone.[2] He hints at this by combining the ethical use of *bebaios*—in which the idea of being fixed in place is applied to a moral quality—with the use of the term in literary contexts to figure the lastingness to which verbal commemoration aspires.[3] Aristotle's closing note has something of the flavor of Horace's boast in a poem closing a lyric collection: "I have brought to completion a monument more lasting than bronze" (*Exegi monumentum aere perennius*, Odes 3.30.1).

The nexus of ideas attaching to ethical *bebaios* can be connected by a short chain of associations to the idea of writing as speech made lasting by being made fixed and tangible. The best known link in this chain is the use of *bebaios* in Plato's *Phaedrus* to describe the presumed stability that writing confers on speech.[4] That supreme writer undermines the pretension of writing to give stable form to thought in order to insist that true understanding is not transcribed in texts but is created in the souls of philosophers by their dialectical conversations (their "dialogues"). This ironic attack on writing in writing is characteristic of Plato, but neither confined to him nor without precedent: earlier commemorative poetry in Greek had hit on the idea that the true monument of a fallen warrior is not the physical marker over his body but the inspiration his example leaves behind for the survivors. Hence I need not assert a direct connection with Plato's *Phaedrus* when I suggest that *bebaios* represents Aristotle's response to the perennial challenge for eulogists—how to make plausible the claim that something of the departed will live on. I suggest that this word's background and emphatic placement in the song indicates that, in promising that Hermias's heroism will be preserved, Aristotle considered whether this preservation will be on people's lips, on stones, or as scripts. Having seen the handwriting on the wall—perhaps having seen an inscribed version of Ariphron's famous paean—he alluded with his last trope to the question of what shape the survival he promised might take.

Memorial: Aristotle's Elegiacs to Eudemus

That Aristotle gave thought to how his commemorative song might become a lasting memorial appears if we consider his other most substantial poetic remnant, three and a half elegiac couplets quoted by Olympiodorus, a sixth-century Neoplatonist philosopher. The poem is only partially quoted, and in speculating about its missing part, it is key to bear in mind that it is adduced as evidence that Aristotle did not quarrel with Plato, contrary to what some had asserted. I will accordingly interpret the fragment as if it constitutes, in Olympiodorus's words, Aristotle's "encomium in praise of Plato" (ἐπαινῶν Πλάτωνα ἐγκωμιάζει):[5]

ἐλθὼν δ' ἐς κλεινὸν Κεκροπίης δάπεδον
εὐσεβέως σεμνῆς φιλίης ἰδρύσατο βωμὸν
   ἀνδρὸς ὃν οὐδ' αἰνεῖν τοῖσι κακοῖσι θέμις,
ὃς μόνος ἢ πρῶτος θνητῶν κατέδειξεν ἐναργῶς
   οἰκείωι τε βίωι καὶ μεθόδοισι λόγων   5
ὡς ἀγαθός τε καὶ εὐδαίμων ἅμα γίνεται ἀνήρ·
   οὐ νῦν δ' ἔστι λαβεῖν οὐδενὶ ταῦτά ποτε.

    .... Coming to Cecrops' glorious plain
he piously established an altar to holy Friendship
   for a man whom the lowly ought not even to praise,
who alone or first of men showed for all to see
   by his conduct in life and his way of speaking   5

that a man becomes good and happy at once;
   now is it not possible for anyone ever to attain these
   things.

Olympiodorus calls the poem "the elegiacs to [πρός] Eudemus" and once again interpretation hangs on a proper name. The question of which Eudemus the poem addresses affects how we decide who it is who is arriving in Athens at the fragment's opening and who is the excellent man commemorated with the altar. In an excellent exegesis, Jaeger inferred from Olympiodorus's use of the preposition πρός in his title that the addressee was alive at the time; he accordingly identified him as Eudemus of Rhodes, a well-known pupil of Aristotle's. If this tiny detail in a very late source is to be pressed, we must discard another far more dramatic candidate, Eudemus of Cyprus: in his youth a friend of Aristotle and pupil of Plato, he died in 354 fighting the tyrant of Syracuse.[6] As this context has been lost to us, we fall back on the text to try to identify its actors.

To begin with the person who dedicates the altar: an early view, now not generally believed, proposed that it was Socrates who showed the path to becoming truly good (*agathos*, the adjective of *aretê*), in which case Plato would naturally have been the dedicator.[7] But "coming to Cecrops' plain" (i.e., Attica) clearly indicates that a non-Athenian is intended, in which case it is natural to think that the dedicator was Aristotle, either subsequent to his arrival to study with Plato in 367 or, more likely, after 334 when he returned to Athens after his sojourn in Asia Minor and Macedon. This is the interpretation proposed by Düring, which I support.[8] It makes sense to think that Aristotle on his return to Athens would have put up a sign of his close connections with the thriving Platonic Academy (and possibly too would have announced that he was back in town). His last will and testament makes several bequests for monuments to be erected for friends and family, showing that he was fully involved with the culture of dedications.

On this view, Aristotle's elegiacs recount his own action in erecting an altar to commemorate his friendship with Plato, whose philosophy, as Jaeger points out, can be seen neatly epitomized in the penultimate line identifying being good and being happy.[9] Now this altar is, for us, an object made purely of discourse, much like Aristotle's Delphic monument to Hermias; but even imaginary altars offer space for inscription, and ancient as well as modern readers have taken vv. 2–3 to be Aristotle's paraphrase of what he had inscribed on the monument. Aristotle's biographical tradition records a number of attempts to reconstruct the original behind the paraphrase, including a version that would have Aristotle write, "on the grounds of august friendship I dedicate this altar to Plato."[10] But if there were an actual altar behind these verses, Aristotle would hardly have flouted convention and dedicated it to Plato; great as is the respect he evinces here, one did not offer altars to mortals.[11] (The Samians dedicated an altar to Lysander along with the paean they sang for him, but Lysander was being given extraordinary honors and 404 was an exceptional time.) The adjective σεμνῆς ("august," "holy") in the paraphrase suggests, as Jaeger observes, that the abstraction "friendship" was being personified and divinized, and this is a far likelier dedicatee of an altar than a person. Jaeger is convincing when he argues that the altar, whether we think of it as real or imaginary, "carried only one word, 'To Friendship.'"[12] The grammar of the paraphrase, however, is dense enough (both "a man" and "friendship" being genitives depending on "altar") to bring the two postulated dedicatees together, suggesting that the goddess Friendship was revealed to mankind in the person and actions of Plato. (Describing such "vivid" apparitions is one common use of the adverb ἐναργῶς in 4.) Such an implication would fit with the impression the complete text gave to Olympiodorus, who claimed it as proof that Aristotle revered (σέβει) Plato as a teacher.[13]

Jaeger is right that the imagined inscription need not have named Plato any more than the elegy to Eudemus does (or than Hermias's song names him). In this case, the fact that Plato was the proper name underlying "man" in v. 3 would have to have been preserved in a para-tradition, either an oral tradition as friend passed the couplets on to friend, or, if the elegiacs were inscribed, by those people to be found around monuments and antiquities who were willing to explain them. In fact, as Jaeger also observes, Aristotle frames his speech as the discourse of such an exegete.[14] This is also, one sees on reflection, the stance he took in the couplets on Hermias's monument at Delphi.

The greatest objection to taking Aristotle as the dedicator of the monument in the poem is that speaking of oneself in the third person is really quite unparalleled in elegiac poetry until well into the Hellenistic age. For this reason, Jaeger concluded that Aristotle describes the dedication of some unknown person, "presumably a pupil of Plato's."[15] But it is hard to imagine such a close friend of Plato's passing unmentioned among these giants, and here we may, as in the case of the possibly *faux* Delphic inscription, allow Aristotle to be near the *avant garde* in verse.

Taking Aristotle as the dedicator in this text gives us a rather multilayered elegy—he commemorates in an elegy his own earlier commemoration of Plato with a monument, itself possibly bearing a message in elegiacs. To write an elegy about an inscribed altar may seem excessively self-referential and "Hellenistic," but can also be seen as a way of broadcasting Aristotle's message more widely: as in the case of the multiform songs praising health, an ability to translate a message from one verbal medium or register to another extended its reach by multiplying the occasions on which it could be suitably performed. It is possible that Aristotle memorialized his friendship with Plato, and with Hermias as well, both on stone and in verse: in this case, the elegy to Eudemus serves as the monument's loudspeaker, replaying its message and extending its reach.[16]

As forms of commemoration, then, we may compare the altar to friendship erected in the words of this poem and Aristotle's ending his song to Hermias on a note of stability (βεβαίου). As the old topos of the funeral oration has it, Aristotle's hymn to *areta* will be Hermias's true shrine, and his steadfastness will be matched by the endurance of the song in remembrance of him. Without imputing postmodern views to Aristotle, we note that his song ends with poetry making everything happen, contradicting Auden's despairing declaration in his elegy for Yeats that "poetry makes nothing happen." The power of perpetuating fame that tradition had symbolized in the Muses really inheres in the song tradition, which is a prime way that values are "grown" from one generation to the next. Aristotle's song ends on a bid to join this tradition: on endless future occasions the prize for "steadfast friendship" will be perennially re-awarded to Hermias in a ceremony that reverence enjoins and memory makes possible. If we take the song at its word and suppose it continued to be performed in the Lyceum after Aristotle died, we can imagine something of the setting where this monument in words would have resounded. Theophrastus's will, as recorded in Diogenes, makes provision for refurbishing a shrine in or near the Lyceum called the *Mouseion*, and it directs that an image of Aristotle be erected there alongside one of Nicomachus; Diogenes also mentions an altar nearby.[17] As James Redfield remarks in an illuminating study of the rise of academic institutions in Athens, "This is not exactly hero cult, but it is something like it: the spirit of the founding philosophers, lingering in the place where they taught, motivates the presence there of their successors and gives those successors a claim on the space."[18] In this sense, the Hymn to Hermias would not only preserve the patron's memory among his friends but also that of its author, keeping the "cult" of Aristotle alive.[19]

The survival of the song was assisted both by creating physical spaces in which it might be re-performed and by investing its language with hymnic, poetic, and rhetorical powers: Aristotle claims the right to name the god, to personify, to recall, to inspire. These powers can be called divine if for no other reason than that through them values last for more than a human generation. The true daughters of Zeus—the true prop and stay of their father's laws—are the songs that manage to get remembered. The immortalization Hermias will obtain depends on a series of human, social actions; the song will survive by being handed down among friends, as if it were a valuable guest gift. And as with guest gifts, each exchange honors both of the principals while affirming the greatness of Zeus *xenios*.[20] Thus Aristotle's song ends on a sophisticated, humane thought, but still piously. Composed, subtle, observing due decorum without forgoing irony, it reinvents the hymn: adopting elements from hymns to praise Hermias, it does not deny the distinctions between mortal and immortal, encomium and hymn. The themes that Aristotle chose make Hermias's song suitable to serve as a *skolion* celebrating fellowship, even as the friendship extends across generations; at the same time, his scrupulousness in expression makes the song appropriate to be re-used, for example as a libation paean, especially when the toasts were to "Zeus, the Olympians, and the heroes." Aristotle composed at a time when genres were in flux, as they always are; his work as poet was simultaneously to create a statement greeting something new, to project an atmosphere of ritually correct form behind the words, and to inflect this statement so as to have an effect, a pointed meaning, both at its first presentation and in its hoped-for afterlife. Exploiting the language of tradition and of his time, he made an utterance that was at once intelligible and memorable, well-behaved and distinctive, tightly compact with thought and free to address the future.

Survival: A Letter from Plato

In the collection of letters ascribed to Plato, the Sixth is addressed to Hermias of Atarneus. It says it was written in Plato's old age (322D), and so may date from the last decade of the tyrant's life. This brief letter recommends two brothers, Erastos and Koriskos, who had studied with Plato and now are in Hermias's area, having returned to their hometown Skepsis in the Troad. Plato vouches for his former students as talented but not very worldly and, addressing all three, urges them to form a mutually beneficial friendship. In other words, he asks Hermias to serve as patron to these promising young philosophers. As a letter of recommendation it seems to have worked, if Jaeger was right to restore Koriskos beside Erastos in Didymus's list of Platonists at Hermias's court (col. 5.53–54).[21]

Lovers of Plato learn to regard the epistles with fascination underlined by worry. Some seem too good to be true, most famously the Seventh, in which Plato discloses the true reasons for his deliciously complex writing. Treasures like the Seventh Letter make it worth bearing in mind that a famous writer's letters were as desirable to an Alexandrian librarian as they were easy to concoct from the author's *oeuvre*. But there are no strong grounds for suspecting the authenticity of the Sixth.[22] It has no obvious, excessive details, and what details it does give do not conflict with what we know from elsewhere: Erastos is easily identified with the Erastos mentioned in Epistle 13 as having assisted Plato in a financial transaction (363B); Philodemus notes that he wrote a memoir of Plato, and Didymus places him with Aristotle at Assos.[23] Koriskos is much better known, especially from numerous incidental references to him in Aristotle's works: they were fellow pupils at the Academy and lifelong friends. The brevity of the letter and its lack of "juiciness" count in its favor. I do not pretend to retry the case, but note that the language in which the tyrant is addressed is, typologically speaking, quite in harmony with the courteous didacticism we have seen in several of our texts. Amid the opening greetings, the author—whom I call Plato—congratulates Hermias: "Now Hermias' power will be increased not by the number of his horse nor by any military alliance, nor even by the addition of gold, so much as by steadfast friends of sound character" (322d: Ἑρμείᾳ μὲν γὰρ οὔτε ἵππων πλῆθος οὔτε ἄλλης πολεμικῆς συμμαχίας οὐδ' αὖ χρυσοῦ προσγενομένου γένοιτ' ἂν μείζων εἰς τὰ πάντα δύναμις, ἢ φίλων βεβαίων τε καὶ ἦθος ἐχόντων ὑγιές). Addressing a prince, Plato is ceremonious as he teaches, and so it is not fortuitous that he sounds like Sappho in deprecating the value of cavalry in a priamel; or that he sounds like Aristotle in putting the value of wealth below friends.[24] A little later, Plato comes up with a gnome that might well have been pronounced by the proto-advisor to tyrants, Simonides, "Nothing is steadfast *[bebaion]* in human affairs" (322e: τὸ γὰρ ἀνθρώπινον οὐ παντάπασιν βέβαιον), a truth which Hermias eventually learned to his cost and of which Greek tyrants at all times seemed to need reminding.

Steadfast and sound friendship is what Hermias lacked in Mentor, but this faint topical point does not prove the letter a fiction. What seems more significant is Plato's using the same word, *bebaios*, that was used by Hermias's other Platonist friends. And the word "friend" itself (*philos*) could have a special sense for this circle, for "friend" was the common manner in which members of the Academy greeted each other: Theophrastus's will refers to members of the Peripatetic community as "friends."[25] More important than the authenticity of the letter as a work of Plato is its allusion to the network of friendship that bound them all. Certainly there is no mistaking the links that joined Plato to Aristotle, Aristotle to Hermias, Hermias to Koriskos, and so on. One noteworthy link here is that between the two Academicians, Aristotle and Koriskos, for it bore fruit of a rare sort in the next generation: the son of Koriskos was Neleus of Skepsis, a close associate of Aristotle's successor Theophrastus. It seems that at Aristotle's death in 322 Theophrastus took over Aristotle's personal library, and when he died in the 280s, his will left "all the books" to Neleus (DL 5.52). The story gets very Romantic—and implausible—from there.

Plutarch and Strabo say that after Koriskos's son inherited Aristotle's library from Theophrastus, he moved it from Athens to Skepsis. They give not wholly harmonious accounts but agree that the works were hidden away underground with the result that they were acquired neither by the Alexandrian library nor by its rival in Pergamon, which rose to prominence in the second century BCE. Only around 90 BCE did Neleus's successors sell the collection, to Apellicon of Teos, a wealthy book collector and devotee of Aristotle. He brought the library back to his home in Athens, where it fell into Roman hands when Sulla conquered the city in 86 BCE. Sulla had the books transported to Rome, where they eventually came to be cared for by Andronicus of Rhodes. Andronicus published works of Aristotle (and Theophrastus) on a better and more authoritative basis than theretofore. In this way, Neleus, the son of Koriskos, contributed to a renaissance in the study of Aristotle in the first century BCE.

This story is not as fully fleshed out as one could wish for in dealing with a corpus of such momentous significance, and Athenaeus gives a contradictory account, according to which Neleus sold the books right off to Ptolemy II Philadelphus (reigned 274–246) for the Alexandrian library.[26] What makes the stories suspicious is that they seem to be taking sides in an argument that either Athens or Alexandria was backward in its knowledge of Aristotle during the centuries after his death. And they seem to contradict indications that some scholars knew Aristotle's writings in the Hellenistic age.[27] One likely alternative channel for knowledge of at least some of Aristotle's works in this period is another close associate, Eudemus of Rhodes; this Eudemus, possibly the addressee of Aristotle's elegiacs on the altar for Plato, was a member of the Lyceum at the time when Theophrastus took over, and may have taken copies of some of the founder's works back to Rhodes. He was later known for his valuable commentaries on Aristotle's works and even, in the case of the eponymously titled *Eudemian Ethics,* for editorial work.

Yet the story about Neleus may contain a relevant truth. Even if the collection he safeguarded was not the only one in circulation, it could have followed more or less the course that Plutarch and Strabo suggest, passing on to Apellicon in Athens, a part of the story attested to by the first-century BCE historian Poseidonios (cited by Athenaeus 214d-e = *FGrH* 87 F 36 = F 253 Edelstein-Kidd = F 247 Theiler). One way or another, it seems that Aristotle's books had to spend time in the care of friends until the Romans rediscovered them. If the sixth Platonic Epistle has any basis in fact, it was a protégé of Hermias whose steadfast son played a key role in ensuring that Aristotle's excellence would be recognized in the new world to come. The honor of Zeus, who honors the obligations of friends, was indeed vindicated long after all the players had died.

The book collector Apellicon also contributed the final chapter to the ancient Hermias story: Aristocles knew a book he wrote about Aristotle's and Hermias's friendship and says of it, "anyone who reads this book will soon cease to speak evil of the two men."[28] As for the song, it survived better than Apellicon's book, though we cannot say who exactly preserved the text so it could be copied by Didymus, Athenaeus, and Diogenes. It is possible that Hermippus recorded the words to Aristotle's song along with the trial story; he could have found the text among the works about Aristotle in Alexandria, if not in the philosopher's corpus itself; but we cannot be sure that Hermippus quoted the text.[29] Alternatively, it may have found its way into the record among those lost works on paeans with which Athenaeus supplemented the material from Hermippus; this was a branch of study that Didymus knew as well, and to which he contributed *On Lyric Poetry*. Finally, Aristotle's opponents may have cited the incriminating lines and so unwittingly kept them alive. I have stressed that songs by themselves did not automatically get transferred to texts, and it is not clear that Aristotle's lyric was included with the corpus of his other writings. Diogenes appends to his *Life* of Aristotle a list of 146 of his works (5.27), as indeed Hermippus had included such a list in his biography. Diogenes' list ends with two books of poems: one is labeled "hexameter poems" (ἔπη, no. 145), whence he cites the hymn to the "pure" goddess (Fr. 671 Rose); the other is elegiac poems (ἐλεγεῖα, no. 146), identified by "O Daughter of a mother with fair children" (Fr. 672 Rose = 672 *IEG*). In his valuable study of the ancient lists of Aristotle's works, Paul Moraux slips in supposing that Aristotle's "celebrated" hymn to Hermias would have been inserted somewhere among these collections.[30] This supposition is excluded by Diogenes' genre terms: certainly the epigram on Hermias or the poem to Eudemus could have been placed in the elegiacs, but the song to Hermias is formally excluded from that book and from the hexameters as well. Another list of Aristotle's works contains a likelier rubric under which to place the hymn: the anonymous catalogue appended to the Hesychian life of Aristotle includes an item that reads, "*enkômia or humnoi. Difference*" (A 180: ἐγκώμια ἢ ὕμνοι διαφορά). Moraux understands "difference" (διαφορά) as a gloss, *differentia*, taking it as a reader's reminder that, as a book on distinguishing the meanings of words put it around 100 CE, "the hymn differs [διαφέρει] from the *enkômion:* for the hymn is for gods and the *enkômion* for men."[31] The song to Hermias would fit well either as a hymn or *enkômion*, and its reception history makes the note about the "difference" between the two all the more relevant. But it may be that Aristotle simply did not compose enough lyric poems to tempt later editors to collect them in a papyrus roll, or that the ones he did compose did not survive in sufficient quantity. There is in any case no trace of a book of *melê* among his output. It is a long shot but perhaps worth remarking in conclusion that the song to Hermias might possibly lie under an otherwise unknown work "On Virtue" that is reported, out of alphabetical order and in the context of sympotic literature, as no. A 163 in the Hesychian list.

By obscure routes such as these, Aristotle's song became available to the scholars and antiquarians of the Roman Empire. In the end, it was a translation from performance piece into text that kept the song alive, but in reading it I have found it helpful to keep in mind that Didymus and company were readers and writers, while Aristotle and his company were singers and composers as well as writers. We know the song now not from hearing it intoned by learned gentlemen at the end of a sociable gathering but because its words were copied into books, much as Didymus copied out a passage from Callisthenes or Athenaeus preserved the old Attic *skolia*. Once singing is replaced by writing, scholarship must take up the tasks of friendship if the song is to survive.

This may be why I find a passing comment that Didymus makes so poignant. In the course of recounting *l'affaire Hermias*, Didymus mentions the song and says "it seems worth recording here since there are not many copies to hand."[32] Despite Aristotle's brave hope for his song's endurance, it was becoming rare even in the greatest center of learning in the ancient world.

Aristotle had shaped his song so that any time it was read, performed, or brought up in discussion, Hermias was repaid once again for his friendship, repaid and more than repaid in the lavish way of the large-minded Greek. But eventually, the community for which the song was composed died out, and the duty of reciprocating friendship fell to scholars and antiquarian readers. The music that had accompanied the song is long gone, its chief residuum being a pattern of long and short vowels in the text; the turbulent social circumstances in which it was performed and received have left some marks on the language, but mostly in the form of ghostly presences. The song has jettisoned a great deal in eking out its path to the twenty-first century, but even at our great historical distance we have been able to notice certain powers that Aristotle built into its words from the first: to draw upon and compress the vast resources of an integrated poetic tradition and to focus them on a new event, giving it meaning for the community called together by that song. At the same time, Aristotle composed a lyric able to respond to new circumstances with fresh appeal and so to renew its promise that, through the steadfastness of friends, excellence may find a reward that lasts through time.

NOTES

Notes to Preface

1. Quoting the version given by Aelian in his (3rd-century CE) *Various History*, 3.36. The reports on Aristotle's parting words are collected in the invaluable work of Düring 1957, T 44a-e.

2. Martindale (2005) urges specificity to the object as the way to make criticism literary, quoting (170) a memorable sentence from Pater's preface to *The Renaissance*: "To define beauty, not in the most abstract but in the most concrete terms possible, to find not its universal formula, but the formula which expresses most adequately this or that special manifestation of it, is the aim of the true student of aesthetics."

Chapter 1

1. Aristotle Fr. 675 Rose/5A Gigon (= 842 *PMG*, which Davies is in the process of re-doing as *PMGF*). Page is the basis of the most scholarly English translation, by David Campbell in the Loeb Library *Greek Lyric*, vol. 5, 214–217. Notable editions include Wilamowitz (1892, 2.406), Macher (1914, 21), Wormell (1935, 62–63), Plezia (1977, 4–5), Marcovich (2009, 308–309); others cited at Harding (2006, 154). The textual questions are relatively minor and will be addressed as they

come up. In general, see Renehan (1982), Dorandi (2007), and among earlier studies, Gerke (1902) and Düring (1957, 59–60).

2. *P. Berol.* 9780 (ed. Diels-Shubart), col. 6.22–43. I cite the papyrus from the edition of Pearson and Stephens (1983).

3. Slightly different colometries are conceivable; see, for example, Rutherford (2001, 92–93), Bermer and Furley (2001, 222), and Dorandi (2007).

4. West (1982, 139).

5. Notable studies of the poem are: Wilamowitz (1893, 2.403–412); Smyth (1906, 468–469 and xxxviii); Wormell (1935, 61–65); Bowra (1938/1953); Jaeger (1948, 117–121); Renehan (1982); Guthrie (1981, 26–36, 44); and more recently Santoni (1999); Furley and Bremer (2001, vol. 1.224–227, 263–266; vol. 2.221–228 [commentary]).

6. See Depew (1997) and the fundamental study of Norden (1913, 143–176).

7. Russell and Wilson (1981, xvi, drawing on Aristotle's *Rhetoric* (1.9, 1366a23–68a37); similarly, *Eudemian Ethics* 2.1, 1220a29–34. The article on *aretê* in *LSJ* suffices to show that it can be used for "goodness" or "excellence" of any kind (e.g., one can speak of the *aretê* of productive land), but in people it especially refers to manly qualities in its first attestations, as befits its root *ar-*, as in ἄρσην, "male" or "masculine"; only later in the history of the word do we find it associated with moral virtue, and applied to the gods and their wondrous works. The traditional translation "virtue" (descending from Latin *virtus* by way of *vir*, "man") has the merit of expressing the Romans' awareness that *aretê* encompassed all the good qualities to which a real man (a *vir*) ought to aspire.

8. On the importance of reciprocity in Greek religious ideas, Parker (1998).

9. See Race (1982), developing Bundy (1969).

10. Wilamowitz (1893, 2.405); Page (1981, 1994) calls the charge absurd, Renehan (1982, 255) a sham, seconded by Furley and Bremer (2001, 1.265).

Chapter 2

1. In framing my attitude to the historical value of poetic texts I take inspiration from Ma's (2000, 20) discussion of how to use epigraphical evidence: "a royal letter might speak of the subjects' loyalty, the king's benevolence and his benefactions. We do not know if the subjects were truly loyal, nor whether the king was truly benevolent ... we do not even know if promised benefactions actually took place. What we can say, in all such cases, is that the letter was written and received. That the king did say these things to the recipients of his missive, that the recipients, the citizens of that supremely articulate body, a Hellenistic *polis*, inscribed the missive and perhaps produced a document of their own: all these things in themselves are very real historical facts which deserve attention."

2. Derrida (1974, 158 [originally 1967]); Derrida (1989, 873) returns to the formula, observing that it can equally be used to demand contextual readings: "An 'internal' reading will always be insufficient. And moreover impossible. Question of context, as everyone knows, there is nothing but context, and therefore: there is no outside-the-text [il n'y a pas de hors texte]."

3. Beyond Didymus, Athenaeus, and Diogenes Laertius, Hermias is mentioned by: Diodorus Siculus 16.52, Polyainos *Strat.* 6.48, Photius *Bibl.* 279, p. 350; Himerius *Or.* (40 Colonna); Anon. [Aristotle] *Economica* 29; Anon. *Vita Aristotelis* Westermann; Dionysius of Halicarnassus *Letter to Ammaeus* 5.262 and the so-called *Index of Academic Philosophers* now attributed to Philodemus (*PHerc.* 1021 col. 5.1–22; 1018 col. 2.7 Dorandi). The Suda lexicon names a Hermias as the author of a treatise on the immortality of the soul (= T24 Düring, see his skeptical remarks, p. 283).

4. For difficulties in literary history, see Perkins (1992). It should be clear that the historical contextualization I pursue has nothing to do with the "genetic fallacy," the dubious attempt to delineate the set of historical circumstances that "generated" Aristotle's song. This ill-considered approach to interpretation rightly fell before the New

Criticism: see Wimsatt and Beardsley (1964) and cf. Wellek and Warren (1956, 241–260).

5. Apart from Theocritus of Chios, studied below, cf. Demetrius of Magnesia *apud* DL 5.3 (= F 15 Mejer), who carried on the anti-Hermias campaign in the first century BCE (*RE* 4, col. 2814; Düring [1957, 58]), and probably Theopompus as quoted by Didymus (at col. 4.69, where Pearson and Stephens [1983, 16.24] read "Bithynian," improving Jacoby 115 *FGrH* F 291). Most scholars infer from Hermias's career that he was Greek, though possibly born in Bithynia: Harding (2006, 128, 138), Flower (1994, 206–208), Jaeger (1948, 112 n. 2), Mulvaney (1926, 151).

6. Noticed by Penella (2007, 57) in an excellent exegesis. Using the adjective *entrophos* ("living in, reared in") as a noun ("nursling") seems to be poetic, and a suggestive precedent is in a lyric from Euripides' *Iphigenia at Aulis*: Ajax, born when his father had been exiled from Aegina to Salamis, is styled "nursling of Salamis" (v. 288: Αἴας δ' ὁ Σαλαμῖνος ἔντροφος). Given that Ajax is soon to be mentioned in Aristotle's poem, the figurative expression here for a complex paternity may be significant. (Aristotle mentions this play several times in his *Poetics*, though Euripides' latest editor, Diggle, suspects interpolation in the passage under discussion.)

7. In his *Nicomachean Ethics*, Aristotle asserts that a man who spends his time in the most virtuous activities "will bear the chances of life most nobly and altogether decorously, if he is 'truly good' and 'foursquare beyond reproach'" (*NE* 1.10, 1100b19–21: καὶ τὰς τύχας οἴσει κάλλιστα καὶ πάντῃ πάντως ἐμμελῶς ὅ the third century's interest in the "song culture" of the archaic age, an age with many centers and patrons, a "rich tapestry of poetic forms" (p. 2), and a performance culture not overshadowed by the dramatic festivals of Athens. γ' ὡς ἀληθῶς ἀγαθὸς καὶ τετράγωνος ἄνευ ψόγου), quoting Simonides 542.1, 3 *PMG*. A little later he adds that, when suffering chances to occur to such men, "their fineness shines through, as when they bear with good temper many great misfortunes not through insensitivity to pain but through nobility and greatness of soul" (*NE* 1.10, 1100b30–3: ὅμως δὲ καὶ ἐν τούτοις διαλάμπει τὸ καλόν, ἐπειδὰν φέρῃ τις εὐκόλως

πολλὰς καὶ μεγάλας ἀτυχίας, μὴ δι' ἀναλγησίαν ἀλλὰ γεννάδας ὢν καὶ μεγαλόψυχος, tr. Ross, modified).

8. Redfield (1974, x).

9. Lives of Hermias: Wormell (1935, 55–92); P. von der Muhl, *RE* Suppl. III, col. 1126–1130. Further bibliography in Trampedach (1994, 1).

10. That Hermias murdered Eubulus is mentioned only by Demetrius of Magnesia (*apud* DL 5.3 = F 15 Mejer). Cf. Ari. *Pol.* 1267b31–37 and Strabo 13.1.57 C610. Rhodes and Osborne 2003 date Hermias's taking over from Eubulus after the latter's death to ca. 350, referring to Diodorus Siculus 16.52.5–6.

11. See Weiskopf (1989, 41–42).

12. Herodotus (1.160) says Cyrus gave Atarneus to the Chians as a reward for their having surrendered Pactyes the Lydian to him. Cf. Theopompus's *Letter to Philip* (115 *FGrH* F 250) and his account of Hermias's execution from the *Philippica* (F 291) from which Flower (1994, 86–89) infers an attempt to appropriate Chian territories, connecting it with Hermias's treaty with Smyrna, discussed below.

13. Notably Callisthenes *FGrH* 124 F 2 (discussed below) and Theophrastus, if he is the source of the interlude favorable to Hermias at Didymus col. 5.53–63 as argued by Milns (1994, 78–81), seconded by Bollansée (2001, 94–95) and Harding (2006, 139).

14. See Owen (1983).

15. Aristocles *apud* Euseb. *Praep. Ev.* 15.2.9 Dindorf (= Fragment 2.9 in Chiesara 2004, superseding the edition of Heiland [1925]).

16. Cf. Trampedach (1994, 66–67).

17. *GHI* 165 Tod; I cite the updated text of Engelmann and Merkelbach 1972, no. 9, Vol. 1. 56–60 (= no. 68 in Rhodes and Osborne 2003, 342–5).

18. Didymus col. 5.57–63; Philodemus *Index Acad.* 5.2–11 Dorandi.

19. Hammond and Griffith (1979, 158–160) compare the "companions" of Philip and Alexander (as referred to in, e.g., Aeschines *Against*

Ctesiphon 89), the Macedonian nobles who served as the king's guard. Cf. J. R. Ellis in *The Cambridge Ancient History*, 2nd ed., ed. D. M. Lewis et al. (Cambridge 1994) 770–771. A Pindaric example of *hetairos* used this way is *Pythian* 5.26, for the "Dorian" autocrat Arkesilaus of Cyrene; cf. Currie 2005, 251.

20. As an example, Griffith in Hammond and Griffith (1979, 518) introduces Hermias thus: "this interesting man, combining practical and political skills with (later in life) a willingness to listen to intellectuals and support them, and even probably put some political theory into practice."

21. See, e.g., Jaeger (1948, 110–111); cf. Lynch (1972, 73). On Aristotle's feuding with the Academy, see Aristocles F 2.12 Chiesara (=T 58j Düring) and, on Speusippus's election, Lynch (1972, 60).

22. Redfield (n.d.) points out that the Academy is one of the first ongoing secular corporations we know of that was not based on kinship or residence.

23. Düring (1957, 459) and Chroust (1967) put Aristotle's departure before Plato's death. Proponents of the political interpretation may point to the testimony of Euboulides, a contemporary rival of Aristotle of the Megarian school (DL 2.168): his attacking Aristotle in a polemical book because he was not in Athens when Plato died may imply an earlier departure: cf. Düring (1957, 276 and earlier studies cited at 392 on T 58j). On Demochares reporting that Aristotle acted as a sycophant after the fall of Olynthus, cf. Düring (1957, 388 on T 58g).

24. Düring (1957, T 58g); more on this speech in ch. 4 below.

25. Strabo 13.1.57 C610, pronounced "surely wrong" by Flower (1994, 206 n. 73); Owen (1983, 10) suggests the report stems from an attempt by opponents of the Academy to associate it with tyrants; alternatively, it may be that a text like Theopompus 115 *FGrH* F 250 on Hermias's associating with Platonists was misconstrued. Plato's Sixth letter (more on which below) makes it clear from its tone and from what is said (at 322E–323A) that he has never met Hermias. The explanation of Wormell (1938, 59), essentially that Hermias did visit the Academy when Plato was out of town, is a stop-gap.

26. Nicanor therefore would have been named after his maternal grandfather Nicomachus: Mulvaney (1926, 159), supported by Gottschalk (1972, 322–323) and Düring (1957, 271). The marriage to Pythias may have occurred after Hermias's death: Gottschalk (1972, 322 n. 1); cf. (Düring 1957, 267–268), Mulvaney (1926, 155). On Pythias junior and Nicanor in Aristotle's will see DL 5.16 (= 4a Plezia [1977]); for scholarship on this document, whose authenticity is defended in Gottschalk (1972, 317), see Bollansée (1999a, 298 n. 1).

27. See Lynch (1972, 70–72) for the little that is known about the arrangements of this "school" at Assos. Apart from a general account in Philodemus *Index Acad.* col. 5.2–11 Dorandi, we depend on a lacunose list of names beginning at Didymus col. 5.52, and the only fellow philosopher that can be confidently be read is Erastos (5.53–4, to whom I will return in the final chapter). Jaeger (1948, 115–116 and n. 1) boldly filled in names: neither Koriskos, Erastos's brother, nor Callisthenes (at Assos according to DL 5.5, 10, 39) is improbable, but objections have been raised to Jaeger's using an unreliable passage from Strabo (13.1.57 C610, cited above) to include Xenocrates of Chalcedon (destined to succeed Speusippus as head of the Platonic Academy); Jaeger would thereby make Aristotle's departure from Athens a virtual "secession" (111) from the Academy. For skepticism, see Milns (1994, 72–73) and Owen (1983, 4–10, esp. 7), challenging the restoration of Xenocrates' name.

28. Didymus col. 5.21–27 Pearson and Stephens (= Theopompus 115 *FGrH* F 250); on the date, see Flower (1994, 86).

29. The distinction between Platonist "Academics" and Aristotelian "Peripatetics" arose in later, not altogether clear circumstances: see Lynch (1972, 73–75) with testimonia in Düring (1957, 404–411).

30. Flower (1994, 88–89) suggests (if Aristotle went to Macedon in 342 and if Theopompus's *Letter to Philip* followed soon after) that "Theopompus was more worried about the growing influence of the Academy at the court of Philip than about the freedom of the Greeks in Asia."

31. Chroust (1967, 1971).

32. Demosthenes *Fourth Philippic* 10.31–32 with scholia. See Flower (1994, 86 n. 60). Bosworth (1988, 18 n. 44) holds that this is pure speculation on Demosthenes' part. Various historical accounts positing some cooperation between Hermias and Philip are surveyed in Harding (2006, 124–125).

33. Kahrstedt, "Mentor (6)," *RE* 15, col. 964–965. On the account of Weiskopf (1989, citing Demosthenes 23.154 ff. and Diodorus 16.52), Artabazus had been installed as satrap of Dascyleum around 363, and around this time married Mentor's sister, thereby making her brother an important ally.

34. The *Fourth Philippic* is usually placed between Hermias's capture and his death: Düring (1957, 276). Most scholars now date Hermias's death to 342/1: Trampgedach (1994, 68–69). Rutherford (2001, 93) dates it without argument to 345/4, reverting to an older tradition based on Dionysus of Halicarnassus, *Letter to Ammaeus* 5.

Chapter 3

1. Diogenes Laertius 5.6 (= Aristotle Fr. 674 Rose). I give the text of Page (1975, 622–626). For discussions, cf. Page (1981, 31–32), Wormell (1935, 61), Dielh (1925, 1.46.3), Wilamowitz (1893, 2.403–404, mainly censuring Aristotle's versification).

2. Herman (1987, 26, 129, where the reference to *Nemean* 7.90–92 should be to vv. 60–63).

3. Of course, in our broad use we follow a use of the term developed by the Greek critics. See Ford (2002, ch. 6).

4. Cf. Young (1983, esp. 40–42) on "inscriptional *pote*" as it applies to the possibility of Pindaric re-performance.

5. A.P. 7.258 (= Page [1975, 879–881]); cf. Page (1981, 268–272). The cowardice of bowmen is a theme that can be found from Homer's *Iliad* (see 11.385 ff.) through Euripides (*Hercules Furens* 157–164); cf. Lissarague (1990, 13–34). The adjective τοξόφορος is not negative when used in archaic and classical Greek poetry for Apollo or Artemis; it apparently began to be used of Easterners in Herodotus (9.43, quoting an oracle) and Simonides.

6. Gow and Page (1965, 2.546) note Theocritus's reply as an early example. Cf. Fantuzzi in Fantuzzi and Hunter (2004, 283–291). On the passage of epigrams "from stone to book" see Gutzwiller (1998, ch. 3, esp. pp. 47–53), placing the rise of a distinctly epigrammatic aesthetic "toward the end of the fourth century and the beginning of the third" (52), Bing (2009, 116–141). To remark the rise of "book epigrams" is not to rule out continuing traditions of oral performance and even impromptu composition: see Cameron (1995, 71–103, esp. 76–84), arguing that many were composed for sympotic contexts; discussion by Bing (2009, 106–116, esp. 113–115). On deixis in Greek funerary inscriptions, see Tsagalis (2008, 216–224).

7. Theocritus's riposte apart, Diogenes is our sole source for the verse, though it is referred to in the pseudo-Aristotelian *Apology* quoted by Athenaeus, discussed below, and by Himerius *Or.* 6.6 when he says "for Hermias alone of his friends Aristotle celebrated his death with an elegy" (καὶ ἐλεγείῳ τὸν θάνατον [so Penella, for θάλαμον of the paradosis] μόνῳ τῶν γνωρίμων ἐκόσμησεν).

8. My text is taken from *SH* 738, except that at v. 4, I read βορβόρου with Diehl (1925, 1.110) rather than Βορβόρου. For discussion, see Wormell (1935, 74–75), Düring (1957, 35, 381), Page (1981, 93–95), and Harding (2006, 157–158) with further bibliography. Translation by Flower (1994, 88, reading βορβόρου).

9. See Wormell (1935, 74 n. 32); Harding (2006, 22).

10. Page (1981, 31) copes with the evidence by assuming there was both a statue at Delphi inscribed with the epigram and a cenotaph ("presumably at Assos or Atarneus") to which Theocritus refers.

11. Aristocles F 2.12 Chiesara (= T 58k Düring); Didymus col. 6.46–49 (T 15h Düring) cites Bryon's *On Theocritus* probably courtesy of Hermippus. Plutarch *Mor.* 603C quotes only from the end of the third line, Diogenes Laertius 5.11 only the first two verses.

12. Flower (1994, 88); cf. Düring (1957, 277), Ruina (1986, 533–534).

13. Page (1981, 95) cites Plato *Phaedo* 69C, where the lot of the uninitiated is to "lie in slime" in Hades. Evidence of its popularity is the exclamation of Dionysus in Aristophanes *Frogs* when he arrives in

the underworld and exclaims, no doubt peering out at the audience, "What a lot of muck and slime!" (Εἶτα βόρβορον πολὺν / καὶ σκῶρ ἀείνων, 140-1). Liapis, *per litteras*, points me to Asius of Samos, who abuses a disgusting old parasite appearing at a feast, "rising like a hero from slime" (1.4 *IEG*). He also notes that it is possible to take *Borborou* as a proper name of a fictional river ("Slime River").

14. The phrase is perhaps mock heroic, resembling a fictional epitaph for the hero Memnon from a collection of "literary" epitaphs Aristotle may have known (Fr. 641.62 Rose): "I Memnon, son of Tithonus and Dawn, here lie / in Syria by the outpourings of the river Belos" (Μέμνων Τιθωνοῦ τε καὶ Ἠοῦς ἐνθάδε κεῖμαι / ἐν Συρίῃ Βήλου πὰρ ποταμοῦ προχοαῖς).

15. Most scholars place the prosecution of Aristotle in the anti-Macedonian atmosphere following Alexander's death; Rutherford (2001, 92-93) would place it in 335, when Aristotle returned to Athens and Alexander acceded to power, though he leaves open the possibility that it influenced Aristotle's final departure from Athens in 323.

16. See *LSJ* s. v. and note s. v. II: a synonym for *prokhoos*, a vessel for pouring libations.

17. See, e.g., Wormell (1938, 75 n. 34), Ruina (1986, 532, 533).

18. An archetypal example is Odysseus in rags in the *Odyssey*: see Pucci (1987, 165-172).

19. Ruina (1986, citing *Timaeus* 73A and *Phaedrus* 238A); like Page, he would include Aristotle's alleged sexual impropriety in the charge; but Xenophon *Mem.* 1.2.1 (cited by Ruina) makes a distinction between sex- and *gastêr*-greed: "Socrates was the most temperate of men as far as sex and the stomach went" (Σωκράτης ... ἀφροδισίων καὶ γαστρὸς πάντων ἀνθρώπων ἐγκρατέστατος ἦν).

20. Aristocles' reading is also the basis for the version of Theocritus in Michael Apostolius, a fifteenth-century Paroemiagrapher (6.38a Leutsch-Schneidewin). Didymus apparently read, ὃς γαστρὸς τιμῶν ἄνομον φύσιν εἵλετο ναίειν, a milder expression.

21. Archelaus is also said to have lured Euripides to his court at the end of his life, but for doubts on this tradition see Lefkowitz (1981, 103), Scullion (2003).

22. Simonides' actual social and economic situation—which there is no reason to doubt may have been remarkable in the mobile sixth century— is too obscurely known; he truly is, for us, no more than a figure of discourse, but one that is beautifully opened up in a study by J. M. Bell (1986).

23. Cephisodorus, noted as a detractor of Aristotle in Athenaeus 354b, is cited by Aristocles F 2.7 Chiesara (= T 58h Düring). Similar abuse in Pseudo-Aristippus, from the first book of the treatise *On Ancient Luxury*, is mentioned below.

24. 115 *FGrH* F 210, 242; further tales are given in [Demetrius] *On Style* 293. Owen (1983, 15–16) refers it to stereotype invective.

25. Mulvaney (1926, 155).

26. Fragments 615–17 Rose. See Christesen (2007, 179–190).

27. SIG^3 275 (= 187 Tod = Callisthenes *FGrH* 124 T 23 = 80 Rhodes and Osborne). See Tod (1985, 2.246–248, esp. 248), and Rhodes and Osborne (2003, 395), who date the inscription to 337–327 BCE. A similar instance of iconoclasm occurred in the wake of Philip's aggression in 340, which provoked the Athenians to smash the stone on which their recent treaty with Macedon had been inscribed (Philochorus *FGrH* 328 F 55A and 55B; cf. Diodorus Siculus 16.77.2).

Chapter 4

1. Wilamowitz (1893, 2.405 with n. 3).

2. Wormell (1935, 76), followed by Düring (1957, 277). The tradition of Callisthenes is questioned by Bosworth (1970), but hypercritically: Lynch (1972, 72), Fox (1986, 112 n. 55, citing Chares 125 *FGrH* T 15).

3. W. Crönert's ἐγκώμιον in *Rheinisches Museum* 62 (1907), 383 is printed by, *inter alios*, Jacoby in *FGrH* 124 F 2, Wormel (1935, 75) and Düring (1957, 274). It is defended by Harding (2006, 144–145, noting

that Crönert was anticipated by Blass in *Archiv für Papyrusforschung* 3 [1906] 290) on the grounds that it fits a tendency elsewhere in Didymus to define works by their genres.

4. On prose encomia, see Velardi (1991); on fourth-century experiments in prose, Ford (2008).

5. So *Evagoras* begins (1: Ὁρῶν, ὦ Νικόκλεις, τιμῶντά σε τὸν τάφον τοῦ πατρός). On "encomiazing the excellence of a man in prose," see the commentary by Nicolai (2004, 88–90).

6. Momigliano (1993/1971, 82) and Russell and Wilson (1981, xv) on Agesilaus. One may suggest that, as if in compensation for giving up stirring poetic devices, prose eulogists ventured some rather extreme topoi of praise, such as Isocrates' declaration in *Evag.* 72 that, "If anyone was ever a god among men, Evagoras deserves that title." The one bit of content from Speusippus's work that we have is also religiously bold, claiming that Plato's real father was Apollo: cf. DL 3.2, also mentioning an *Encomium of Plato* by Clearchus (2a Wehrli).

7. Didymus col. 5.64–6.18 (*FGrH* 124 F 2). Supplements are generally as in Pearson and Stephens, but for legibility's sake I have thought it safe to follow Harding's readings (2006) at lines: 5.69 (reverting to Diels-Schubart's αὐτῶι τῶι θανάτωι for αὐτ[ῶι τῶι δεινοτάτ]ωι of P-S), 5.71 (παρ' for Körte's περί), 6.8 (δικάζων Harding), and 6.9 (παρ' αὐτῶι). On Pearson-Stephens see the discussion by Rusten (1987).

8. Jacoby, *Komm.* to 124 F 2, p. 416.

9. Didymus col. 6.50–59 reports the controversy, citing (at col. 6.51–53) Hermippus's *On Aristotle* apropos the tradition that Hermias died in prison (44 Wehrli = *FGrH* 1026 F 31); cf. Bollansée (2001, 83–89). Flower (1994, 209) finds it likely that Callisthenes, the eulogist, euphemizes. See further Rusten (1987, 268) and Harding (2006, 151). The *Athenian Constitution* that was produced in Aristotle's school has in ch. 18 a grisly account of the torture and death of the heroic Aristogeiton by Hippias, the tyrant he had been conspiring against.

10. Rusten (1987, 268–269); Harding (2006, 152). Jaeger (1948, 117) suggests Hermias summoned Artaxerxes himself to be his witness.

11. In an anthropological account integrating Achaemenid practices of torture into their religious, legal, and political ideals, Lincoln (2007, 90–91) notes that a show of beneficence on the part of the torturers could be a significant part of the spectacle.

12. On the terms, see Ford (1992, 13).

13. Cf. Furley and Bremer (2001, 2.228): "The very fact that Aristotle thought this allusive naming [sc. "nursling of Atarneus"] to be sufficient, is ample proof that he composed this poem for private use only" (though one may query their "only").

14. On mimetic hymns, Hopkinson (1984, 32–43), Depew (1997).

15. Guthrie (1981, 44) thinks the detail that the song to Hermeias was sung daily at dinner was "added for the sake of artistic verisimilitude." But while "daily" may be an exaggeration, performance in the Lyceum was apt to have been seized on by the prosecution as an inflammatory detail, suggesting that Aristotle's school was a secret, pro-Macedonian cabal. It plausible in itself that Aristotle would have had the song performed at common meals (*sussitia*) he took care to provide for the Lyceum. (Athenaeus lists Aristotle among philosophers who held symposia: 186b, cf. Lynch [1972, 112]). In his *Politics* he recommended *sussitia* as something a well-run city ought to support: 7.10 (1330a13–15); cf. 7.11.1 (1331a19 ff.) and Ford (2006, 313). By the time of Theophrastus's successor, Strato, the school property included "furniture for *sussitia*, couch-covers, and cups" (as reported by DL 5.62: καταλείπω δ' αὐτῷ καὶ τὰ βιβλία πάντα, πλὴν ὧν αὐτοὶ γεγράφαμεν, καὶ τὰ σκεύη πάντα κατὰ τὸ συσσίτιον καὶ τὰ στρώματα καὶ τὰ ποτήρια).

16. Cited in the scholium on Plato *Gorgias* 451E, quoted below. On the etymological question: Teodorsson (1989) and Liapis (1996).

17. Athen. 694b-c: τηνικαῦτα γὰρ τῶν σοφῶν ἕκαστον ᾠδήν τινα καλὴν εἰς μέσον εἰσφέρειν ἠξίουν. καλὴν δὲ ταύτην ἔλεγον ὡς παραίνεσιν καὶ γνώμην ἔχουσαν τῷ βίῳ χρησίμην.

18. On "paeanic idiom," Rutherford (2001, 94 n. 10).

19. Making the refrain obligatory: [Plut.] *De Musica* 1134d-e, with Harvey (1955, 172–173).

20. On the use/absence of refrains in paeans, see Käppel (1992, 10–13, 65–70, 84–85, with his chart on 66–67); Rutherford (2001, 68–83, 96).

21. Evidence may appear in the transmission of Aristophanes *Wasps* where the strophe of a hymn petitioning Apollo's help ends in an *extra metrum* add-on, ἰήιε Παιάν (874), but the antistrophe (890) does not. Cf. Willi (2003, 45–47) and Ford (2006, 286–268).

22. Duris *FGrH* 76 F 71 and F 26; see Habicht (1970, 3–6 and 243–4) for epigraphical evidence that a Lysandreia continued to be celebrated in the fourth century.

23. Alexinus F 91 Döring (= 40 *SH*). Pace Jacoby, "Krateros," *RE* XI 2, col. 1617 who takes the Craterus here as the son of the general (321–250). Bollansée's (2001, 73 n. 17) compendious discussion includes suggestive speculation about the possibility of festival performances of the "paean" for Crateros at Apollo's site, Delphi. This musical show of magnificence was matched with one in stone by Craterus the younger, who commissioned the famous statuary Lysippus to represent his father and Alexander in a lion hunt (despite Plutarch *Alexander* 40.4–5, who attributes the dedication to the elder Craterus). The work was, like Hermias's cenotaph, dedicated at Delphi, and its influence did not stop there: the image seems to have been reproduced back in Macedonia in a mosaic found in Pella. See discussion in Bollansée. Another notable contemporary case of memorialization in speech and stone is by Mausolus of Caria, who in 353/2 took occupancy of the so-called Mausoleum, one of the Seven Wonders of the Ancient World. His funeral was graced by a contest in prose eulogy among three orators of Isocrates' school—Theopompus, Theodectes, and Naucrates.

24. Περὶ λυρικῶν ποιητῶν. See Schmidt (1854, 386–396). On Athenaeus's sources here, cf. Wilamowitz (1893, 2.403), Bowra (1938, 182), Wehrli (1974, 75). Hermippus's fragments are now available in the superb continuation of Jacoby's *Die Fragmente der Griechischen Historiker* as 1026 in Bollansée (2001), *FGrHist* IV A 3.

25. *On Aristotle* is FGrH 1026 F 28–33; Athenaeus 696a-697b is given as Hermippus *FGrH* 1026 F 30 (= Fr 48 Wehrli = Test. 7 Käppel), though Bolansée (2001, 74–75) concludes that Hermippus was not Athenaeus's sole source.

26. Hermippus has often been identified as Didymus's chief source, perhaps through intermediaries: Diels-Schubart (1904, xxxvi–xliii, esp. xxxviii), Wormell (1935, 78–82); Düring (1957, 275). Reservations in Wehrli (1974, 75–76), Yunis (1997, 1052), Bollansée (1999b, 64–65 with n. 135 for bibliography), and Harding (2006, 35, 37–38).

27. Düring (1957, 79) calls Hermippus a "main source" for Diogenes, but Mejer (1978, 32–34) cautions about oversimplifying the tradition. Against the assumption of Wilamowitz (1893, 2.403 with n. 1) that, "what is common to Diogenes Laertius and Athenaeus goes back to Hermippus" see Bollansée (1999b, 65–69 and 56 n 1).

28. On Hermippus's reputation: Diels in Diels-Schubart (1904, xxxviii–xli), Heibges in *RE* 8, Wehrli (1974, 75), Bollansée (1999b, xii–xv, 54).

29. Bollansée (1999a, 312); critiques of Hermippus in Wehrli (1974, 75) and Momigliano (1993, 79, 114) are possibly overdone: Mejer (1978, 32 n. 1).

30. Derenne (1930, 198). We know of Socratic Ἀπολογίαι composed by Plato, Xenophon, Crito, Lysias, Theodectes, and Demetrius of Phalerum (an associate of Aristotle's); a version of the *Accusation of Socrates* was produced by the rhetorician Polycrates: Ford (2008, 32–33).

31. σῶμα is Kaibel's supplement to the text of Athenaeus, which gives εκοσμήσατο (A)/ ἐκόσμουν (C, E); without an object for the verb the grammar is a little rough, and σῶμα (better than Düring's [1957] 281 ἐκόσμησα αὐτόν) reinforces clausular balance (ἐκόσμησα τὸ σῶμα recalls, chiastically, the end of the first clause μνῆμα κατεσκεύαζον) and structures its own clause with a φύσιν /υῶμα opposition.

32. DL 5.5, just before citing Favorinus on Demophilus, on which see below. Cf. Düring (1957, 374), Bollansée (2001, 69–70 n. 6).

33. Aristocles F 2.8 Chiesara (=T 58i Düring, possibly from Hermippus: Düring [1957, 464]). On the tale, cf. Wormell (1935, 87) and Mulvaney

(1926, 156–157), who suggests it may contain some truth. It may be relevant that in his will Aristotle provided for a "Demeter" to be dedicated on his mother's behalf at Nemea (DL 5.16.1–2 = 4b Plezia [1977]). On Lycon of Iasos, a rather obscure figure, see 1110 *FGrH* F 1 (= 57 T 4 DK) and W. Capelle, "Lykon (15)" in *RE* s. v. col. 2308–2309. On the complicated testimonia about Aristotle's marital relations, Bollansée (1999a, 298–304).

34. Athenaeus may be attempting to reconcile varying traditions. In his version (696b), the hierophant Eurymedon stirred the politician Demophilus to act. Diogenes Laertius says (5.5) that Aristotle was indicted for impiety by Eurymedon, on account of both the paean and the inscription, but adds that Favorinus in his history named Demophilus as the indicter (= F 68 Barrigazzi / 36 Mensching). We do not know whether (a) Diogenes and Athenaeus both used Favorinus or (b) whether Favorinus and Athenaeus used the same source: Düring (1957, 279). Clinton (1974, 21) notes that a Eurymedon is recorded as chairman of the *hieropoioi* of the Eleusinian *Boulê* in 329/8. Demophilus may be the one named by Plutarch (*Phocion* 38.1) as one of the accusers who in 318 brought about the execution of Phocion, an Athenian associate of Demetrius of Phaleron, for advising accommodation with Macedon. In general, the attention to the teamwork between Eurymedon and Demophilus recalls the use of Anytus and Meletus in Socratic literature to represent different constituencies within the prosecution.

35. DL 5.3–4 (= T 10e Düring): Ἀρίστιππος δ' ἐν τῷ πρώτῳ Περὶ παλαιᾶς τρυφῆς φησιν ἐρασθῆναι τὸν Ἀριστοτέλην παλλακίδος τοῦ Ἑρμίου. τοῦ δὲ συγχωρήσαντος ἔγημέ τ' αὐτὴν καὶ ἔθυεν ὑπερχαίρων τῷ γυναίῳ, ὡς Ἀθηναῖοι τῇ Ἐλευσινίᾳ Δήμητρι· τῷ τε Ἑρμίᾳ παιᾶνα ἔγραψεν, ὃς ἔνδον γέγραπται. I take it that Diogenes' paraphrase extends through ἔγραψεν at least, because of the close way that τῷ τε Ἑρμίᾳ is linked to τῷ γυναίῳ. That is, I take it that pseudo-Aristippus mentioned Hermias as well as the sacrifice. At the end of the quoted block, it is safer to attribute "which is written out below" to Diogenes (since he actually goes on to transcribe the text) than to Aristippus, but the possibility that he quoted it as well cannot

be excluded. On the dating of pseudo-Aristippus see Wormell (1935, 85 n. 59); cf. Düring (1957, 268).

36. Something like the reconstruction attempted in this paragraph must be, as far as I can see, the basis of Wilamowitz's summary declaration (1893, 2.403): "Before Hermippus, the poem had been noticed in the defense speech of Aristotle that he himself suspected (Ath. 979a), in pseudo-Aristippus (Diog. 5.4), and perhaps in Lycon the Pythagorean from Iasos . . . from which one can suppose that the scoundrel who charged Aristotle with impiety had not so much abused the poems as the fact of their existence." ("Vor Hermippos hatten die gedichte berücksichtigung gefunden in der von diesem selbst bezweifelten verteidigunsrede des Aristoteles (Ath. 697a), bei dem falschen Aristippos (Diog. 5.4) und vielleicht dem Pythagoreer Lykon von Iasos . . . denen man wohl so viel glauben kann, dass der schurke, der den Aristoteles wegen religionsfrevels belangte, nicht sowohl die gedichte als die tatsache ihrer existenz misgebraucht hatte.") I differ from Wilamowitz only in his final point, for the passage from Aeschines *Against Timarchus* 135–137, discussed below, shows that the actual words of a defendant's poetry could have been thrown in his face during a political wrangle.

37. Rose (1886, 599). See Wormell (1935, 86 n. 62).

38. Aristocles F 2.5 Chiesara (= T 58f Düring).

39. Mulvaney 1926, 156, adopted by Döring (F 60) and Düring (1957, 388) with n. 124; Vayos Liapis achieves the same result more simply by deleting ὡς as dittography (*per litteras*). Wormell (1935, 86) considers it probable that Euboulides refers to forged "incriminating evidence" that was produced in reaction to *l'affaire Hermias*.

40. As noted by Chiesara (2001, 72).

41. Wehrli (1974, 76). Wehrli also thinks one may doubt whether Hermippus took over the entire text of the song in his work, see below.

42. So Düring (1957, 343–344), citing Derenne (1930, 200). Cf. O'Sullivan (1997, 136–139).

43. As Lord (1986) notes, citing: Diodorus Siculus 20.45.2–5, DL 5.78–79, Strabo 9.1.20; skeptical are Pfeiffer (1968, 87–104) and Bagnall (2004, 349–351).

44. DL 5.38. More on Sophocles' law: Athenaeus 610b-f (including a telling fragment from the comic poet Alexis); Pollux 9.42 (368–9 Bekker). Cf. Regenbogen RE *Suppl.* 7, col. 1360.

45. Aristocles F 2.6 Chiesara (= T 58g Düring). On Demochares, cf. Athenaeus 215c, 508b, 610f. On the speech: Düring (1957, 343–344, 388); Lynch (1972, 103–104, 117–118); Chroust (1973, 1.149–151); Habicht (1988); Brunt (1993, 332–334); Bollansée (1999a, 505 n. 221).

Chapter 5

1. The charge was, in effect, as Kevin Clinton (1974, 21) puts it "worshipping in public a god whose cult was not officially authorized by the state," citing Rudhardt (1960, 92–93); cf. Parker (1996, 214–217, 276–277).

2. This is a main theme of Ford (2002).

3. Harvey (1955). My sketch is also indebted to the fine account of Lowe (2007, 167–176).

4. See Heath's 1985 very rich study of "receiving the *kômos*" in epinician. Pindar *Nem.* 4.78 (ἐπινικίοισν ἀοιδαῖς) and Bacchylides *Ode* 2.13 are likely to have provided the scholars with the idea for the technical term. Note that at *Ol.* 8.75 μναμοσύναν ... ἐπινίκιον refers in the first instance to the "memory of victory" that Pindar's song will arouse.

5. Harvey (1955, esp. 162–164) on *skolion* and *enkômion*; Lowe (2007, 169). An early example of an *enkômion* in prose is Plato's *Symposium*, where the littérateur Phaedrus implicitly contrasts *enkômia* with songs for divinities: "we have numerous hymns and *paeans* composed by poets to the other gods, but for Eros we have not even an encomium" (177A-B). The underlying distinction between songs for gods and songs for mortals is elaborated in *Laws* 700A-E, discussed below.

6. Cf. *Eudemian Ethics* 2.1, 1219b8ff., esp 1219b8–9: ἔτι δ' οἱ ἔπαινοι πῆς ἀρετῆς διὰ τά ἔργα, καὶ τὰ ἐγκώμια τῶν ἔργων.

7. On the canonical Alexandrian editions of Pindar (by Callimachus, Aristophanes of Byzantium and his predecessors including Apollonius the eidographer), Rutherford (2001, 152–158).

8. Though the paean was traditionally associated with Apollo and his sister Artemis, from the classical period one finds paeans generalized to other gods, as Sophocles' paean to Sleep in *Philoctetes* 827–832. See Käppel (1992, 341–349), Schröder (1999, 22–31), Ford (2006, 285).

9. *Laws* 700C: (βακχεύοντες καὶ μᾶλλον τοῦ δέοντος κατεχόμενοι ὑφ' ἡδονῆς, κεραννύντες δὲ θρήνους τε ὕμνοις καὶ παίωνας διθυράμβοις ... καὶ πάντα εἰς πάντα συνάγοντες. For a discussion, see Käppel (1992, 36–38) and Ford (2002, 258–260). Nagy (1990, 109–110) insightfully places such responses in the context of the infusion of Panhellenic lyric genres into the classical Athenian theater. For recent perspectives on the "musical revolution" see, e.g., Csapo (2004) and LeVen (2008), with bibliography.

10. For the interplay between cult occasions and song types, cf. the anecdote (noted by Chroust [1973, 146 n. 7]) about Xenophanes of Colophon cited by Aristotle in the *Rhetoric* (2.23, 1400b5–8): when asked by the Eleans whether or not they should sacrifice and sing dirges to their Leucothea, he advised them that if they supposed her a god not to sing a dirge, and if they supposed her mortal, not to offer sacrifice. (οἷον Ξενοφάνης Ἐλεάταις ἐρωτῶσιν εἰ θύωσι τῇ Λευκοθέᾳ καὶ θρηνῶσιν ἢ μή, συνεβούλευεν, εἰ μὲν θεὸν ὑπολαμβάνουσιν, μὴ θρηνεῖν, εἰ δ' ἄνθρωπον, μὴ θύειν).

11. *Poetics* 1448b25–27: οἱ μὲν γὰρ σεμνότεροι τὰς καλὰς ἐμιμοῦντο πράξεις καὶ τὰς τῶν τοιούτων, οἱ δὲ εὐτελέστεροι τὰς τῶν φαύλων, πρῶτον ψόγους ποιοῦντες, ὥσπερ ἕτεροι ὕμνους καὶ ἐγκώμια.

12. Aristotle uses *paian* as a metrical term in the *Rhetoric* (3.8), where it seems to be a neologism, for he says that orators "began using the paean from the time of Thrasymachus, but without being able to say what its name was" (so I take 1409a1–3: λείπεται δὲ παιάν, ᾧ ἐχρῶντο μὲν ἀπὸ Θρασυμάχου ἀρξάμενοι, οὐκ εἶχον δὲ λέγειν τίς ἦν).

13. Dichaearchus *On Musical Competitions* Frr. 88–89 Wehrli; cf. Reitzenstein (1883, 5), Rutherford (2001, 51), Aristoxenus Fr. 125

Wehrli; cf. Reitzenstein (1893, 3–13, 16 n. 28), Färber (1936, Pt. I, 57–63), Harvey (1955, 162–163, 174).

14. On Aristotle's library, see Dziatzko (1899, 408–409); testimonies in Düring (1957, T 42a-d and T 66), esp. Strabo 13.1.54 C608 and Plutarch *Sulla* 26 with Athenaeus 3a-b.

15. On Sappho in Alexandria, Yatromanolakis 1999 and Ferrari (2010, 116-123) on the *epithalamia*.

16. See Lowe 2007 for details. Simonides' epinicians may have been classed primarily by event, as Lobel inferred from *P. Oxy.* 2431.

17. Barthes (1988, 85).

18. Proclus *apud* Photius *Bib.* cod. 239.319b ff. Proclus to some extent relied on Didymus: cf. Schmidt (1854, 390), Severyns (1938, 114), Rutherford (2001, 105–107 n. 39). Russell and Wilson (1981, 227–228) compare the very similar (though not identical) list of hymnic genres that is found (possibly interpolated) in Menander Rhetor, I: *Division*, 331.20–332.7.

19. On the persistent hymns-gods/encomia-mortals distinction in the rhetorical tradition, cf. R. Wünsch, "Hymnos" *RE* 9.1 col. 181.28–182.52; on Didymus, see 181.64ff. Lowe (2007, 172) notes that Proclus's distinction between *prosodia* sung in procession and *humnoi* performed while standing (as, e.g., around an altar) may derive from Didymus's use of the mobile/static opposition to distinguish *prosodia* and *humnoi*.

20. Pfeiffer (1968, 127–134), Bagnall (2004, 356, n. 36). Moraux (1951, 221–222) argues that Hermippus relied on the *Pinakes*. Bollansée (1999b, 1–14) stresses Hermippus's association with Callimachus over the tradition that would make him a (distant) student of Aristotle's.

21. "Dithyramb" Fr. 23 Maehler, who associates the song with a Bacchylidean "dithyramb" mentioned by the scholium on Pindar *Pythian* 1.100; cf. Porphyry on Horace *Odes* 1.15.

22. *P. Oxy.* 2368 (= Bacchylides p. 128 Snell-Maehler = Test. 3 Käppel 1992): "Aristarchus says this song is dithyrambic because it includes the story of Cassandra, and titles it *Cassandra*; and he says that Callimachus

erred in ranging it among the Paeans because he did not understand that the refrain is shared between dithyrambs [sc. and paeans]." I give the text as in Callimachus Fr. 293 SH: ταύτην τ]ὴν ᾠδὴν Ἀρίσταρχ(ος) [..... διθ]υραμβικὴν εἶ[ναί φησι]ν διὰ τὸ παρειλῆ[φθαι ἐν α]ὐτῇ τὰ περὶ Κασ[σάνδρας,] ἐπιγράφει δ' αὐτὴν [... Κάσσ]ανδραν, πλανη[θέντα δ' αὐτὴν κατατάξαι [ἐν τοῖς Π]αιᾶσι Καλλίμαχον [.......] οὐ συνέντα ὅτι [..επίφθ]ε{γ}μα κοινόν ἐ[στι καὶ δ]ιθυράμβου κτλ. Rutherford (2001, 97-98) supports Lobel's restoration, as does the logic of the argument: see Käppel and Kannicht (1988) on the text and, on the debate generally, Käppel (1992, 38-42), *contra* Schröder (1999, 110-119). Käppel (2000) discusses Plato's *obiter dictum* in *Rep.* 394B-C that associates narrative and dithyramb.

23. Jaeger (1948, 117).

24. For Simonides, see Ford (2002, 110-111 and 128-130) on Simonides 531 *PMG*; see Fantuzzi (2001) and Boedekker (2001) on the "new" Plataea elegy of Simonides (11 *IEG*), which pushes the tradition by making the recently dead Greek soldiers equivalent to Homeric heroes. The most important passage of that song for present purposes is its transitional invocation to the Muses in which Simonides, having recounted the death of Achilles and mentioned its glorification by Homer, turns to those who showed valor (*aretê*) in the battle of Plataea and prays for help in making their fame "immortal" (11.28 *IEG*). For "Pericles," see Thucydides 2.43 and Stesimbrotos of Thasos, a contemporary, who recalled him saying in an encomium for those who had died in Samos that they had become immortal like the gods: "for we do not see these but reckon that they are immortal from the honors they receive and the benefits they bestow" (107 *FGrH* F 9 = Plut. *Pericles* 8.5: οὐδὲ γὰρ ἐκείνους αὐτοὺς ὁρῶμεν, ἀλλὰ ταῖς τιμαῖς ἃς ἔχουσι καὶ τοῖς ἀγαθοῖς ἃ παρέχουσιν ἀθανάτους εἶναι τεκμαιρόμεθα).

25. Momigliano (1987, 97). Ruler cult appears not to be directly dependent from hero cult, which is attested for living figures in the fifth century: e.g., the cult for Brasidas in 422 at Amphipolis; cf. Cleomedes, the mad boxer who was ca. 500 given cult at Astypulaea after "disappearing" in a homicidal bout.

26. Momigliano (1987, 94), quoting Simon Price. Cf. Habicht (1970, 17–25, 243, 245). On Philip, see Fredricksmeyer (1979). Ma (2000, 219–226) carries the analysis further with a case study from Hellenistic Teos.

27. See Bosworth (1977).

28. Arrian, *Anabasis* 4.10–12, 13–14. See Rhodes and Osborne (2003, 395) who put it in the context of the "conspiracy of pages" in 327.

29. Aelian, *Various History* 2.19, cf. Athenaeus 251b. On the divinity of Alexander, a trenchant discussion is Bosworth (1988, 278–290); cf. Hammond and Wallbank (1988, 82). It is controversial whether Alexander actually, as was said, wrote to the Greeks demanding divine cult or merely let it be known that he would regard such gestures on the part of Greek cities with favor: see, e.g., Badian (1981), Fredricksmeyer (1981), Cawkwell (1994), and Bosworth's discussion (1988, 288).

30. Athenaeus 251b, Aelian *Various History* 5.12. The charge may have been a *graphê paranomos*: see O'Sullivan (1997, 138–139), Derenne (1930, 185–188; to be used with caution). On such trials generally, which go back to the fifth century, see Parker (1996, 206–207).

31. The quotation is from Hermocles' "ithyphallic" processional: Powell, *CA* pp. 173–175, quoted by Athenaeus 253d-f; cf. 697a citing Philochorus (328 *FGrH* 165) on a contest in composing paeans for Demetrius and his father. On poems of this kind (e.g. *SH* 491, 492), cf. Mikalson (1998, ch. 3), Gelzer (1993). Michael Flower points me to a powerful statement of Athenian resentment of such practices from around 322. Hyperides' *Funeral Oration* deplores Macedonian arrogance for having imposed on Greece such spectacles as "sacrifices being performed for men, the statues and altars and temples of the gods being neglected while those for men are carefully established, and we are forced to honor the servants of these men as heroes" (6.21, the final reference being to Hephaestion, Alexander's comrade who died in 324 and for whom Alexander instituted heroic cult).

32. Currie (2005, esp. 159–172) is a rich study that succeeds at least in showing that Pindar's epinicians often raise the idea of heroic honors

as a reward to victors, even if actual cult for living athletes remained exceptional.

33. Duris of Samos *FGrH* 76 F 71 (=Plut. *Lysander* 18.2–4): πρώτῳ μὲν γάρ, ὡς ἱστορεῖ Δοῦρις, Ἑλλήνων ἐκείνῳ βωμοὺς αἱ πόλεις ἀνέστησαν ὡς θεῷ καὶ θυσίας ἔθυσαν, εἰς πρῶτον δὲ παιᾶνες ᾔσθησαν, ὧν ἑνὸς ἀρχὴν ἀπομνημονεύουσι τοιάνδε. This evidence has been subject to dispute, notably by Badian (1981), but see the discussion of Flower (1988, 131–133), and Habicht (1970, 244–245, 271) for epigraphical evidence for a fourth-century Lysandreia. Plutarch (*Lysander* 18.7) names a number of poets who composed such paeans to mortals—for lavish rewards at times: Antilochus, Antimachus, and Niceratus the Heracleote, all in *SH* 51, 325, 565.

34. I take the verb as a short-vowel subjunctive, as commonly in hymnic song; the meaning is not much different if we take it, also in conformity with hymnic use, as a "performative future" whose resolve is being fulfilled at the moment it is expressed: cf. Bundy (1969, 21).

35. Derenne (1930, 190) compares the bringing to trial of the courtesan Phryne for violating the Eleusinian mysteries and of Demades in 324/3 for proposing that Alexander be made the thirteenth Olympian. See Fredricksmeyer (1979, 59–60), O'Sullivan (1997) and Worthington (2004, 266–267). Clinton (1974, 21) finds it more probable that Eurymedon was acting from political or personal reasons than that Aristotle in any way actually denigrated the Eleusinian cult. On the type of religious prosecutor, see Gagné (2009).

36. Aeschines *Against Timarchus* 135–7. For discussion, see Ford (1999a, 251).

37. Demosthenes *On the False Embassy* 162–163, cf. 128 and Rutherford (2001, 67, 93). *On the Crown* 287 attacks Aeschines' paean-singing after Chaeronea. Rutherford (2001, 92–93) supposes the prosecution's case was that the "hymn" was a sympotic paean, and as part of the preliminary rites belonged among the praises of the gods. The evidence we have suggests that the procedures for holding a "proper" symposium were adaptable to different households and occasions and so I doubt

that the prosecution would have based their charge on such a fine point of party-planning.

38. Though Hermippus may have proposed that Aristotle's song was a *skolion*, its additional qualification as a *skolion sui generis* may be Athenaeus': in the context of the *Deipnosophists*, the added point makes sense as an explanation of why the song differs in meter and dialect from the Attic *skolia* and the poem to Hybrias recited just before.

39. Cf. Wormell (1935, 85); Düring (1957, 58 on DL 5.4); Bollansée (1999a, 312 n. 50).

40. Wilamowitz (1893, 405). So too Chroust (1973, 146).

41. Reitzenstein (1893, 42).

42. Smyth (1899, 469).

43. Jaeger (1934, 108). Cf. Derenne (1930, 192), Wormell (1935, 76), Guthrie (1981, 33, 44), Bollansée (2001, 72 n. 16).

44. Extensively argued in LeVen (2008, ch. 4) and by Vayos Liapis *per litteras*. Cf. Furley and Bremer (2001, I.265). While recognizing in Aristotle many common epinician elements (ranging from dialect and meter to the use of mythic exempla, themes of *ponos*, commemoration in song, etc.), I hold the difference in postulated occasions is decisive: Hermias has won no victory. (It would obviously be anachronistically Christian to take Hermias's death as a triumph.) The similarities are due to the fact that both songs are lyrics honoring mortals and so exploit traditional praise forms. It is also worth noting that epinician in lyric meter seems to have been a moribund form after Pindar (apart from the dactylo-epitritic epinician to Alcibiades tentatively ascribed to Euripides by Plurarch, *Alibiades*. 11.3 = 755 *PMG*); Callimachus's poetic notices of victory are in elegiacs (the *Victoria Berenicis*, 254–268C *SH*, and the "victory of Sosibios," Fr. 384 Pf.) or iambics (*Iambi* 8), on which see Fuhrer (1993).

45. Renehan (1982, 254) quoting Harvey (1955, 173, cf. 153). Critiqued by Käppel (1992, 1–7).

46. See Rutherford (2001, 95).

47. So Santoni (1991, 194–195).

48. Santoni (1991).

49. Renehan (1982); cf. Bowra (1938), seconded by Düring (1957, 57–58).

50. For a discussion of the critical price paid by uncompromising anti-intentionalism, see Hinds (1998, esp. 47–51).

Chapter 6

1. Schröder (1999) unpersuasively denies that Ariphron's song is a paean, on the grounds that it has more "hymnische Sprechhaltung" than "gebetshafte Sprechhaltung." *Contra*, see Käppel (1992, 68), Rutherford (2001, 19–23), Furley and Bremer (2001, 1.225).

2. Lucian, *A Slip of the Tongue in Salutation* 6.26: τὸ γνωριμώτατον ἐκεῖνο καὶ πᾶσι διὰ στόματος. For the sources of the text, see Wagman (1995, 149–159) and Furley and Bremer (2001, 1.224–227, 2.175–180).

3. The similarities were first extensively noted by Wilamowitz (1893, 2.406) and examined by Bowra (1938). For commentary, Wagman (1995, 160–178).

4. Cf. West (1985, 76).

5. Hesiod, *Works and Days* 760–763, much-discussed lines (e.g., Aeschines 1.127–130, 2.144), see A. Rzach's *Hesiodi Carmina*, editio *maior* (Leipzig, 1902). For personified Health on vases, cf. Shapiro (1993, 125–131), Furley and Bremer (2001, 1.225) and, on "new" gods, Parker (1996, 152–187, 227–237). Simonides, who had helped prepare the way for Aristotle in praising a personified *Areta*, also sang in praise of health, though not necessarily personified: 604 *PMG*.

6. Foe πρέσβιστος with the sense "oldest," cf. its use as an epithet of Eros as primordial deity in Plato's *Symposium* 178C-E and of Earth in the Homeric *Hymn to Gaia* (both discussed below). For this reason I would not flatten out the epithet in Ariphron to "august," as Wagman (1995, 173) suggests. A later example of the epithet with the sense "oldest" is Mesomedes hailing "The beginning and source of all, oldest Mother of the universe" (Fr. 35.2 *CA*): Ἀρχὰ καὶ πάντων γέννα, / πρεσβίστα Κόσμου μᾶτερ).

7. As Aristotle says in *Metaphysics* (983b32: τιμιώτατον μέν γὰρ τὸ πρεσβύτατον). Euripides praises moderation (*sophrosunê*) by declaring that nothing is "more venerable" (*presbuteron*) than she (Fr. 959 Nauck = Kannicht).

8. Furley and Bremer (2001, 1.47), tracing the tradition back to the hymns to *Anagkê* (Necessity) in Euripides' *Alcestis* 962–1005 and to *Hosia* (Holiness) in *Bacchae* 370–433. Looking forward, Russell and Wilson (1981, 230–231) point to the rhetorical category of "fictitious hymns" to personified abstractions, for which Mendander Rhetor cited as a prototype a hymn Simonides addressed to "Tomorrow" (*Aurion*, 615 *PMG*).

9. See Ford (2009, 139–141).

10. Santoni (1991, 187 n. 42) cf. Aeschylus *Choe*. 372. Pindar *Isthmian* 5.1–3 refers to the popularity of leading off priamels with gold.

11. *Pace* Page's comment ("*vix credibile*"), the importance of noble ancestry as a topos of encomiastic rhetoric suggests that we take *goneôn* (v. 11) in this way. Cf. Aristotle *Pol*. 1283a7 where *eugeneia* is defined as "excellence of breeding," *aretê genous*; so, e.g., Jaeger (1948), Santoni (1999, 189–191). Bowra (1938) takes it as referring to children; Renehan (1982, 260–262) to parents. Biographism approaches absurdity here if we consider how tactless praise of progeny would have been if Hermias were in fact a eunuch.

12. In Aristotle, the epic termination of sleep's epithet, μαλακαυγήτοιο (v. 8, Atticized to *-ou* in Didymus), may bring a subtle association with sexual pleasure by recalling the priamel on satiety in *Il*. 13.636–637: "there is a time when one has had enough of everything—of sleep and love, and sweet singing and fair dancing" (πάντων μὲν κόρος ἐστὶ καὶ ὕπνου καὶ φιλότητος / μολπῆς τε γλυκερῆς καὶ ἀμύμονος ὀρχηθμοῖο). Pindar has a compressed version at *Nem*. 7.52–53: κόρον δ' ἔχει / καὶ μέλι καὶ τὰ τέρπν' ἄνθε' Ἀφροδίσια ("there is enough even of honey and of the delightful flowers of Aphrodite") and closes a strophe by mentioning sleep (*Pythian* 9.24–25). Cf. the association of "sweetest sleep" (ἂν μαλακώτατα καθεύδοις) with "being with young boys" (παιδικοῖς ὁμιλῶν) climaxing the priamel in Prodicus (Xen. *Mem*.

2.1.24.1). The "dithyrambic" qualities of μαλακαυγήτοιο are analyzed below.

13. The syntax of Ariphron's v. 9 may be easier if we follow Wagman (1995, 177) and read ὄαροι in a *schema Pindaricum*.

14. With the rhetoric of Ariphron's v. 10, compare again Prodicus (in Xen. *Mem.* 2.1.32.1), who has *Aretê* say: "there is no fine work of man or god without me" (ἔργον δὲ καλὸν οὔτε θεῖον οὔτ' ἀνθρώπειον χωρὶς ἐμοῦ γίγνεται). Cf. Pindar's *Olympian* 14.9–10, studied in the following section.

15. See Pulleyn (1997, 42–55) on the distinction. An example of a paean with attested cult function is the so-called Erythraean paean to Asclepius (934 *PMG* = 136–7 *CA*), on which see Käppel (1992, 189–200, 370–374) and Graf (1985, 250–257).

16. Such a scenario is suggested by Demochares (75 *FGrH* F 2) when he sneers that the Athenians were so obsequious that they sang a hymn to Demetrius the Besieger (*CA* 173–174, noted above) "not just in public but in their homes" (οὐ δημοσίᾳ μόνον, ἀλλὰ καὶ κατ' οἰκίαν: Athenaeus 253b).

17. E.g., *Tukhê* (Fortune) beginning *Ol.* 12, *Hêsukhia* (Peace) in *Pyth.* 8, *Theia* (Divinity) in *Isth.* 5; such abstractions in Pindar, called by Bundy (1969, 36) "hypostasizations of aspects of success," are listed in Farnell (1932, 467); cf. Furley and Bremer (2001, 1.265); Burnett (2005, 93 ff).

18. The text is from B. Snell and H. Maehler, commentary in McLachan (1993, 42–55). For the cult of the Graces, see Farnell (1909, 5.427–431); on their festival at Orchomenos, the *Charitesia*, Schachter (1981, 1.140–144).

19. With Pindar's σὺν γὰρ ὔμμιν (v. 5), cf. Ariphron's μετὰ σεῖο (8); with his οὐδὲ Χαρίτων ἄτερ (8), cf. Ariphron's σέθεν δὲ χωρὶς οὔτις (10).

20. The wider fame of the Graces is already acknowledged by the epithet ἀοίδιμοι in v. 3: possibly they are called "sung of" because Hesiod sang their praises in *Theogony* 907–9, where the three Graces have the same names and appear in the same order as in Pindar. Various traditions about their number and names are recorded in Pausanias 9.35.

21. On possible Pythagorean overtones in ἀέναον, see Ford (2002, 108–111). It may also be, as scholars have suggested, that the image of flowing prepares Pindar's turn to Asopichos, who was named after another river of Orchomenos, the Asopos.

22. For a possible parallel, consider the third stasimon of Euripides' *Medea* in which the first strophic pair (824–845) contains general praise of Athenian culture usable at any time, whereas the second pair (846–865) ruminates, in a slightly different meter, on the specific problem of how Athens can take in the infanticidal heroine.

23. The mention of "Pythian Apollo" has been thought to point to a fact on the ground: ancient commentators on v. 10 say that in Delphi statues of the Graces (enthroned?) were situated next to Apollo. But such information may be speculation derived from Pindar's text or a text like the *Homeric Hymn to Apollo* 194–196, which represents the Graces dancing in Apollo's train at Delphi.

24. E.g. Lucian, *A Slip of the Tongue* 6.26, who reasons that "if Health is *presbistê*, so her work of healing must be ranked before all other goods" (ὥστε εἰ πρεσβίστη ἐστὶν ὑγίεια, καὶ τὸ ἔργον αὐτῆς τὸ ὑγιαίνειν προτακτέον τῶν ἄλλων ἀγαθῶν). Maximus of Tyre (7.1.e-f) also justifies the epithet. A similarly ambiguous use of the superlative is *Iliad* 4.59–61, where Hera (who has the epithet πρέσβα in epic) seems to declare herself the "eldest" as well as "most venerable" (πρεσβυτάτην, 4.59) of Cronus's daughters, "both in birth and because I am the wife of Zeus" (ἀμφότερον γενεῇ τε καὶ οὕνεκα σὴ παράκοιτις / κέκλημαι, 4.60–61). The idea of Hera as "eldest" has been thought to be a mirage created by interpolation from her more intelligible claim (in 17.365-6) to be the "best" (ἀρίστη) among goddesses in γενεῇ (descent) and marriage. See the *Lexicon des Frügriechischen Epos* s. v. πρεσβύτερος, 2αβ. Solmsen (1960) argues that this passage generated a response in the fifth *Homeric Hymn* to Aphrodite (possibly the earliest composition in the collection): there Hestia is the one called πρέσβειρα (*H. Hom.* 6.32; cf. *Hymn* 29.3) and Hera's aretology (6.40–42) seems expanded in compensation. Cf. Faulkner (2008, 101–102, 125–126), who is skeptical.

25. See Calame (2005, 19–35) for an overview of the genre.

26. Bowra (1953, 30). On the date of *Homeric Hymn* 30, Janko (1982, 275 n. 12). My attention was drawn to this poem by LeVen (2008).

27. V. 19 is exactly repeated in *To Demeter* 495, *To Apollo* 546, etc.; similar formulae: *To Hermes* 580, *To Aphrodite* 21, etc. The third Platonic epistle (315B) quotes a hexameter line that began a hymn composed by Plato's tyrant-patron, Dionysius of Syracuse. Plato notes that the hymn was intended for performance at Delphi, and claims to know it from having been informed by "those who were attending the festival" (ὡς ἤγγειλαν οἱ τότε θεωροῦντες). Plato quotes the line to quibble with it for deploying, as hexameter hymns could, the χαῖρε formula as an introduction: "Rejoice, and keep safe the life of the tyrant in pleasure" (χαῖρε καὶ ἡδόμενον βίοτον διάσῳζε τυράννου). The epistle discourses on the inaptness of this traditional way of greeting a god; Lucian (*Slip of the Tongue* 4) summarizes: "Plato reproves Dionysius for commencing a hymn to Apollo with 'Rejoice,' which he maintains is unworthy of the Pythian, and not fit even for men of any discretion, not to mention Gods" (tr. Fowler, adapted). Plato proposes to say "do well" instead (εὖ πράττειν, 315A). (Doubting the authenticity of the letter, Bury in the Loeb aptly compares a similar discussion of what is wrong in the *khaire* formula in *Charmides* 164D-E, where note the context is also Delphic piety.)

28. The epithet was pliant enough that Sophocles could use it to mean "all mother, mother through and through" (Sophocles *Ant.* 1282).

29. On the variant in *Iliad* 14.259, see Janko (1992, ad loc). In accord with cosmogonies in which Night figured as the first thing created, Zenotodus, Aristophanes, and a papyrus call Night the mother (μήτειρα) of gods and men. Callimachus's μήτειρα(ν) in *SH* 301 seems to confirm the form in the Homeric hymn as a variant of "mother," even though etymologically παμμήτειρα might be construed as "all knowing." (Just to keep things interesting, the form δαμάτειρα, "subduer," cannot be ruled out from *Iliad* 14.259 since it is also found in Callimachus, Fr. 267 Pf.).

30. *Theogony* 116–117. Aristotle and his contemporaries pored over these Hesiodic lines to get clues about the first principles in earlier cosmogonies: *Physics* 4.1 (208b27–33); *Metaphysics* A4 (984b23–32); so too Plato, *Symposium* 178B. Details in Ford (2009, 141–144).

31. Artemis: *Od.* 5.123, 18.202, and 20.71, where ἁγνή is taken as "virginal" by the Aristotelian *Problems* 894b34. Demeter: *Works and Days* 465. Aristotle knew ἅγνος as the name of the "chaste tree" (*Vitex Agnus-castus*, *History of Animals* 627a9), the branches of which had a ritual function for matrons during the Thesmophoria.

32. The same passage of Diogenes (2.42) also quotes from Socrates' Aesopic poem, revealing that it was in elegiac couplets ([1] *IEG*). See the testimonia of West on Socrates in *IEG* for variation in the tradition in references to Socrates' "paean" or "prooimion" to Apollo.

Chapter 7

1. *Politics* 8.3 (1337b23 ff.), cf. 7.13–15 and Ford (2004, 313). Two independent but convergent analyses of this discourse genre are Ford (1999b) and Pelliccia (2002).

2. *Gorgias* 451E: οἴομαι γάρ σε ἀκηκοέναι ἐν τοῖς συμποσίοις ᾀδόντων ἀνθρώπων τοῦτο τὸ σκολιόν, ἐν ᾧ καταριθμοῦνται ᾄδοντες ὅτι ‹ὑγιαίνειν μὲν ἄριστόν› ἐστιν, τὸ δὲ ‹δεύτερον καλόν γενέσθαι, τρίτον δέ›, ὥς φησιν ὁ ποιητὴς τοῦ σκολιοῦ, ‹τό πλουτεῖν ἀδόλως› Dodds's great commentary on *Gorgias* opened up the significance of this verse for me.

3. 890 *PMG*. Cf. Athenaeus 693f-694c. For other sympotic examples, see Schmid (1964, 105–109).

4. *Rhetoric* 2.21, 1394b13, with oral variants in the text.

5. Aristotle *Eudemian Ethics* 1.1, 1214a5; cf. *Nicomachean Ethics* 1.8.14, 1099a27.

6. Fr. 16 Voigt (= 16 L-P, with Page's supplement at v. 8). I take the song to be complete after verse 20. For a recent analysis see Calame (2005, 55–69).

7. As Most (1991) notes in a valuable analysis, Aristotle cites Sappho's use of the Helen myth here in his *Rhetoric* as an example of the "proof from authority"; the woman who excels all others in beauty (*kallos*, v. 7) can be assumed to know what is *kalliston*.

8. A prose example that Plato devised to be spoken in the persona of Socrates is worth quoting for its great renown, and for its broad relevance to the milieu for which Aristotle's poetry was suited: "I say, and it happens to be true, that the greatest good thing for a human being is this: to spend time each day discussing *aretê* and the other things you have heard me talking about, to clarify my own ideas and those of others; the unexamined life is not worth living for a human being" (λέγω ὅτι καὶ τυγχάνει μέγιστον ἀγαθὸν ὂν ἀνθρώπῳ τοῦτο, ἑκάστης ἡμέρας περὶ ἀρειῆς τοὺς λόγους ποιεῖσθαι καὶ τῶν ἄλλων περὶ ὧν ὑμεῖς ἐμοῦ ἀκούετε διαλεγομένου καὶ ἐμαυτὸν καὶ ἄλλους ἐξετάζοντος, ὁ δὲ ἀνεξέταστος βίος οὐ βιωτὸς ἀνθρώπῳ, *Apology* 38A).

9. Page (1955, 135 n. 1). Anagora, but not Anactoria, is listed in the Suda lexicon (S 107, iv 322s Adler) among Sappho's female students (μαθήτριαι). Ferrari (2010, 37 n. 16) would emend. Apart from Sappho 16 Voigt, we hear of Anactoria in Ovid, *Heroides* 15.17, and Maximus of Tyre 18.9.

10. Bundy (1969, 5); cf. Race (1982, 63–64).

11. Euripides personified *areta* at the beginning of a choral ode in *Orestes* 807–808, though in the nominative, not vocative case.

12. As when Castor, in an epiphany, declares that even the gods feel "pity for toiling mortals" (οἶκτος θνητῶν πολυμόχθων, Eurpides *Electra* 1330).

13. Athenaeus's version of v. 12, σὰν ἀγρεύοντες δύναμιν ("tracking down your power"), reprises the metaphor, if right: Diogenes Laertius has ἀναγορεύοντες; Didymus is unclear. Renehan (1982, 257) compares a Euripidean phrase, "to track down excellence is a great thing" (μέγα τι θηρεύειν ἀρετάν, *Iphigeneia at Aulis* 568), noting it has a "sophistic," we can say protreptic, background. The metaphor is mock-heroic in Ariphron's periphrasis for sex, "longings we hunt with Aphrodite's sweet and secret snares" (πόθων οὓς κρυφίοις Ἀφροδίτας ἕρκεσιν

θηρεύομεν, 5). The attempt by Crosset (1967, 148 n. 7) to make the hunting metaphor the "burden" of the song seems to me a warning example of excessive New Criticism.

14. On philosophical protreptic at this time, see Slings (1995 and 1999, 67–95).

15. It was popularly thought that repeated exposure to Homer's encomia of heroic warriors, for example, inculcated in the young an appetite for valorous action (*aretê*): Isocrates *Panegyricus* 4.159; cf. Lycurgus *Against Leocrates* 102–103 and cf. Aristophanes *Frogs* 1034–1036 for Homer as a teacher of *aretê*.

16. This is the message, often not fully appreciated, of *Politics* 7–8; see Ford (2004).

17. On epinician *ponos*, see Bundy (1969) and Kurke (1991, indexes s.v.). A biographical reading might suggest that Aristotle has chosen *mokhthos* because, encompassing more passive travails than *ponos*, it is a broad enough term to include Hermias's tortures among his pursuit of Virtue. Of the two uses of μόχθος in Homer, *Il.* 2.723 concerns the suffering Philoctetes, on whom see below.

18. Jaeger (1948, 118, 140, 153), followed by Crosset (1967, 148–149) (who yet usefully compares the "hymn to beauty" in Isocrates *Helen* 54–58); so too Wilamowitz (1893, 2.410–411). Against seeking out such issues in the poem, Bowra (1938, 188), followed by Düring (1957, 59–60), Renehan (1982, 268–274), Guthrie (1981, 34).

19. Norden (1913, 159–160).

20. With Aristotle's placement of the vocative, cf. the hymn-style opening of Pindar *Isthmian* 5.6: διὰ τεάν, ὤνασσα, τιμὰν.

21. On reading καρπόν here, see Renehan (1982, 259–260), Dorandi (2007, 24–25).

22. For the semantics of ἰσαθάνατον, cf. the common epic epithet ἰσόθεος, "godlike," used only of mortals; for the formation, cf. Ariphron's ἰσοδαίμονος βασιληίδος ἀρχᾶς (v. 4) of royal power "a fortune like that of the gods." Lyric antecedents include ἰσοδαίμων

βασιλεύς in a lament for the Great King in Aeschylus's *Persians* 634 (cf. ἰσόθεος Δαρεῖος of the decidedly mortal Darius at 857).

23. Aristotle refers to the play at *NE* 1146a20 and 1150b9.

24. Text by Lloyd-Jones and Wilson (1990), except that I have retained οὐ γὰρ ηὐσέβεια συνθνῄσκει at 1443, see the discussion.

25. A euphemism for "kill" comparable to Aristotle's "left the rays of the sun bereft" (v. 16).

26. In the *LSJ*, *Philoctetes* 1420 is cited as the earliest example (followed by Plato's *Symposium* 208D, quoted below) of *aretê* being used in an extended sense not for "excellence" but for excellence's reward—distinction, fame, glory.

27. E.g. Isocrates *To Demonicus* (49–50): "Zeus made [Heracles] immortal because of his *aretê* while subjecting [Tantalus] to the greatest torments because of his baseness." (τὸν μὲν διὰ τὴν ἀρετὴν ἀθάνατον ἐποίησεν, τὸν δὲ διὰ τὴν κακίαν ταῖς μεγίσταις τιμωρίαις ἐκόλασεν). Cf. *Evagoras* 70: "those in the past who have become immortal on account of their *aretê*" (τινες τῶν γεγενημένων δι' ἀρετὴν ἀθάνατοι γεγόνασιν); also *On the Peace* 94, and Hyperides' *Funeral Oration* 19.10.

28. Jebb (1932) notes on v. 1420 that the seer Diotima makes the same point in Plato's *Symposium* 208D-E: this prose encomium resembles Aristotle's in offering a trio of heroic exemplars who nobly accepted death (Alcestis, Achilles, capped by the Athenian Codrus) to argue that everyone is moved by the hope of "immortal *aretê* and a glorious (*eu-kleous*) reputation of the sort we here now sustain [i.e. by recalling these very stories]" (ὑπὲρ ἀρετῆς ἀθανάτου καὶ τοιαύτης δόξης εὐκλεοῦς ἦν νῦν ἡμεῖς ἔχομεν).

29. Webster (1970, 157) takes it as "the excellence of an immortal as distinct from a mortal," suggesting Heracles appeared as divinely youthful; similarly, Kamerbeek (1980, 195).

30. On Asclepius, Jebb (1932, 205, 221) gives details (on vv. 1333, 1437); cf. Kamerbeek (1980 *ad loc.*). In the background may be, as Mitchell-Boyask (2007, 85–114) argues, a reference to the cult of Asclepius, introduced in Athens a decade earlier. The ancient biography

of Sophocles reports that he served as a ministrant of the cult in recognition of which he was given heroic (NB not divine) honors after his death.

31. In place of ἡ γὰρ εὐσέβεια at 1443, Lloyd-Jones and Wilson (1990) and other recent editors print Dawes's οὐ γὰρ ηὐσέβεια. Kamerbeek (1980) has the fullest discussion, supporting the conjecture and Linforth's interpretation.

32. Linforth (1956, 149 n. 30), approved by Lloyd-Jones and Wilson: "it is the fame resulting from piety that the poet has in mind."

33. Wilamowitz's explanation is cited by Kamerbeek (1980, 191); similarly, Campbell (1881, vol. 2. 477) ("Follows men in their Death"). A parallel to the eschatological thought is Sophocles' *Electra* 291–292, where I take Clytemnestra to say, "may you [Electra] perish miserably, and may the gods below never release you from your present lamenting" (*pace* Jebb and others; cf. Finglass [2007: 186]).

34. Aristotle approaches this idea in his ethical works, declaring that "no function of man has so much permanence as virtuous activities; these are thought to be more durable even than scientific knowledge" (*NE* 1.10 1100b12–14: περὶ οὐδὲν γὰρ οὕτως ὑπάρχει τῶν ἀνθρωπίνων ἔργων βεβαιότης ὡς περὶ τὰς ἐνεργείας τὰς κατ' ἀρετήν· μονιμώτεραι γὰρ καὶ τῶν ἐπιστημῶν αὗται δοκοῦσιν εἶναι).

35. Jebb (1932, 221–222) argues that Sophocles should say "the effect of piety is imperishable, bringing happiness to the pious in Hades and an example to those who survive." Rejected by Kamerbeek (1980 *ad loc.*).

36. Sophocles composed a renowned paean to Asclepius (Philostratus *The Life of Apollonius of Tyana* 3.17 = T 73a *TrGF* Radt; see Testimonia 67–73) and, as noted, experimented in *Philoctetes* by directing a paean to Sleep (827–832): see Haldane (1963).

37. Pickard-Cambridge (1988, 276), citing Theophrastus *Char.* 15,10, 27.2; see also Aeschines 1.168; Menander *Epitrepontes* 767–768.

38. On Sophoclean epiphanies, see Pucci (1994) and Parker (1999, 11–13); on tragic epiphanies, see Sourvinou-Inwood (2003, 459–512) who, like Pucci, characterizes the *Philoctetes* as Euripidean in

its stress on the disjunction between the divine and mortal worlds (482–484).

Chapter 8

1. For "divining resemblances" see *Poetics* 1459a5-8: "The most important thing by far [for a poet] is to be good at metaphor. For this alone is not possible to get from another person but is a sign of inborn talent. Making good metaphors is the ability to discern similarities" (πολὺ δὲ μέγιστον τὸ μεταφορικὸν εἶναι. μόνον γὰρ τοῦτο οὔτε παρ' ἄλλου ἔστι λαβεῖν εὐφυΐας τε σημεῖόν ἐστι· τὸ γὰρ εὖ μεταφέρειν τὸ τὸ ὅμοιον θεωρεῖν ἐστιν). So too *Rhetoric* 3.8 (1409a8-10). For "deviations from ordinary language" (ξενικὸν δὲ λέγω γλῶτταν καὶ μεταφορὰν καὶ ἐπέκτασιν καὶ πᾶν τὸ παρὰ τὸ κύριον, *Poet*. 1458a22-23) see *Poetics* 1458a18-1459a17.

2. Aristotle *Poetics* 1459a19, *Rhetoric* 3.3, 1406b2. Wilamowitz (1893, 1.407), followed by Smyth and Bowra. On compound epithets in the "new" dithyramb of the later classical age, see Ford (forthcoming). The poem's most outstanding example is the epithet "soft-beamed" sleep (μαλακαυγήτοιο, v. 8). The word seems to be a coinage blending a more straightforward lyric compound like "soft-eyed" (μαλακόμματος, 929(g)1 *PMG*) with the kind of expression to be found in the dithyrambist Licymnius, a poet whose style Aristotle admired (*Rhet*. 3.11, 1413b12-16); Licymnius said that Sleep used to put Endymion to sleep with his eyes open because he so enjoyed the "beams of his eyes" (ὀμμάτων αὐγαῖς, 771.2 *PMG*).

3. Mastronarde (1994), on Euripides *Phoenissae* v. 784. Santoni (1991, 180 n. 4 and 181 n. 9) collects earlier uses, noting that, outside of a few uses in Sophocles and Euripides, πολύμοχθος is common in Orphic hymns and Sibylline oracles.

4. Bundy (1969, 91) notes that a number of epinician odes "turn in conclusion to the inevitability of death in order to define and illuminate the essence of *areta*," citing Bacchylides' lines among the examples and characterizing his as "the least stylized and allusive" version of the topos. As Bundy notes, the underlying ethical idea is expressed in Aristotle's

Rhetoric (1.9, 1367a1-3): "the preeminently praiseworthy actions are those which it is possible for a man to possess after death rather than during his lifetime, for the latter involve more selfishness."

5. On Philip's interest in Heracles, see Hammond and Griffith (1979, 514–515) and Markle (1976). Among the evidence is Isocrates *To Philip* (5.76–77, where the hero is cited as an ancestor of Philip), and the prominence of Heracles in the Letter to Philip written by Speusippus of the Academy (*Epist. Socrat.* 30). Heracles had been "ethicized" in writings of Prodicus and Antisthenes and, at the end of the fifth century, Herodorus of Heraclea Pontica (e.g., *FGrH* 31 F 14—where it is noteworthy that Virtue is symbolized by the apples of the Hesperides). Plato used Heracles as a figure for Socrates' life (and death?): *Apology* 22A; cf. *Theaet.* 175A, *Lysis* 205C.

6. Galinsky (1972, 107) speaks of Aristotle's song as continuing "the traditional Pindaric praise of Herakles as the embodiment of *aretê*."

7. On these myths in mystery religions, Boyancé (1937, 307); on the Alexander historians, Harding (2006, 155), citing Bosworth. Of course, philosophers had their own interpretations of the stories, e.g., Xenophon's Socrates "mythologizing" at a symposium that Heracles and the Dioskouroi are symbolic of beauty of mind and that of body (*Symposium* 8.28–30). These exempla, and the elusiveness with which they suggest immortality, were still in use much later: Menander Rhetor (414.23–27) advises eulogists to cite traditions ("they say") that Helen, the Dioskouroi, and Heracles share the community of the gods, and on that basis to "praise [the deceased] as a hero, or rather bless him as a god." For commentary, see Russell and Wilson (1981, *ad loc.*).

8. On Achilles' cult in the Black Sea area, Burgess (2009, 111–131); Hooker (1988) is skeptical; on Ajax, Henrichs (1993, 175–177).

9. For "look upon," *Il.* 16.188; Mimnermus 1.8 *IEG*; Theognis 426. "Leaving the light of the sun," *Il.* 18.11, cf. *Od.* 11.93. Smyth (1906, 471) suggests Aristotle's χήρωσεν is equivalent to a middle ("bereft himself"), but in favor of taking it transitively is a passage Smyth cites from Euripides *Cyclops* 440, rightly characterizing the expression's "dithyrambic extravagance."

10. E.g., in Pindar *Pyth.* 5.96 the periphrase λαχόντες Ἀΐδαν ("winning Hades as their lot") coexists with the explicit and emphatic (triad-ending) κεῖται θανών in 5.93, describing the heroized founder of Cyrene, Battos. For the motif in fourth-century Attic tombstones, see Tsagalis (2008, 77–85).

11. Aristotle's accusers could have construed ἀθάνατόν τε μιν αὐξήσουσι Μοῦσαι in 18 as "will make him increase until he is immortal," and could have compared Pindar *Pythian* 9.35, which describes immortalization by applying nectar and ambrosia to the lips as "making him deathless" (θήσονταί τε νιν ἀθάνατον).

12. See Ford (1992, 59–67).

13. Ibycus S151 *PMGF*; 282(a) *PMG*, on which see Budelman (2009) and Hutchinson (2001). For other self-referential signatures ("seals," *sphrêgides*) closing a lyric, cf. Pindar *Pyth.* 4. 298–299, Bacchylides 3.96–98.

14. The *enkômion* is usually assumed to be a genre for solo performance, while the triadic composition of Ibycus's song is assumed to indicate choral performance; but I see no reason why these short triads could not have been performed by a soloist; we simply do not know what forms lyric encomium might have taken before our first (fragmentary) examples from Pindar.

15. Sonnet 18. Shakespeare's irony is in drawing attention to the media in which the song will be preserved: for the object of praise to survive requires breath to sing the sonnet or eyes to read it (read, not behold, because in the future the only object of beauty actually before admiring eyes will be the text). With Ibucys's blending praise of patron and self, cf. Pindar *Paean* 6.61.

16. Santoni (1991, 187) aptly compares the conclusion of the speech of Aretê in Prodicus's *Heracles at the Crossroads* (Xenophon *Memorabilia* 1.2.33–34) which strikes many of the same themes as Aristotle: "And when the appointed time may come, they [Virtue's devotees] do not lie unhonored and in oblivion, but through memory they flourish in songs (ὑμνούμενοι θάλλουσι) for all time. If you toil after such things (διαπονησαμένῳ), Heracles, you stripling of noble

parents, you may come to obtain the most blessed form of happiness" (ὅταν δ' ἔλθῃ τὸ πεπρωμένον τέλος, οὐ μετὰ λήθης ἄτιμοι κεῖνται, ἀλλὰ μετὰ μνήμης τὸν ἀεὶ χρόνον ὑμνούμενοι θάλλουσι. τοιαῦτά σοι, ὦ παῖ τοκέων ἀγαθῶν Ἡράκλεις, ἔξεστι διαπονησαμένῳ τὴν μακαριστοτάτην εὐδαιμονίαν κεκτῆσθαι).

17. For representative texts and discussion, see Cole (2003, esp. 202–207), and Johnston in Graf and Johnston (2007, esp. 117–120).

18. See *The American Heritage Dictionary of the English Language*, 4th ed. (Houghton Mifflin, 2000), Appendix s.v. aug-. At Athens there was a cult to Auxô, as a form of the Graces: Pausanias 9.35, Farnell (1909, 428).

19. A metaphorical fruit "withers" in a noteworthy phrase by Pindar *Isthmian* 8.48: ἐπέων δὲ καρπός οὐ κατέφθινε: "the fruit of [Zeus'] words did not wither away" (i.e. prove ineffectual).

20. Cf. Tsagalis (2008, 149–150) for the (infrequent) use of αὐξάνειν in early Greek funerary inscriptions; a notable late example is *CEG* 599.4.

21. There is not a great deal of difference between the force of γένει βροτείῳ in v. 1 and βίῳ in v. 2, and the song repeats a number of roots: αυγ- 8, 16, τλη- 5, 11, αθανατ- 7, 18, μορφ- 3, 15, ἐργ- 11, 17; and possibly the hunting metaphor in 1 and 12. Note that Ibycus 151S *PMGF* also exhibits a good deal of repetitiveness in diction. Other arguments against Wilamowitz's change: Renehan (1982, 267–268).

22. Furley and Bremer (2001, 2.43) note that αὐξάνειν in Aristonoos's hymn to Hestia (CA 163–4, v. 10) combines a musical sense ("raise a song about") with an encomiastic one ("raise in stature," cf. Lat. *magnificare*).

23. Cf. the *Rhetoric to Alexander* 3.35. For a neat and trenchant discussion of "Rhetoric and Lyric Poetry" see Race (2007).

24. Cf. Cassius Dio 53.16: Octavian "was styled Augustus, as if he were a being superior to the mortal race. For all things [among the Romans] which are considered most honorable and sacred are called 'august,' wherefore the Greeks rendered the word Augustus by sebastos, as if 'venerable' [*quasi venerandum dicas*]." The account of Augustus's names in Suetonius differs in some aspects but confirms the association of Augustus with the divine, as does Ovid (*Fasti* I. V. 609).

25. As Renehan (1982, 255) notes, "The only explicit reference to [Hermias] is oblique—[Atarneus' nursling]—scarcely an honorific description appropriate to a god." Nor is Hermias named in Aristotle's dedicatory monument at Delphi (though Theocritus knew to whom it referred). On the role of names in real and fictional grave epigrams, see the fascinating discussion of Fantuzzi in Fantuzzi and Hunter (2004, 291–306).

Chapter 9

1. *NE* 7.8, esp. 1158a27–b5: see Broadie and Rowe (2002, 413).

2. On the connection, see Ford (2002, 115–119). Cf. Pulleyn (1997, 55): a hymn "is a sort of negotiable ἄγαλμα [offering], which generates χάρις [a feeling of reciprocity] whereas a [prayer] is not."

3. The idea of excellence leaving behind a *deathless* memorial is a cliché of encomiastic rhetoric: e.g., Isocrates *Panegyricus* 84 (τῆς δ' ἀρετῆς ἀθάνατον τὴν μνήμην ἐποίησαν); Lysias Epitaphios 81 (ἐπειδὴ θνητῶν σωμάτων ἔτυχον, ἀθάνατον μνήμην διὰ τὴν ἀρετὴν αὐτῶν κατέλιπον) and Xenophon *Agesilaus* 6.2.

4. The word *bebaios* recurs when Plato denies there can be any plain and stable meaning (τι σαφὲς καὶ βέβαιον) in a piece of writing (*Phaedrus* 275C) and says it is impossible to leave behind a written text with stability and clarity (277D: βεβαιότητα... καὶ σαφήνειαν).

5. Olympiodorus *In Gorg.* 41.3 (= Aristotle Fr. 673 Rose = *IEG*); also partly quoted in the *Vita Marc.* 26 (= T 34c Düring). Cf. Jacoby *FGrH* III B 2, p. 482. For claims that Aristotle quarreled with Plato, see Guthrie (1981, 25 n. 1).

6. Jaeger (1927, 14). Further discussion in Renehan (1991, 256–258).

7. Bernays (1878), rejected by Wilamowitz (1893, 2.413).

8. Düring (1957, 315). So too (Immisch 1906). Renehan (1991, 258) withholds judgment.

9. Jaeger also notes that this line recalls the interpretation that Plato gave an old poem on *aretê* by Tyrtaeus (cf. 12 IEG) cited in his last work, *Laws* 660E: "Shall we not enjoin poets to say that the good man, if he

be temperate and just, is also happy and blessed, no matter if he be big and strong or small and weak, rich or not" (*Laws* 601E: τοὺς ποιητὰς ἀναγκάζετε λέγειν ὡς ὁ μὲν ἀγαθὸς ἀνὴρ σώφρων ὢν καὶ δίκαιος εὐδαίμων ἐστὶ καὶ μακάριος, ἐάντε μέγας καὶ ἰσχυρὸς ἐάντε μικρὸς καὶ ἀσθενὴς ᾖ, καὶ ἐὰν πλουτῇ καὶ μή). Thus Aristotle's epitome of Platonic philosophy in v. 7 would have pleased his teacher.

10. The "vulgar" *Lives* give different reconstructions, usually incorporating something from vv. 2–3. See testimonia printed at West's *IEG*, 2.45, where note that a late commentary on Porphyry by David identifies Aristotle as the dedicator in his version of the inscription: βωμὸν Ἀριστοτέλης ἱδρύσατο τόνδε Πλάτωνος. Cf. Immisch (1906, 11–12), Jaeger (1948, 107 n. 2).

11. The reconstruction by Wilamowitz (1893, 413–414), followed by Immisch (1906, 15–16), is rejected by Renehan (1991, 260–261), who points to, *inter alia*, Aristotle's inclusion of Plato among "mortals" (θνητῶν, v. 4). I agree, and note that the reasoning is reminiscent of the importance to Athenaeus and others of the mention of Hermias's death in the alleged paean to him.

12. Jaeger (1948, 109) (adopting a suggestion of Blass). *Pace* Wilamowitz's objection (1893, 2.414), who would take φιλίης as a genitive of cause.

13. Jaeger (1948, 108). I would construe the end of the poem differently from Jaeger: I doubt it refers to a philosophical conception of the impossibility of embodying the ideal (see 109, with n. 2); putting weight on "first" in v. 4, the more widely intelligible statement would be that Plato can never be displaced as the "first discoverer" of the moral truth enunciated in v. 7. So Renehan (1991, 265–266).

14. Jaeger (1948, 109) rightly remarks that Aristotle's poem is phrased a fictional speech "interpreting the inscription in the manner of a pious exegete before a sacred object."

15. Jaeger (1927, 14). Boyancé (1937, 250–257) posits a "stranger" from the East, since he sees the poem and altar as rendering religious homage to Plato.

16. There may possibly have been a prose version as well: Olympiodorus remarks that Aristotle "not only composed an encomium in praise of him [sc. Plato] but also praises him in the elegiacs for Eudemus." Düring (1957, 317), who does not have a high opinion of Olympiodorus as a historian, suggests he might be confusing Callisthenes' encomium for Hermias.

17. DL 5.51-2. Cf. Lynch (1972, 100-105 and 114-115) on the (not technically religious) term *mouseion* for such schools.

18. Redfield (n.d.) refers to Speusippus's aforementioned *Funeral-feast of Plato* in showing that "Hero cult is indeed one of the many institutional ancestors of the philosophical schools."

19. Notwithstanding my view that the poem should not be treated as versified philosophy, it is hardly surprising that compatible ideas can be found in the famous chapter from *Nicomachean Ethics* on the best life (*NE* 10.7, 1177b31 ff.). Aristotle argues that since the mind is something godlike in us, a life lived in accordance with it makes "human life godlike" (εἰ δὴ θεῖον ὁ νοῦς πρὸς τὸν ἄνθρωπον, καὶ ὁ κατὰ τοῦτον βίος θεῖος πρὸς τὸν ἀνθρώπινον βίον); he thus recommends going beyond the archaic advice that mortals should think mortal thoughts and "as far as possible become immortal" (ἐφ' ὅσον ἐνδέχεται ἀθανατίζειν). That pursuing *arête* is the way to do so is clear from a passage like *NE* 7.1 (1145a15-25), in which Aristotle opposes to the vice of brutishness (θηριότης) a "heroic and godlike excellence" (ἀρετήν ἡρωικήν τινα καὶ θείαν) "like the ultimate excellence that people suppose allows men to become gods" (εἰ, καθάπερ φασίν, ἐξ ἀνθρώπων γίνονται θεοὶ δι' ἀρετῆς ὑπερβολήν).

20. Herman (1987, 69): "ritualised friendship was thought to outlast the individual actors and, conspicuously mimicking kinship ties, pass on to their descendents. Thus, a person could die, but the role of *xenos* could not."

21. See discussion in ch. 2 above.

22. Against authenticity: Trampgedach (1994, 70-72). Defending it: Wilamowitz (1920, 2.281), Wormell (1935, 59-61), Guthrie (1975, 400-401), Post (1921, 127), and Harward (1932, 186), observing that a forger

might have been expected to drag Aristotle into the letter. As noted in my earlier reference to the letter, Strabo's unsupported claim (13.1.57 C610) that Hermias knew Plato at Athens does not condemn the letter's denial that Plato's had personal knowledge of Hermias (323A).

23. DL 3.46; Philodemus *Index Acad.* col. 6.10 Dorandi; Didymus col. 5.53–54.

24. Cf. *Eudemian Ethics* 7,2 1238a11 ff.

25. Lynch 1972, 76; cf. 87.

26. Athenaeus (3a-b). Discussions include: Gottschalk (1972, 335–342 and 1987, 1083–1088); Moraux (1973, 3–94), reviewed by Leonardo Tarán in *Gnomon* 53 (1981, 721–750, esp. 725–731); Barnes (1997, esp. 1–16), and Bollansée (1999b, 234–243); brief remarks in Fraser (1972, 1.320 and 2a.473 n. 100), with critique in Tarán (above, 727), and Guthrie (1981, 59–65). For possible connections between Neleus and the Attalids of Pergamon, see Kosmetatou (2003). Finally, Lord (1986, 140–145) sees behind the story credible measures for safekeeping the collection in light of the Peripatetics' changing political fortunes in the later fourth century.

27. Lynch (1972, 144–149).

28. Trans. Chiesara, Aristocles F 2.13 Chiesara (= T 581 Düring).

29. Diels-Schubart (1904, 24–25) suggest Hermippus may have transmitted the song to Didymus; see further Bollansée (1999b, 313–314, and 2001). But Wehrli (1974, 75), citing Jacoby *FGrH* 3b Suppl. 1, *Text* 329, notes that there is no evidence that Hermippus included long verbatim quotations; so too Harding (2006, 35, 37–38). If Athenaeus copied the song from Hermippus, the differences between his text and the one in Didymus—tabulated by Gerke 1902—may be due to the latter's having got his version from another source, Favorinus according to Wilamowitz (1892, 2.403 n.1); cf. Harding (2006, 154).

30. Moraux (1951, 144–145). For the list in Diogenes, see text in Düring (1957, 41–50, 67–69). It seems that the catalog preserved in Diogenes is not closely related to what Hermippus did: Moraux (1951, 211–233), Bollansée (1999b, 163–182).

31. [Ammonius] 482 Nikau: <ὕμνος ἐγκωμίου> διαφέρει. ὁ μὲν γὰρ ὕμνος ἐστὶ θεῶν, τὸ δὲ ἐνκώμιον ἀνθρώπων. See Moraux (1951, 261-262) and cf. R. Wünsch, "Hymnos" RE 9.1 col. 181. On Aristotle's "On Virtue" (A 163), see Moraux (1951, 254, 269). For the *appendix Hesychiana* (Moraux's *l'Anonyme de Ménage*), see Düring (1957, 82-92).

32. Didymus col. 6.21-22: κοὐκ ἄν [ἔ]χ[ο]ι φαύλως αὐτὸν ἀναγρά[ψαι δι]ὰ τὸ μὴ πολλοῖς πρὸ χειρὸς (εἶναι).

BIBLIOGRAPHY

Badian, Ernst. 1981. "The Deification of Alexander the Great." In *Ancient Macedonian Studies in Honor of C. F. Edson*, ed. H. J. Dell, 27–71. Thessaloniki: Institute for Balkan Studies.

Bagnall, Roger S. 2004. "Library of Dreams." *Proceedings of the American Philosophical Society* 146: 348–362.

Barigazzi, Adelmo. 1966. *Favorinus. Opere*. Florence: Le Monnier.

Barnes, Johnathan. 1997. "Roman Aristotle." In *Philosophia Togata*. Vol. II, *Plato and Aristotle at Rome*, ed. Johnathan Barnes and Miriam Griffin, 1–69. Oxford: Oxford University Press.

Barthes, Roland. 1988. "The Old Rhetoric: An Aide-mémoire." In the *Semiotic Challenge*, tr. R. Howard, 11–94. New York: Hill and Wang.

Bell, J. M. 1978. "*Kimbix kai sophos*: Simonides in the Anecdotal Tradition." *Quaderni Ubinati di Cultura Classica* 28: 29–86.

Bernays, Jacob. 1878. "Aristoteles' Elegie an Eudemos." *Rheinisches Museum* 33: 232–237.

Bing, Peter. 2009. *The Scroll and the Marble: Studies in Reading and Reception in Hellenistic Poetry*. Ann Arbor: University of Michigan Press.

Bloom, Harold. 1975. *A Map of Misreading*. New York: Oxford University Press.

Boedeker, Deborah. 2001. "Heroic Historiography." In *The New Simonides*, ed. D. Boedeker and D. Sider, 120–134. Oxford: Oxford University Press.

Bollansée, Jan. 1999a. *Hermippos of Smyrna. Die Fragmente der Griechischen Historiker Continued IV*. A. Leiden: Peeters.

Bollansée, Jan. 1999b. *Hermippos of Smyrna and his Biographical Writings, a Reappraisal* (Studia Hellenistica 35). Leiden: Peeters.

Bollansée, Jan. 2001. "Aristotle and the Death of Hermias of Atarneus: Two Extracts from Hermippos' Monograph on Aristotle." *Simblos* 3: 67–98.

Bosworth, A. B. 1970. "Aristotle and Calisthenes." *Historia* 19: 407–413.

Bosworth, A. B. 1977. "Alexander and Ammon." In *Greece and the Eastern Mediterranean in History and Prehistory*, ed. K. H. Kinzl, 51–75. Berlin: W. de Gruyter.

Bosworth, A. B. 1988. *Conquest and Empire: The Reign of Alexander the Great*. Cambridge: Cambridge University Press.

Bowra, C. M. 1938. "Aristotle's Hymn to Virtue." *Classical Quarterly* 37: 182–189. (Reprinted in *Problems in Greek Poetry*, Oxford: Oxford University Press, 1953, 138–150).

Boyancé, Pierre. 1937. *Le Culte des muses chez les philosophes grecs*. Paris: E. de Boccard.

Broadie, Sarah, and Christopher Rowe. 2002. *Aristotle: Nichomachean Ethics*. Oxford: Oxford University Press.

Brunt, P. A. 1993. *Studies in Greek History and Thought*. Oxford: Oxford University Press.

Budelman, Felix, ed. 2009. *The Cambridge Companion to Greek Lyric*. Cambridge: Cambridge University Press.

Bundy, E. L. 1969. *Studia Pindarica*. Berkeley: University of California Press. Reprint, 1986.

Burgess, Jonathan S. 2009. *The Death and Afterlife of Achilles*. Baltimore: The Johns Hopkins University Press.

Calame, Claude. 2005. *Masks of Authority: Fiction and Pragmatics in Ancient Greek Poetics*, tr. Peter M. Burke. Ithaca and London: Cornell University Press.

Cameron, Alan. 1995. *Callimachus and His Critics*. Princeton: Princeton University Press.
Campbell, David. 1993. *Greek Lyric*, Vol. 5. Loeb Classical Library. Cambridge, Mass.: Harvard University Press.
Campbell, Lewis. 1881. *Sophocles*. 2 vols. Oxford: Oxford University Press.
Cawkwell, G. L. 1994. "The Deification of Alexander the Great: A Note." In *Ventures into Greek History*, ed. Ian Worthington, 292–306. Oxford: Oxford University Press.
Chiesara, Maria Lorenza. 2001. *Aristocles of Messene: Testimonia and Fragments*. Oxford: Oxford University Press.
Christesen, Paul. 2007. *Olympic Victor Lists and Ancient Greek History*. Cambridge: Cambridge University Press.
Chroust, Anton-Hermann. 1966. "Aristotle's Flight from Athens in the year 323 B.C." *Historia* 15: 185–192.
Chroust, Anton-Hermann. 1967. "Aristotle Leaves the Academy." *Greece and Rome* 14: 39–44.
Chroust, Anton-Hermann. 1971. "Aristotle's Sojourn in Assos." *Historia* 21: 170–176.
Chroust, Anton-Hermann. 1973. *Aristotle: New Light on His Life and on Some of His Lost Works*. 2 vols. Notre Dame: University of Notre Dame Press.
Clinton, Kevin. 1974. *The Sacred Officials of the Eleusinian Mysteries*. Transactions of the American Philosophical Society, v. 64, pt. 3. Philadelphia: American Philosophical Society.
Cole, Susan G. 2003. "Landscapes of Dionysus and Elysian Fields." In *Greek Mysteries: The Archaeology and Ritual of Ancient Greek Secret Cults*, ed. Michael B. Cosmopoulos, 193–217. London and New York: Routledge.
Csapo, Eric. 2004. "The Politics of the New Music." In *Music and the Muses: The Culture of 'Mousike' in the Classical Athenian City*, ed. P. Murray and P. Wilson, 207–248. Oxford: Oxford University Press.
Currie, Bruno. 2005. *Pindar and the Cult of Heroes*. Oxford: Oxford University Press.

Crosset, John. 1967. "Aristotle as Poet: The Hymn to Hermeias." *Philological Quarterly* 46: 145–155.
Davies, M., ed. 1991. *Poetarum melicorum Graecorum fragmenta.* Oxford: Oxford University Press.
Depew, Mary. 1997. "Reading Greek Prayers." *Classical Antiquity* 16: 229–258.
Derenne, Eudore. 1930. *Les procès d'impiété intentés aux philosophes à Athènes au Vme et au IVme siècles avant J.-C.* Liège: H. Vaillant-Carmanne. Reprint, New York: Arno Press, 1976.
Derrida, Jacques. 1974. *Of Grammatology*, tr. G. Spivak. Baltimore: The Johns Hopkins University Press.
Derrida, Jacques. 1989. "Biodegradables: Seven Diary Fragments," tr. Peggy Kamuf. *Critical Inquiry* 15: 812–873.
Diehl, E. 1925. *Anthologia lyrica Graeca.* 2 vols. Leipzig: Teubner.
Diels, H., and W. Schubart. 1904. *Didymos Kommentar zu Demosthenes.* Berliner Klassikertexte I. Berlin: Weidmann.
Dindorf, G., ed. 1867–1871. *Eusebius.* 4 vols. Leipzig: Teubner.
Dodds, E. R. 1959. *Plato: Gorgias.* Oxford: Oxford University Press.
Döring, Klaus, ed. 1972. *Die Megariker. Kommentierte Sammlung der Testimonien.* Studien zur antiken Philosophie, Bd. 2. Amsterdam: Grüner.
Dorandi, T. 1991. *Storia dei filosofi. Platone e l'Academia (PHerc. 1021 e 164).* Naples: Bibliopolis.
Dorandi, T. 1994. *Storia dei filosofi. La Stoà da Zenone a Panezio (PHerc. 1018).* Philosophia antiqua, v. 60. Leiden and New York: Brill.
Dorandi, T. 2007. "Note sulla tradizione e sul testo del poema di Aristotele in onore di Ermia di Atarneo." *Zeitschrift für Papyrologie und Epigraphik* 161: 21–26.
Drachmann, A. B., ed. 1969. *Scholia vetera in Pindari carmina.* 3 vols. Amsterdam: Adolf M. Hakkert.
Düring, Ingomar. 1957. *Aristotle in the Ancient Biographical Tradition.* Göteborg: Elander.
Dziatzko, K. F. O. 1899. "Bibliotheken." *RE* 3 col. 409–23.
Engelmann, Helmut, and Reinhold Merkelbach. 1972–1973. *Die Inschriften von Erythrai und Klazomenai.* Bonn: R. Habelt.

Fairbanks, Arthur. 1900. *A Study of the Greek Paean*. Cornell Studies in Classical Philology XII. New York: Macmillan.

Fantuzzi, Marco. 2001. "Heroes, Descendants of *Hemitheoi*: The Proemium of Theocritus 17 and Simonides 11^2 W." In *The New Simonides*, ed. D. Boedeker and D. Sider, 232–241. Oxford: Oxford University Press.

Fantuzzi, Marco, and Richard Hunter. 2004. *Tradition and Innovation in Hellenistic Poetry*. Cambridge: Cambridge University Press.

Färber, Hans. 1936. *Die Lyrik in der Kunsttheorie der Antike*. Munich: Neuer Filser-Verlag.

Farnell, L. R. 1909. *The Cults of the Greek States*. 5 vols. Oxford: Oxford University Press.

Farnell, L. R. 1932. *The Works of Pindar II: Critical Commentary on Pindar*. London: Macmillan.

Faulkner, Andrew. 2008. *The Homeric Hymn to Aphrodite*. Oxford: Oxford University Press.

Ferrari, Franco. 2010. *Sappho's Gift: The Poet and her Community*, trans. B. Acosta-Hughes and L. Prauscello. Ann Arbor: Michigan Classical Press.

Finglass, P. J., ed. 2007. *Sophocles: Electra*. Cambridge: Cambridge University Press.

Flower, Michael A. 1988. "Agesilaus of Sparta and the Origins of the Ruler Cult." *Classical Quarterly* 38: 123–134.

Flower, Michael A. 1994. *Theopompus of Chios*. Oxford: Oxford University Press.

Ford, Andrew L. 1992. *Homer: The Poetry of the Past*. Ithaca and London: Cornell University Press.

Ford, Andrew L. 1999a. "Reading Homer from the Rostrum: Poetry and Law in Aeschines, *In Timarchus*." In *Performance Culture and Athenian Democracy*, ed. S. Goldhill and R. Osborne, 281–313. Cambridge: Cambridge University Press.

Ford, Andrew L. 1999b. "Odysseus after Dinner: *Od*. 9.2–11 and the Traditions of Sympotic Song." In *Euphrosune: Studies in Ancient Epic and Its Legacy in Honor of Dimitrios Marinatos*, ed. A. Rengakos and J. Kazazis, 109–123. Stuttgart: Franz Steiner.

Ford, Andrew L. 2002. *The Origins of Criticism: Literary Culture and Poetic Theory in Classical Greece*. Princeton: Princeton University Press.

Ford, Andrew L. 2004. "Catharsis: The Power of Music in Aristotle's Politics." In *Music and the Muses: The Culture of 'Mousike' in the Classical Athenian City*, ed. P. Wilson and P. Murray, 309–336. Oxford: Oxford University Press.

Ford, Andrew L. 2006. "The Genre of Genres: Paeans and *Paian* in Early Greek Poetry." *Poetica* 38: 277–296.

Ford, Andrew L. 2008. "The Beginnings of Dialogue: Socratic Discourse and Fourth-Century Prose." In *The End of Dialogue in Antiquity*, ed. Simon Goldhill, 29–44. Cambridge: Cambridge University Press.

Ford, Andrew L. 2009. "Plato's Two Hesiod's." In *Plato and Hesiod*, ed. G. R. Boys-Stones and J. H. Haubold, 133–154. Oxford: Oxford University Press.

Ford, Andrew L. (forthcoming). "The Poetics of Dithyramb." In *Dithyramb and Society: Texts and Contexts in a Changing Choral Culture*, ed. Barbara Kowalzig and Peter Wilson. Oxford: Oxford University Press.

Fox, R. Lane. 1986. "Theopompus of Chios and the Greek World." In *Chios: A Conference at the Homereion in Chios*, ed. J. Boardman and C. Vaphopoulou-Richardson, 111–120. Oxford: Oxford University Press.

Fredricksmeyer, E. A. 1979. "Divine Honors for Philip II." *Transactions of the American Philological Association* 109: 39–61.

Fredricksmeyer, E. A. 1981. "On the Background of the Ruler Cult." In *Macedonian Studies in Honor of Charles F Edson*, ed. H. J. Dell, 145–156. Thessaloniki: Institute for Balkan Studies.

Fuhrer, Therese. 1993. "Callimachus' Epinician Poems." In *Callimachus*, ed. M. A. Harder, R. F. Retguit, and G. C. Wakker, 79–97. Groningen: Forsten.

Furley, William D., and Jan Maarten Bremer. 2001. *Greek Hymns. A Selection of Greek Religious Poetry from the Archaic to the Hellenistic Poetry*. Vol. 1: *The Texts in Translation*. Vol. 2: *Greek Texts and Commentary*. Tübingen: Mohr Siebeck.

Gagné, Renaud. 2009. "Mystery Inquisitors: Sacrilege and Authority at Eleusis." *Classical Antiquity* 28: 211-47.

Gaiser, Konrad. 1966. "Die Elegie des Aristoteles an Eudemos." *Museum Helveticum* 23: 84–106.

Galinsky, G. Karl. 1972. *The Herakles Theme: The Adaptations of the Hero in Literature from Homer to the Twentieth Century*. Oxford: Oxford University Press.

Gelzer, Thomas. 1993. "Transformations." In *Images and Ideologies: Self-definition in the Hellenistic World*, ed. A. W. Bulloch et al., 130–151. Berkeley: University of California Press.

Gercke, A. 1902. "Die Überlieferung des Diogenes Laertios." *Hermes* 37: 424–425.

Gibson, Craig A. 2002. *Interpreting a Classic: Demosthenes and His Ancient Commentators*. Berkeley: University of California Press.

Gigon, O. 1958. "Interpretationen zu den antiken Aristotles-Viten" *Museum Helveticum* 15: 147–193.

Gigon, O., ed. 1962. *Vita Aristotelis Marciana*. Berlin: W. de Gruyter.

Gottschalk, H. B. 1972. "Notes on the Wills of the Peripatetic Scholarchs." *Hermes* 10: 314–342.

Gottschalk, H. B. 1987. "Aristotelian Philosophy in the Roman World." *Aufstieg und Niedergang der römischen Welt* 36 pt. 2: 1089–1112.

Graf, Fritz. 1985. *Nordionische Kulte*. Rome: Schweizerisches Institut in Rom.

Graf, Fritz, and Sarah Iles Johnston. 2007. *Ritual Texts for the Afterlife: Orpheus and the Bacchic Gold Tablets*. London and New York: Routledge.

Guthrie, W. C. K. 1975. *Plato—the Man and His Dialogues: Earlier Period. (A History of Greek Philosophy IV)*. Cambridge: Cambridge University Press.

Guthrie, W. C. K. 1981. *Aristotle: An Encounter. (A History of Greek Philosophy VI)*. Cambridge: Cambridge University Press.

Gow, A. F. S., and D. L. Page. 1965. *The Greek Anthology. Hellenistic Epigrams*. Cambridge: Cambridge University Press.

Gutzwiller, Kathryn J. 1998. *Poetic Garlands: Hellenistic Epigrams in Context*. Berkeley: University of California Press.

Habicht, Christian. 1970. *Gottmenschentum und griechische Städte*, 2nd ed. Munich: Book.
Habicht, Christian. 1988. *Hellenistic Athens and Her Philosophers*. Princeton: Princeton University Press.
Haldane, J. A. 1963. "A Paean in the *Philoctetes*." *Classical Quarterly* 13: 53–56.
Hammond, N. G. L., and G. T. Griffith. 1979. *A History of Macedonia* II. Oxford: Oxford University Press.
Hammond, N. G. L., and F. W. Wallbank. 1988, *A History of Macedonia* III. Oxford: Oxford University Press.
Harding, Phillip. 2006. *Didymos: On Demosthenes*. Clarendon Ancient History Series, translation, text, and commentary. Oxford: Oxford University Press.
Harvey, A. E. 1955. "The Classification of Greek Lyric Poetry." *Classical Quarterly* 49: 157–175.
Harward, J. 1932. *The Platonic Epistles*. Cambridge: Cambridge University Press.
Heath, Malcolm. 1988. "Receiving the *Kômos*, the Context and Performance of Epinician." *American Journal of Philology* 109: 180–195.
Heibges, J. S. 1912. "Hermippos (6)." *RE* 8.1 col. 848–852.
Heiland, H. 1925. *Aristoclis Messenii reliquiae*. Giessen: Otto Meyer.
Henrichs, Albert. 1993. "The Tomb of Aias and the Prospect of Hero Cult in Sophokles." *Classical Antiquity* 12: 165–180.
Herman, Gabriel. 1987. *Ritualised Friendship and the Greek City*. Cambridge: Cambridge University Press.
Hinds, Stephen. 1998. *Allusion and Intertext: Dynamics of Appropriation in Roman Poetry*. Cambridge: Cambridge University Press.
Hooker, J. T. 1988. "The Cults of Achilles." *Rheinisches Museum* 131: 1–7.
Hopkinson, N. 1984. *Callimachus: Hymn to Demeter*. Cambridge: Cambridge University Press.
Hutchinson, G. O. 2001. *Greek Lyric Poetry: A Commentary on Selected Larger Pieces*. Oxford: Oxford University Press.
Immisch, O. 1906. "Ein Gedichte des Aristoteles." *Philologus* 65: 1–23.

Jaeger, W. 1927. "Aristotle's Verses in Praise of Plato." *Classical Quarterly* 21: 13–17.

Jaeger, W. 1948. *Aristotle: Fundamentals in the History of His Development*, trans. R. Robinson, 2nd ed. Oxford: Oxford University Press.

Janko, Richard. 1982. *Homer Hesiod and the Hymns: A Study in Diachronic Development*. Cambridge: Cambridge University Press.

Janko, Richard. 1992. *The Iliad: A Commentary. Books 13–16*. Cambridge: Cambridge University Press.

Jebb, R. C. 1932. *Sophocles. The Plays and Fragments VI: The Philoctetes*. Cambridge: Cambridge University Press.

Käppel, Lutz. 1992. *Paian: Studien zur Geschichte einer Gattung*. Untersuchungen zur antiken Literatur und Geschichte 37. Berlin: W. de Gruyter.

Käppel, Lutz, and R. Kannicht. 1988. "Noch einmal zur Frage 'Dithyrambos oder Paian?'" *Zeitschrift für Papyrologie und Epigraphik* 73: 19–24.

Kamerbeek, J. C. 1980. *The Plays of Sophocles VI: The Philoctetes*. Leiden: E. J. Brill.

Kosmetatou, Elizabeth. 2003. "The Attalids in the Troad An Addendum: An Episode in the Perils of the Aristotelian Corpus." *Ancient Society* 33: 53–60.

Kurke, Leslie. 1991. *The Traffic in Praise*. Ithaca and London: Cornell University Press.

Lefkowitz, M. R. 1981. *The Lives of the Greek Poets*. Baltimore: The Johns Hopkins University Press.

LeVen, Pauline. 2008. *The Many-Headed Muse: Tradition and Innovation in Fourth-Century B.C. Greek Lyric Poetry*. PhD. dissertation, Princeton University / Paris IV, Sorbonne.

Liapis, V. 1996. "Double Entendres in Attic Skolia: The Etymology of Skolion." *Eranos* 94: 111–122.

Lincoln, Bruce. 2007. *Religion, Empire, and Torture: The Case of Achaemenian Persia, with a Postscript on Abu Ghraib*. Chicago: University of Chicago Press.

Linforth, I. M. 1956. "Philoctetes the Play and the Man." *University of California Publications in Classical Philology* 15.3. 95–156.

Lissarrague, F. 1990. *L'autre guerrier*. Paris: La Découverte.
Lord, Carnes. 1986. "On the Early History of the Aristotelian Corpus." *American Journal of Philology* 107: 137–161.
Lowe, N. J. 2007. "Epinician Eidography." In *Pindar's Poetry, Patrons, and Festivals*, ed. Simon Hornblower and Catherine Morgan, 167–176. Oxford: Oxford University Press.
Lloyd-Jones, Hugh, and P. Parsons. 1983. *Supplementum Hellenisticum*. Berlin: W. de Gruyter.
Lloyd-Jones, Hugh, and N. G. Wilson. 1990. *Sophoclis Fabulae*. Oxford: Clarendon Press.
Lobel, E., and D. L. Page, eds. 1955. *Poetarum Lesbiorum fragmenta*. Oxford: Clarendon Press.
Lynch, J. P. 1972. *Aristotle's School. A Study of a Greek Educational Institution*. Berkeley: University of California Press.
Ma, John. 2000. *Antiochus III and the Cities of Western Asia Minor*. Oxford: Oxford University Press.
Macher, Engelbert. 1914. *Die Hermiasepisode im Demostheneskommentar des Didymos*. Brünn.
Maehler, H. 1982–1997. *Die Lieder des Bakchylides*, 2 vols. Leiden: E. J. Brill.
Markle, Minor M., III. 1976. "Support of Athenian Intellectuals for Philip: A Study of Isocrates' *Philippus* and Speusippus' Letter to Philip." *Journal of Hellenic Studies* 96: 80–99.
Martindale, Charles. 2005. *Latin Poetry and the Judgment of Taste: An Essay in Aesthetics*. Oxford: Oxford University Press.
Mastronarde, D. 1994. *Euripides. Phoenissae*. Cambridge: Cambridge University Press.
McLachan, Bonnie. 1993. *The Age of Grace: Charis in Early Greek Poetry*. Princeton: Princeton University Press.
Mensching, E. 1963. *Favorin von Arelate*, Vol. 1 Berlin: W. de Gruyter.
Mejer, Jørgen. 1978. *Diogenes Laertius and His Hellenistic Background*. (*Hermes* Einzelschriften 40.) Wiesbaden: Steiner.
Mikalson, Jon D. 1998. *Religion in Hellenistic Athens*. Berkeley: University of California Press.

Mitchell-Boyask, Robin. 2007. "The Athenian *Aesklepion* and the End of the *Philoctetes*." *Transactions of the American Philological Association* 137: 85–114.

Milns, R. D. 1994. "Didymea." In *Ventures into Greek History*, ed. Ian Worthington, 70–88. Oxford: Oxford University Press.

Moraux, Paul. 1951. *Les listes anciennes des ouvrages d'Aristote*. Louvain: Éditions universitaires de Louvain.

Moraux, Paul. 1973. *Der Aristotelismus bei den Griechen I: von Andronikos bis Alexander von Aphrodisias. Die Renaissance des Aristotelismus im I. Jh. v. Chr.* Berlin: W. de Gruyter.

Momigliano, Arnaldo. 1987. *On Pagans Jews and Christians*. Scranton, Pa.: Wesleyan University Press.

Momigliano, Arnaldo. 1993. *The Development of Greek Biography*, 2nd ed. Cambridge, Mass.: Harvard University Press.

Most, Glenn. 1981 "Sappho Fr. 16.6–7 L-P." *Classical Quarterly* 31: 11–17.

Mulvaney, C. M. 1926. "Notes on the Legend of Aristotle." *Classical Quarterly* 66: 155–167.

Nagy, Gregory. 1990. *Pindar's Homer: The Lyric Possession of an Epic Past*. Baltimore: The Johns Hopkins University Press.

Nickau, K. ed. 1966. *[Ammonius] Gramm., De adfinium vocabulorum differentia*. Leipzig: Teubner.

Nicolai, Roberto. 2004. *Studi su Isocrate*. Quaderni dei Seminari Romani di Cultura Greca 7. Rome: Quasar.

Norden, E. 1913. *Agnostos Theos: Untersuchungen zur Formengesschichte religiöser Rede*. Leipzig: Teubner.

O'Sullivan, L.-L. 1997. "Athenian Impiety Trials in the Late Fourth Century B. C." *Classical Quarterly* 47: 136–152.

Owen, G. E. L. 1983. "Philosophic Invective." *Oxford Studies in Ancient Philosophy* 1: 1–25.

Page, Denys. 1955. *Sappho and Alcaeus*. Oxford: Clarendon Press.

Page, Denys, ed. 1962. *Poetae melici Graeci*. Oxford: Clarendon Press.

Page, Denys, ed. 1975. *Epigrammata Graeca*. Oxford: Clarendon Press.

Page, Denys. 1981. *Further Greek Epigrams*. Cambridge: Cambridge University Press.

Parker, Robert. 1996. *Athenian Religion*. Oxford: Oxford University Press.

Parker, Robert. 1998. "Pleasing Thighs: Reciprocity in Greek Religion." In *Reciprocity in Ancient Greece*, ed. C. Gill, N. Postlethwaite, and R. Seaford, 105–125. Oxford: Oxford University Press.

Parker, Robert. 1999. "Through a Glass Darkly: Sophocles and the Divine." In *Sophocles Revisited*, ed. J. Griffin, 11–30. Oxford: Oxford University Press.

Pavese, C. 1961. "Aristotele e i filosofi ad Asso." *La parola del passato* 16: 113–119.

Pearson, Lionel, and Susan Stephens. 1983. *Didymi in Demosthenem commenta*. Stuttgart: Teubner.

Pelliccia, Hayden. 2002. "The Interpretation of *Iliad* 6.145–9 and the Sympotic Contribution to Rhetoric." *Colby Quarterly* 38: 197–230.

Penella, Robert J. 2007. *Man and the World: The Orations of Himerius*. Berkeley: University of California Press.

Perkins, David. 1992. *Is Literary History Possible?* Baltimore: The Johns Hopkins University Press.

Pfeiffer, Rudolph. 1968. *History of Classical Scholarship I: From the Beginnings to the End of the Hellenistic Age*. Oxford: Oxford University Press.

Pickard-Cambridge, A. W. 1988. *The Dramatic Festivals of Athens*, 2nd ed. revised with a new supplement by J. Gould and D. M. Lewis. Oxford: Clarendon Press.

Plezia, Marianus, 1977. *Aristotelis privatorum scriptorum fragmenta*. Leipzig: Teubner.

Post, L. A. 1921. *Thirteen Epistles of Plato*. Oxford: Clarendon Press.

Powell, J. U., ed. 1925. *Collectanea Alexandrina*. Oxford: Clarendon Press.

Pucci, Pietro. 1987. *Odysseus Polutropos: Intertextual Readings in the Odyssey and the Iliad*. Ithaca and London: Cornell University Press.

Pucci, Pietro. 1994. "Gods' Interventions and Epiphany in Sophocles." *American Journal of Philology* 115: 15–16.

Pulleyn, Simon. 1997. *Prayer in Greek Religion*. Oxford: Oxford University Press.

Race, William. 1982. *The Classical Priamel from Homer to Boethius.* Leiden: Brill.

Race, William. 2007. "Rhetoric and Lyric Poetry." In *A Companion to Greek Rhetoric,* ed. I. Worthington, 509–525. Oxford: Blackwell.

Redfield, James. 1974. *Nature and Culture in the Iliad.* Chicago: University of Chicago Press.

Redfield, James. n.d. "Theophrastus' Will and Plato's Academy."

Reitzenstein, R. 1883. *Epigram und Skolion.* Giessen: Ricker.

Renehan, R. 1982. "Aristotle's as Lyric Poet: The Hermias Poem." *Greek Roman and Byzantine Studies* 23: 251–74.

Renehan, R. 1991. "Aristotle's Elegiacs to Eudemus." *Illinois Classical Studies* 16: 255–267.

Rhodes, P. J., and R. Osborne. 2003. *Greek Historical Inscriptions 404–323 BC.* Oxford: Oxford University Press.

Rose, V. 1863. *Aristoteles pseudepigraphus.* Leipzig: Teubner.

Rose, V. 1886. *Aristotelis qui ferebantur librorum fragmenta.* Leipzig: Teubner.

Rudhardt, Jean. 1960. "La Définition du délit d'impiété d'après la législation attique." *Museum Helveticum* 17: 87–105.

Ruina, D. T. 1986. "Theocritus of Chios' Epigram Against Aristotle." *Classical Quarterly* 36: 531–534.

Russell, D. A., and N. G. Wilson. 1981. *Menander Rhetor.* Oxford: Clarendon Press.

Rusten, Jeffrey. 1987. Review of Pearson-Stephens, *Classical Philology* 82: 265–269.

Rutherford, Ian. 2001. *Pindar's Paeans: A Reading of the Fragments with a Survey of the Genre.* New York: Oxford University Press.

Santoni, Anna. 1991. "L'Inno di Aristotele per Ermia di Atarneo." In *La Componente Autobiographica nella poesia Greca e Latina,* ed. G. Arrighetti and F. Montanari, 179–195. Pisa: Giardini.

Severyns, A. 1938. *Recherches sur la "Chrestomathie" de Proclos,* vol. 2. (Bibliothèque de la faculté de philosophie et lettres de l'université de Liège fascc. 78). Paris: E. Droz.

Schachter, Albert. 1981. *Cults of Boiotia.* 4 vols. London: Institute of Classical Studies.

Schmid, Ulrich. 1964. *Die Priamel der Werte im Griechischen von Homer bis Paulus*. Wiesbaden: Harrassowitz.

Schmidt, Maurice. 1854. *Didymi Chalcenteri Grammatici Alexandrini Fragmenta*. Leipzig: B. G. Teubner.

Schroeder, Otto. 1925. "Aristoteles als Dichter." *Neue Jahrbücher für Wissenschaft und Jugendbildung*, n.s. 1: 31–35.

Schröder, Stephan. 1999. *Geschichte und Theorie der Gattung Paian*. Stuttgart: Teubner.

Scullion, S. 2003. "Euripides and Macedon, or the Silence of the *Frogs*." *Classical Quarterly* 53: 389–400.

Shapiro, H. A. 1993. *Personifications in Greek Art*. Zürich: Akanthus.

Slings, S. R. 1995. "Protreptic in Ancient Theories of Philosophical Literature." In *Greek Literary Theory after Aristotle*, ed. J. G. J. Abbenes, S. R. Slings, and I. Sluiter, 173–192. Amsterdam: VU University Press.

Slings, S. R. 1999. *Plato Clitophon*. Cambridge: Cambridge University Press.

Smyth, H. W. 1906. *Greek Melic Poets*. London and New York: Macmillan.

Solmsen, F. 1960. "Zur Theologie im grossen Aphrodite-Hymnus." *Hermes* 88: 1–13.

Sourvinou-Inwood, Christiane. 2003. *Tragedy and Athenian Religion*. Lanham, Md.: Routledge.

Teodorsson, S. T. 1987. "The Etymology of Scolion." *Eranos* 87: 127–132.

Tod, Marcus N. 1985. *Greek Historical Inscriptions*, 2 vols. (Arno reprint of the 2nd ed., Oxford, Clarendon Press, 1946).

Trampedach, Kai. 1994. *Platon, die Akademie und die zeitgenössische Politik*. Stuttgart: Steiner.

Tsagalis, Christos. 2008. *Inscribing Sorrow: Fourth-century Attic Funerary Epigrams*. Berlin: W. de Gruyter.

Velardi, Roberto. 1991. "Le origini dell'inno in prosa." In *L' inno tra rituale e letteratura nel mondo antico* (AION 13), Albio Cassio ed., 205–231. Roma: Gruppo Editoriale Internazionale.

Völker, Harald. 2003. *Himerios, Reden und Fragmente*. Wiesbaden: Reichert.

von der Muhl, P. 1918. "Hermias." *RE Suppl*. III col. 1126–1130.

Webster, T. B. L. 1970. *Sophocles Philoctetes*. Cambridge: Cambridge University Press.
Wehrli, F. 1974. *Hermippos der Kallimacheer. Die Schule d. Arist.*, Supplbnd. 1. Basel: Schwabe.
Weiskopf, Michael, 1989. *The So-called "Great Satraps' Revolt,"* 366–360 B.C. *Historia* Einzelschriften 63. Stuttgart: F. Steiner.
Wellek, René and Warren, Austin. 1956. *Theory of Literature*, 3rd ed. New York: Harcourt, Brace & World.
West, M. L. 1982. *Greek Metre*. Oxford: Clarendon Press.
West, M. L., ed. 1992. *Iambi et elegi Graeci*. 2nd ed. Oxford: Clarendon Press.
Wilamowitz-Moellendorff, Ulrich von. 1893. *Aristoteles und Athen.* Vol. 2. Berlin: Weidmann.
Wilamowitz-Moellendorff, Ulrich von. 1920. *Platon*. Berlin: Weidmann.
Willi, Andreas. 2003. *The Languages of Aristophanes*. Oxford: Oxford University Press.
Wimsatt, W. K. and Monroe Beardsley. 1964. "The Intentional Fallacy." In *The Verbal Icon*, 1–21. Lexington: University of Kentucky Press.
Wagman, Robert S. 1995. *Inni di Epidauro*. Biblioteca di studi antichi 75. Pisa: Giardini.
Wormell, D. E. W. 1935. "The Literary Tradition Concerning Hermias of Atarneus." *Yale Classical Studies* 5: 57–92.
Yatromanolakis, Dimitrios. 1999. "Alexandrian Sappho Revisited." *Harvard Studies in Classical Philology* 99: 179–195.
Young, David C. 1983. "Pindar *Pythians* 2 and 3: Inscriptional *Pote* and the 'Poetic Epistle.'" *Harvard Studies in Classical Philology* 87: 31–48.
Yunis, Harvey. 1997. "What Kind of Commentary is the *peri Dêmosthenous* of Didymus?" *Archiv für Papyrusforschung* 3: 1049–55.
Zeller, Eduard. 1897. *Aristotle and the Earlier Peripatetics*. 2 vols. London and New York: Longmans, Green.
Zuntz, Günther. 2005. *Griechische philosphische Hymnen*, ed. H. Cancik and L. Käppel. Tübingen: Mohr Siebeck.

GENERAL INDEX

abstractions, hymns to 87, 91, 93–4, 97, 122, 140, 162, 197 n. 8, 199 n. 7
Academy 21–4, 35, 40, 47, 161, 167–8, 177 n. 21
Achilles 2, 5–7, 12–13, 127, 144–5, 193 n. 24, 205 n. 28
agalma 142, 158; *see also* memorials
Alexandrian library, *see* Library of Alexandria
altars 83, 93, 132, 160, 164, 169, 194 n. 31
Anactoria 120–1, 145, 148, 203 n. 9
aoidimos ("celebrated in song") 7, 142, 147, 149, 150
Apellicon of Teos 168, 169
aphthitos ("unwithering") 143, 148, 150, 153–4

apologia (defense speech) 60–3, 65, 66, 85
of [Aristotle] 60–1, 66, 181 n. 7, 188 n. 39
areta (*aretê*), definition of 4, 174 n. 7
Aristocles of Messene 19, 37–8, 40, 41, 62–7, 169
[Aristippus] *On Ancient Luxury* 62, 86
Asclepius 129, 131, 206 n. 36
Artaxerxes II 18, 25
Artaxerxes III Ochus 25, 51
Atarneus 2, 6, 10–15, 18–20, 22–5, 39, 42, 47, 56–7, 82, 145, 154, 166
Athenaeus 2, 12, 54–63, 67, 69, 70, 77, 79, 82–9, 115, 125, 168–9, 170–1, 186 n. 21, 195 n. 38
Attic *skolia* 54–6, 59, 69, 70, 73–4, 77–80, 86–9, 96,

233

Attic *skolia*—Cont'd
  101, 114–119, 145,
  165, 171
  name of 55
Augustus, name of 152, 154,
  155, 210 n. 24
auxanein 143, 152–4, 209 n. 20,
  210 n. 22

Bacchylides 73, 78–9, 138,
  141–3, 149, 152, 153,
  156, 158, 159, 190 n. 4,
  192 n. 22
bebaios ("steadfast, stable")
  142, 157–9, 164, 167,
  211 n. 4
book epigrams, *see* epigrams

Callimachus 53, 59, 78–9,
  109, 192 n. 20,
  196 n. 44; *see also*, hymns,
  mimetic
Callisthenes of Olynthus 20,
  23–4, 43–53, 82
Castor and Pollux, *see*
  Dioskouroi
Craterus of Macedon 57, 58,
  186 n. 23

defense speech *see apologia*
deictics 32, 34–5, 38, 43,
  53, 103
Delphi 18, 29, 31, 33, 38, 43,
  53, 57, 61, 81, 83, 158,
  162, 163
Demades 83, 195 n. 35

Demeter 94, 108
  rites of 62, 187 n. 33,
  201 n. 37
Demetrius of Phaleron 66,
  188 n. 34
Demetrius the Besieger
  (*Poliorcetes*) 66–7, 83,
  194 n. 31, 199 n. 16
Demochares 22, 67, 189 n. 45
Demosthenes 3, 22, 25–26, 67,
  80, 85
Didymus 3, 12, 17–24, 32,
  36–8, 45, 46, 48, 59,
  63–4, 86, 126, 152, 166,
  169–171, 186 n. 21, n. 27
  On Lyric Poetry 59, 170
Diogenes Laertius 3, 12, 23, 29,
  34–40, 59, 61, 62, 86,
  108–10, 125, 164, 169,
  170, 181 n. 7
Dioskouroi (Castor and Pollux)
  6, 144–5, 208 n. 7
dirge (*thrênos*) 71, 75, 81, 86–7,
  191 n. 10
dithyramb 74–9, 87, 193 n. 23
  dithyrambic style 125–6,
  133, 138–9, 207 n. 2,
  208 n. 9
do ut des 5, 156

elegiacs 29, 31, 33, 36, 51–3, 87,
  109, 116–7, 119, 160–3,
  169, 170, 196 n. 44
enargeia (vividness) 53, 93, 162
encomium (*enkômion*) 6–7, 43,
  45–7, 72–4, 76, 78, 89,

94, 148, 152, 154, 160, 165, 170–1, 190 n. 5, 193 n. 24, 209 n. 14
name of 70, 73
of Hermias (?) 45–7
of Plato 47, 160, 184 n. 6
epigrams 27–30, 33, -36 81, 170
book 34–6, 40–43, 180 n. 6
epinician 7, 72–3, 78, 87, 97, 99, 101, 124, 141, 142, 149, 190 n. 5, 204 n. 17
name of 73
epiphany 121, 125, 127, 133–4, 145, 206 n. 38
epitaphios logos 61, 210 n. 3
name of 61
epitaphs 30–2, 35–9, 52
fictional 38, 181 n. 14, 210 n. 25
epithalamia (wedding songs) 77, 191 n. 15
epithet 5, 33, 61, 84, 91, 93–4, 100, 105, 107–8, 114, 121–2, 124–6, 130–3, 138–41, 146, 150–1, 207 n. 2
transferred 84, 139
epos/melos distinction 31–2, 51–53, 110, 126; see also verse
Erastos 23, 166
ethos 14, 55, 113–4, 126, 134
Euboulides, of Megara (?) 63–65
Eubulus 18, 35, 37, 38, 176 n. 10

Eudemus of Rhodes 160–4, 169, 170
Euripides 12, 133, 138–41, 143, 153, 182 n. 21, 197 n. 8

fame, *see kleos*
friend (*philos*), friendship 19, 20, 31, 50, 64 142, 152, 154–5, 157–8, 162–4, 167–9, 172;
see also xenia

genre 4, 6, 28, 34, 35, 38, 46, 50, 54–60, 69–79, 86–8, 97, 100, 104, 110, 111, 114, 124, 134, 141, 148, 151, 156, 165, 170
dependence on context 87–9

Heracles 2, 5, 6, 12, 82, 116, 123, 125–34, 142–6, 150, 154, 207 n. 5, 208 n. 7
Hermippus of Smyrna 7, 54, 57–60, 63, 65, 79, 86, 170
hero cult 82, 83, 145, 164, 194 n. 32
Hermotimus of Pedasa 41–2
hexameters, dactylic 7, 31, 53, 100, 104–10, 170
humneô ("to sing") 84, 153, 210 n. 2
husteron proteron 15–16

hymn (n.) (*humnos*) 4, 6, 75–6,
    171; see also *humneô*
    "Homeric" 100, 105–6,
    "mimetic" 53
    name of 80

impiety trials 8, 56–9, 61,
    62, 65–7, 154–5,
    194 n. 30
inscription 9, 17–20, 29, 31, 33,
    36, 43, 53, 162, 163
integration of poetic tradition
    105, 143, 172

kleos ("fame, glory") 33, 130,
    142, 147–9, 153
kômos ("revel song") 6, 73,
    190 n. 4
Koriskos 23, 166–8

lament *see* dirge
Library of Alexandria 3, 59, 66,
    71–4, 77, 79, 89, 108,
    166–170
Lyceum 23, 54, 81, 123,
    164, 169
  common meals (*sussitia*) 54,
    56, 86, 87, 185 n. 15
Lycon the Pythagorean 62–3,
    188 n. 36
lyric poetry 2, 10, 14, 27, 28, 33,
    51–2, 59, 70, 85, 86, 110,
    113, 138, 159
  genres of 71–80, 89–90,
    191 n. 9

transcriptions of 3, 103, 113,
    159; see also song,
    epos/melos distinction
Lysander of Sparta 57, 58, 80,
    83–4, 162

melos (song) 51, 73, 76; see also
    song, *epos/melos*
    distinction
memorials 34, 37–8, 45, 61, 88,
    129, 156, 160, 186 n. 23,
    210 n. 3
memory personified, *see*
    Mnamosuna
Mentor of Rhodes 25, 30
mimêsis 76
mnêma / mnêmaion, *see*
    memorials
Mnamosuna ("Memory")
    150–1, 155
monuments *see* memorials
morphê ("shape") 124, 144
Muses 2, 7, 81, 143, 149–155,
    164, 193 n. 24

names, proper 12–14, 39, 45,
    120, 161, 163, 181 n. 13
naming 16, 33, 156, 184 n. 13,
    210 n. 25
Neleus of Skepsis 168, 169

paeans 8, 55–62, 69, 70, 72,
    75–91, 94–7, 101, 109,
    110, 116, 160, 162, 165,
    170, 206 n. 36
  at libations 96, 165,
    195 n. 37

name of 72
sympotic 88, 101
phthinein ("withering") 143
Pindar 7, 20, 73, 78, 97–105, 152, 190n7, 198 n. 12
Plato 19–24, 40, 41, 47, 64–6, 71, 74–80, 85–8, 94, 97, 110, 114–7, 124, 158–69
Symposium 94, 158
Poetics of Aristotle 75–6, 137
polumokhthos ("of much toil") 138–41
priamel 5, 6, 91, 95, 100, 119–20, 154, 167, 198 n. 10, n. 12
Prodicus 94, 207 n. 5
Heracles at the Crossroads 123–5, 130
protreptic 121, 123–4, 126, 133, 141
Proxenus of Atarneus 22–3
Pythias, daughter of Aristotle, 23, 42

refrains 57–58, 72, 79, 86, 185 n. 19, 192 n. 22
re-performance 4, 31–6, 71, 97, 101–4, 147–51, 156–7, 165, 171, 180 n. 4
reverence (*eusebeia/sebas*) 2, 99, 132, 150, 151, 154, 163–4

Sappho 77–8, 113–4, 117–21, 149, 167
seal (*sphrêgis*) 208 n. 13

sebas, *see* reverence
Simonides 29, 33–34, 41, 81, 116, 122, 123, 167
skolion 55, 59, 74, 80, 86, 165, 190 n. 5, 195 n. 38; *see also* Attic *skolia*
song (*melos*) xvi, 3, 28, 31–2, 51–2, 54, 70, 81, 101
books 117, processional 104
Sophocles of Sounion 67
Speusippus (of Athens) 21–2, 47, 177 n. 21, 184 n. 6
sphrêgis see seal
suggramma ([prose] composition) 46, 49, 50, 52
sussitia (common meals) *see* under Lyceum
symposia 47, 54, 88, 89, 101, 114–6, 148, 185 n. 15, 195 n. 37
literary 47, 94

Theocritus of Chios 27, 29, 35–42
Theognis 116–7
Theophrastus of Eresos 23, 66–7, 164, 167–9
Theopompus of Chios 18, 21, 24–5, 39, 42, 47, 50
thrênos see dirge
toil 92, 121–4, 130, 138–45, 204 n. 17

unwithering fame, *see aphthitos*

verse (*epos*) 117, 163–4;
see also *epos/melos*
distinction
vividness see *enargeia* 53, 162
virtue, see *areta*

waxing, see *auxanein*
withering, see *phthinein*

xenia ("guest friendship"), *xenos*
("guest-friend") 20,
30–31, 155; see also Zeus
xenios

Zeus *xenios* (god of
guest-friends) 30, 151,
154, 165

INDEX OF PASSAGES DISCUSSED

AELIAN
  2.19: 51
  14.1: 43
ALEXINUS (*SH*)
  Fr. 40: 186 n. 23
AMBRYON (Bryon?)
  On Theocritus: 37
ANON. *skolia* (*PMG*)
  890: 115–6
  894: 145
ARIPHRON (*PMG*)
  813: 57–58, 91–97, 116
ARISTOCLES of Messene
  (Chiesara)
  Fr. 2.5: 63–65
  Fr. 2.7: 41, 182 n. 23
  Fr. 2.8: 62
  Fr. 2.9: 19
  Fr. 2.12: 37–8
  Fr. 2.13: 169
ARISTOPHANES
  Frogs
    50: 41
    140–1: 181 n. 13
    1034–6: 203 n. 15
ARISTOTLE
  Eudemian Ethics
    1219b8–9: 190 n. 6
  Nicomachean Ethics
    1100b12–14: 206 n. 34
    1100b19–21: 176 n. 7
    1100b30–3: 176 n. 7
  Fragments (Rose)
    Fr. 615–17: 43
    Fr. 641: 181 n. 14
    Fr. 645: see [Aristotle]
    Fr. 671: 108–109, 170
    Fr. 672: 109, 170
    Fr. 674: 29–33
    Fr. 673: 160–4
    Fr. 675 (= 842 *PMG*): *passim*
  Politics
    1283a7: 198 n. 11
  Poetics

ARISTOTLE—Cont'd
   1447a14–27: 76
   1448b4–27: 76
   1448b25–7: 76
   1449b21–50b20: 75
   1454b2: 131
   458a18–59a17: 206
   1459a5–8: 137, 206 n. 1
   1459a19: 139
   1458a22–23: 206 n. 1
   1459a5–8: 137, 206 n. 8
   Rhetoric
   1366a23–68a37: 4, 124
   1367a1–3: 207 n. 4
   1367b26–9: 74
   1368a: 154
   1388b21: 74
   1394b13: 116
   1400b5–8: 191 n. 10
   1406b2: 139
   1409a1–3: 191 n. 12
   1413b12–16: 207 n. 2
[ARISTOTLE]
   Fr. 645 Rose: 60–63, 66
ARISTOXENOS (Wehrli)
   Fr. 125: 77
ATHENAEUS
   610f: 67
   692f: 54,
   693f-694c: 55
   694a: 54, 55
   694c-695e: 55
   695f-696a: 55
   696a-697b: 55, 56
   696e: 56–58
   697a: 57

BACCHYLIDES (Maehler)
   Epin. 1.178–84: 141–3, 158
   2.13: 190 n. 4
   3.90–92: 153
   Fr. 23: 192 n. 21
   Fr. dub. 56: 152

CALLIMACHUS (*SH*)
   293: 192 n. 22
CALLISTHENES of Olynthus
   (124 *FGrH*)
   Fr. 2: 48–51
CLEARCHUS (Werhli)
   2a: 184 n. 6

DEMETRIUS of Magnesia
   (Mejer)
   Fr. 15: 175 n. 5, 174 n. 10
DEMOCHARES (75 *FGrH*)
   Fr. 2: 199 n. 16
DEMOSTHENES
   Fourth Philippic 32: 25
DICHAEARCHUS (Wehrli)
   Fr. 88–89: 76–7
DIDYMUS
   On Demosthenes
   (Pearson-Stephens)
   4.60–65: 18
   5.23: 18
   5.53–4: 166
   5.53–63: 177 n. 13
   5.63: 22, 64
   5.64: 46, 183 n.3
   6.2: 49, 157
   6.15–16: 20
   6.21–22: 171, 214 n. 32
   6.46–49: 37–8

DIOGENES LAERTIUS
  2.42: 109–10
  3.2: 184 n. 6
  3.4–5: 188 n. 35
  5.3: 40
  5.5.1–2: 164
  5.6: 29–30
  5.6.10: 86
  5.27: 108, 170, 175
DURIS of Samos (76 FGrH):
  Fr. 71: 83–4, 194 n. 33

Erythraean paean to Asclepius
  (943 PMG): 198 n. 15
EURIPIDES
  Iphigeneia at Aulis
  288: 176 n. 6
  568: 203 n. 13
  Orestes
  807–8: 203 n. 11
  Medea
  824–45: 199 n. 22
  Phoen.
  784–5: 139–40
  Fragments (TrGF)
  Fr. 645a: 140–1, 153
  Fr. 734: 133
  Fr. 916: 140, 143
EURIPIDES (?) *PMG*
  755: 196 n. 44
EUSEBIUS
  Praep Ev. (Mras)
  15.2.11:19

GHI (Tod)
  165: 19–20
  187: 43, 183 n. 27

HERMIPPUS of Smyrna (1026
  FGrH)
  Fr. 30: 186 n. 25
  Fr. 31: 184 n. 9
  Fr 65: 59
  Fr 67: 59
HERMOCLES (*CA*)
  pp. 173–5 Powell: 83,
    194 n. 31
HERODOTUS
  1.86–87: 51
  8.104–6: 42–3
HESIOD
  Theogony:
  116–117: 108, 201 n. 30
  117: 107
  120: 94
  907–9: 199 n. 20
  Works and Days:
  287–92: 121–2
  760–63: 93, 197 n. 5
HIMERIUS (Colonna)
  40.2–3: 12, 20
  40.40:13
HOMER
  Iliad
  4.59–61: 200 n. 24
  6.358: 147
  9.189: 7
  13.636–7: 198 n. 12
  Odyssey
  24.196–8: 146–7
[HOMER] *Hymns*
  30 (*to Gaia*): 105–9
HYPERIDES
  Funeral Oration
  6.21: 194 n. 31

IBYCUS (*PMG*)
   S151: 148–9
ION of Chios (*PMG*)
   742: 93, 95
ISOCRATES
   Evagoras
      8: 46–7
      70: 205 n. 27
   To Demonicus
      49–50: 205 n. 27
   Panegyricus
      159: 203 n. 15

LICYMNIUS (*PMG*)
   771: 207 n. 2
LUCIAN
   A Slip of the Tongue in Salutation
      6.26: 92
LYCUYRGUS
   Against Leocrates 102–3: 203 n. 15

MENANDER Rhetor (Russell and Wilson)
   331.20–332.7: 192 n. 18
   414.23–7: 208 n. 7
MESOMEDES (*CA*)
   Fr. 35: 197 n. 6

PINDAR
   Isth. 8.48: 209 n. 19
   Nem. 4.78: 190 n. 4
   8.40–42: 152
   Ol. 10.95: 153
   Ol. 14: 97–104

PLATO
   Apol.
      19C: 66
      38A: 202 n. 8
   Laws
      601E: 211 n. 9
      700A-E: 74–5
      700C: 75, 190 n. 9
   Phaedo
      60C-61B: 110
      69C: 181 n. 13
   Phaedrus
      275C-277D: 211 n. 4
   Symp.
      177A-B: 94, 190 n. 5
      178A-C: 94–5
      208D-E: 204 n. 26, 205 n. 28
      209C: 158
PLATO (?) *Epistles*
   3.315B: 200 n. 27
   3.322D: 167
   3.322E: 167
   6: 166–9
PLUTARCH
   On Exile
      603C: 39
[PLUTARCH] *De Musica* 1134d-e: 185 n. 19
PRODICUS
   Choice of Heracles (84 B 2 DK), see Xenophon, *Mem.* 2.1–21–34
PROCLUS
   Chrestomathy (*apud* Proclus *Bib.*)
      319b: 78

SAPPHO (Voigt)
   16: 117–21
SIMONIDES (IEG/PMG)
   11 (IEG): 193 n. 24
   531 (PMG): 81, 193 n. 24
   579 (PMG): 122
   604 (PMG): 197 n. 5
   615 (PMG): 197 n. 8
   651 (PMG): 116
SIMONIDES (?) A.P. 7.258 33–4
SOCRATES (?) 1 IEG: 202 n. 32
   2 IEG: 109–110
SOPHOCLES
   Test. 73a (TrGF): 206 n. 36
   Philoctetes
   827–32: 190 n. 8, 206 n. 36
   1409–1471: 127–34
   1420: 130–1
   1437: 131
   1442: 130, 142
   1443–4: 132
STRABO
   C608: 77, 191 n. 14
   C610: 22, 178 n. 25

THEOCRITUS of Chios (SH)
   Fr. 738: 5–41
THEOGNIS (IEG)
   255–6: 116–7, 119
THEOPOMPUS (115 FGrH)
   Fr. 250: 18, 24–5, 39
   Fr. 291: 18, 50
TYRTAEUS (IEG)
   12: 211 n. 9

XENOPHON
   Memorabilia
   1.2.1: 182 n. 19
   2.1.21–34: 123
   2.1.24: 198 n. 12
   2.1.32: 198 n. 14
   2.1.33–4: 209 n. 16
   Symposium
   8.28–30: 208 n. 7